24-99

Using Moodle

SECOND EDITION

Using Moodle

Jason Cole and Helen Foster

O'REILLY®

Beijing · Cambridge · Farnham · Köln · Paris · Sebastopol · Taipei · Tokyo

Using Moodle, Second Edition
by Jason Cole and Helen Foster

Published by O'Reilly Media, Inc., 1005 Gravenstein Highway North, Sebastopol, CA 95472

O'Reilly books may be purchased for educational, business, or sales promotional use. Online editions are also available for most titles (*http://safari.oreilly.com*). For more information, contact our corporate/institutional sales department: (800) 998-9938 or *corporate@oreilly.com*.

Editor:	Isabel Kunkel	**Indexer:**	Joe Wizda
Production Editor:	Sarah Schneider	**Cover Designer:**	Karen Montgomery
Proofreader:	Sada Preisch	**Interior Designer:**	David Futato
		Illustrator:	Robert Romano

Printing History:

July 2005:	First Edition.
November 2007:	Second Edition.

RepKover.™

This book uses RepKover™, a durable and flexible lay-flat binding.

ISBN-13: 978-0-596-52918-5

[M] [04/08]

Table of Contents

Preface

What Is Moodle?

Moodle is an open source Course Management System (CMS) that universities, community colleges, K–12 schools, businesses, and even individual instructors use to add web technology to their courses. More than 30,000 educational organizations around the world currently use Moodle to deliver online courses and to supplement traditional face-to-face courses. Moodle is available for free on the Web (*http://www.moodle.org*), so anyone can download and install it. More on that later in this preface.

The name Moodle has two meanings. First, it's an acronym (what isn't these days?) for Modular Object-Oriented Dynamic Learning Environment. Moodle is also a verb that describes the process of lazily meandering through something, doing things as it occurs to you to do them, an enjoyable tinkering that often leads to insight and creativity.

Moodle was created by Martin Dougiamas, a computer scientist and educator who spent time supporting a CMS at a university in Perth, Australia. He grew frustrated with the system and learned that engineers, not educators, had built it. Martin realized that a system built by someone who started with the educational process, rather than an engineering process, would be infinitely better than what he had to work with. He put his postgraduate degrees in Education and Computer Science to work and started developing Moodle as an alternative. Martin now works on Moodle full-time. A community of dedicated open source developers from around the world works with him in a collaborative effort to make Moodle the best CMS available. Martin lives in Australia with his wife, daughter, and son.

Who Is This Book For?

This book is for people who want to teach a course using Moodle. You can use Moodle to teach a fully online course or to supplement a face-to-face course in a traditional setting. It doesn't matter if you teach at a primary school, a secondary school, in higher education, or in a corporate setting; you can use the tools and features available in Moodle to create an effective class.

The first edition of this book was written for Moodle 1.4. This second edition has been updated to cover all the features in Moodle 1.8, such as the new roles and permissions system, blogs, messaging, and the database module.

Also included in this second edition are references to the Moodle Teacher Certificate (MTC) skills. The Moodle Teacher Certificate is a way for people to demonstrate their skills in using Moodle as a teacher through a course project, a narrative document, and an online exam. The content of the certification is designed by the Moodle community, and the certification process is administered worldwide by Moodle Partners. Further details of the MTC can be found in the MTC area on Moodle.org: *http://moodle.org/course/view.php?id=48*.

Prerequisites—What Do You Need Before You Start?

To use this book, you will need the following:

- Moodle installed and configured on a server. You can download Moodle via *http://download.moodle.org/* and can find installation instructions in the Moodle documentation at *http://docs.moodle.org/en/Installing_Moodle*.
- A computer with Internet access.
- A web browser such as Internet Explorer, Mozilla Firefox, Safari, or Opera.
- Teacher access to a course on Moodle, or administrator access to the Moodle site.

About Us

Jason: Since we're going to be spending some time together, I'd better introduce myself. I've been working in the field of educational technology for 10 years. I've been a school district technology administrator, developed commercial web-based training, and written supplemental CDs for inclusion with textbooks. I have been involved in San Francisco State University and the Open University UK's moves to Moodle. I currently have my own instructional design and e-learning consultancy, The eLearning Hub.

I've spent a lot of time working with teachers to incorporate technology into their classes. I've seen what works, what doesn't, and some of the pitfalls to avoid.

I'm an education geek at heart. I love living at the intersection of technology and learning theory. There are so many new and exciting opportunities in this area that I can see myself doing this for at least another 10 years.

Helen: Ten years ago I was teaching mathematics in Botswana, in a village school with hardly any educational technology!

I discovered Moodle in December 2004, when researching virtual learning environments for Alton College in the UK. I gained a great deal from the forums on *Moodle.org*, learning from other Moodle users' experiences, and increasing my understanding by explaining things for others. I went on to implement Moodle at Alton College and also supported local schools' use of Moodle.

I'm now Moodle documentation steward and facilitator for the Using Moodle course on *Moodle.org*. It's great being a member of the worldwide Moodle community and being able to contribute to the development of such powerful educational technology.

How to Use This Book

This book is written for instructors learning how to use Moodle. It's not just a how-to manual, however. Every chapter includes suggestions, case studies, and best practices for using Moodle effectively. Using Moodle won't make your course better by itself. Only by applying effective educational practices can you truly leverage the power of Moodle.

The Moodle interface can be customized a great deal. The descriptions and screenshots in this book illustrate the default interface without any customization. If you have changed the order of the blocks in your course or if the system administrator has changed the look and feel of the main interface, your system will look different from the screenshots here.

Chapter 1 discusses what Course Management Systems have to offer and what makes Moodle special.

Chapter 2 gets us started using Moodle. We'll sign up for an account, review the basic interface, get used to some of the conventions, and start a course.

Chapter 3 covers how to add content to your course.

Chapter 4 delves into course management, including understanding and using roles, arranging students into groups, and how to obtain reports of student activity.

Chapters 5 to 14 cover individual tools in the basic Moodle package. We'll discuss how and when to use forums, hold chat sessions, send messages, give quizzes, set assignments, develop shared glossaries and databases, create pathed lessons, collaboratively develop web pages, create blogs, set up surveys and polls, and record student grades. Each chapter covers how to add the tool to your course, discusses the options available, and gives you some creative ideas for effectively using the tool in your class.

Chapter 15 pools all the disparate tools into a comprehensive whole and shows some of the creative ways teachers have used Moodle.

Chapter 16 covers how to administer an entire Moodle site. A system administrator usually handles these functions, but if you're on your own, there's a lot of power behind the curtain.

You can use this book in a couple of different ways. First, you can read it cover to cover. Hopefully, you'll find it so compelling that you won't be able to put it down until you've finished it. Or you can use it like a reference manual. The beginning of each tool chapter covers the how-tos and the options. If you get lost, flip to the appropriate chapter and take it from the beginning. If you're looking for inspiration, Chapters 3 and 15 and the end of each tool chapter should fuel the creative fire. Happy Moodling!

Conventions Used in This Book

The following typographical conventions are used in this book:

Italic
> Indicates new terms, URLs, email addresses, filenames, and file extensions.

`Constant width`
> Used for program listings, as well as within paragraphs to refer to program elements such as variable or function names, databases, data types, environment variables, statements, and keywords.

 This icon signifies a tip, suggestion, or general note.

 This icon indicates a warning or caution.

Safari® Enabled

 When you see a Safari® Enabled icon on the cover of your favorite technology book, that means the book is available online through the O'Reilly Network Safari Bookshelf.

Safari offers a solution that's better than e-books. It's a virtual library that lets you easily search thousands of top tech books, cut and paste code samples, download chapters, and find quick answers when you need the most accurate, current information. Try it for free at http://safari.oreilly.com. (*http://safari.oreilly.com*)

Acknowledgments

Jason: I am indebted to several people in the writing of this book: first, my wife Jeanne for her constant love and support—this book would not be possible without her; Bryan Williams and Michelle Moore at Remote Learner for promoting the first edition in their Moodle workshops; Jon Allen and Jim Farmer at Instructional Media and Magic have been instrumental in promoting the book to a wide audience; Martin Dougiamas for creating Moodle and becoming a good friend and support; Kevin Kelly for doing yeoman's work at SFSU while I gallivanted around the world.

Helen: I would like to thank the following people: Martin Dougiamas and Moodle's "Knight in Shining Armor," Eloy Lafuente, for their friendship and support; members of the worldwide Moodle user community for their discussion and documentation contributions, many of which have been included in this book; colleagues and students at Alton College, in particular Andrew Walker, from whom I learnt a great deal; and a special thanks to my partner, Koen, for being wonderful.

CHAPTER 1

Introduction

If you teach, you've probably heard for years about the revolution the Internet was supposed to bring to teaching and learning. As with so many promises of revolution, the changes haven't materialized. Instead, there has been a slow evolution toward using the Web to enhance teaching and learning. A suite of tools called Course Management Systems (CMSs) supports this new practice. You can use CMSs to enhance your teaching by taking advantage of the Internet without replacing the need for a teacher.

What Is a Course Management System?

CMSs are web applications, meaning that they run on a server and are accessed by using a web browser. Your Moodle server is probably located in your university or department, but it can be anywhere in the world. You and your students can access the system from any place with an Internet connection.

At their most basic, CMSs give educators tools to create a course web site and provide access control so only enrolled students can view it. CMSs also offer a wide variety of tools that can make your course more effective. They provide an easy way to upload and share materials, hold online discussions and chats, give quizzes and surveys, gather and review assignments, and record grades. Let's take a quick look at each of these features and how they might be useful:

Uploading and sharing materials
> Most CMSs provide tools to easily publish content. Instead of using an HTML editor and then sending your documents to a server via FTP, you simply use a web form to store your syllabus on the server. Many instructors upload their syllabus, lecture notes, reading assignments, and articles for students to access whenever they want.

Forums and chats
> Online forums and chats provide a means of communication outside of classroom meetings. Forums give your students more time to generate their responses and can lead to more thoughtful discussions. Chats, on the other hand, give you a way

to quickly and easily communicate with remote students. They can be used for project discussions between groups of students or for last-minute questions the day before an exam.

Quizzes

Online quizzes can be graded instantaneously. They are a great tool for giving students rapid feedback on their performance and for gauging their comprehension of materials. Many publishers now provide banks of test questions tied to book chapters. A professor teaching a marketing class at San Francisco State uses weekly mini-tests to keep students engaged with the lectures and reading. He then uses proctored online testing to give the final exam using the same question banks.

Gathering and reviewing assignments

Online assignment submissions are an easy way to track and grade student assignments. In addition to grading student assignments yourself, research indicates that using an online environment for student peer reviews increases student motivation and performance.

Recording grades

An online gradebook can give your students up-to-date information about their performances in your course. Online grades can also help you comply with new privacy rules that prohibit posting grades with personal identifiers in public places. CMS gradebooks allow students to see only their own grades, never another student's. You can also download the grades into Excel for advanced calculations.

While you could find or write programs to do all of these things on your own site, a CMS combines all of these features in one integrated package. Once you've learned how to use a CMS, you'll be free to concentrate on teaching and learning instead of writing and maintaining your own software.

Over the past eight years, CMS systems have matured rapidly and are now considered critical software for many colleges and universities. The CMS market is now a multi-million dollar market and is growing quickly.

Why Should You Use a CMS?

Good question. After all, we've run classes for thousands of years without the use of computers and the Web. "Chalk and talk" is still the predominant method of delivering instruction. While traditional face-to-face meetings can still be effective, applying the tools listed above opens up new possibilities for learning that weren't possible twenty years ago. Currently, there is a lot of research into how to effectively combine online learning and face-to-face meetings in what are called "hybrid" courses or "blended learning."

Hybrid courses combine the best of both worlds. Imagine moving most of your content delivery to an online environment and saving your course time for discussion, questions, and problem solving. Many instructors have found they can save time and increase student learning by allowing students to engage in the material outside of class. This allows them to use face-to-face time for troubleshooting.

Online discussions give many students the opportunity to express themselves in ways they couldn't in a regular class. Many students are reluctant to speak in class because of shyness, uncertainty, or language issues. It's a boon to many students to have the ability to take their time to compose questions and answers in an online discussion, and instructors report much higher participation levels online than in class.

There are a number of other reasons to think about using a CMS in your courses:

Student demand
Students are becoming more technically savvy, and they want to get many of their course materials off the Web. Once online, they can access the latest information at any time and make as many copies of the materials as they need. Having grown up with instant messaging and other Internet communication tools, many students find that online communication is second nature.

Student schedules
With rising tuition, many students are working more hours to make ends meet while they are in school. About half of all students now work at least 20 hours a week to meet school expenses. With a CMS, they can communicate with the instructor or their peers whenever their schedules permit. They can also take quizzes or read course material during their lunch breaks. Working students need flexible access to courses, and a CMS is a powerful way to give them what they need.

Better courses
If used well, CMSs can make your classes more effective and efficient. By moving some parts of your course online, you can more effectively take advantage of scheduled face-to-face time to engage students' questions and ideas. For example, if you move your content delivery from an in-class lecture to an online document, you can then use lecture time to ask students about what they didn't understand. If you also use an online forum, you can bring the best ideas and questions from the forum into your classroom. We'll discuss lots of strategies and case studies for effective practice throughout the book.

You probably heard all of this in the early '90s. So, what's changed? Today, CMSs are more mature and easier to use than they've been at any time in the past. The underlying technology is becoming more robust, and programmers are writing good web applications. In the past, most systems were built as departmental or even personal projects and then commercialized. The leading commercial package, Blackboard, started out as a small college project and has since grown to be a market leader.

However, market leadership does not automatically mean that a given application is the best or most reliable piece of software. Driven by the need for increased profitability, the market leader has struggled to manage its growth, and some would argue that product quality has suffered as a result.

What Makes Moodle Special?

We've both spent time researching different CMSs, and we have become fans of Moodle because it is open source, is built on a sound educational philosophy, and has a huge community that supports and develops it. It can compete with the big commercial systems in terms of feature sets and is easy to extend. Let's take a closer look at some of these advantages and why they are important to you and your institution.

Free and Open Source

The phrase "open source" has become a loaded term in some circles. For those who are outside of the techie culture, it's hard to understand how powerful this idea has become, and how it has forever changed the world of software development. The idea itself is simple: *open source* simply means that users have access to the source code of the software. You can look under the hood, see how the software works, tinker with it, share it with others, or use parts of it in your own product.

So why is this important? For one, open source software is aligned with the academic community's values of freedom, peer review, and knowledge sharing. Just as anyone can download and use Moodle for free, users can write new features, fix bugs, improve performance, or simply learn by seeing how other people solved a programming problem.

Secondly, unlike expensive proprietary CMSs that require license fees and maintenance contracts, Moodle costs nothing to download and you can install it on as many servers as you want. No one can take it away from you, increase the license cost, or make you pay for upgrades. No one can force you to upgrade, adopt features you don't want, or tell you how many users you can have. They can't take the source code back from users, and if Martin Dougiamas decides to stop developing Moodle, there is a dedicated community of developers who will keep the project going.

Educational Philosophy

Martin's background in education led him to adopt social constructionism as a core theory behind Moodle. This is revolutionary, as most CMS systems have been built around tool sets, not pedagogy. Most commercial CMS systems are tool-centered, whereas Moodle is learning-centered.

Social constructionism is based on the idea that people learn best when they are engaged in a social process of constructing knowledge through the act of constructing an artifact for others. That's a packed sentence, so let's break it down a bit. The term "social process" indicates that learning is something we do in groups. From this point of view, learning is a process of negotiating meaning in a culture of shared artifacts and symbols. The process of negotiating meaning and utilizing shared artifacts is a process of constructing knowledge. We are not blank slates when we enter the learning process. We need to test new learning against our old beliefs and incorporate it into our existing knowledge structures. Part of the process of testing and negotiating involves creating artifacts and symbols for others to interact with. We create artifacts and in turn negotiate with others to define the meaning of those artifacts in terms of a shared culture of understanding.

So how does that relate to Moodle? The first indication is in the interface. While tool-centric CMSs give you a list of tools as the interface, Moodle builds the tools into an interface that makes the learning task central. You can organize your Moodle course by week, topic, or social arrangement. Additionally, while other CMSs support a content model that encourages instructors to upload a lot of static content, Moodle focuses on tools for discussion and sharing artifacts. The focus isn't on delivering information; it's on sharing ideas and engaging in the construction of knowledge.

Moodle's design philosophy makes this a uniquely teacher-friendly package that represents the first generation of educational tools that are truly useful.

Community

Moodle has a very large, active community of people who are using the system and developing new features and enhancements. You can access this community at *http:// moodle.org/* and enroll in the Using Moodle course. There you'll find people who are more than willing to help new users get up and running, troubleshoot, and use Moodle effectively. As of this writing, there are over 300,000 people registered on Moodle.org and over 30,000 Moodle sites in 195 countries. The global community has also translated Moodle into over 70 languages.

The Moodle community has been indispensable to the success of the system. With so many global users, there is always someone who can answer a question or give advice. At the same time, the Moodle developers and users work together to ensure quality, add new modules and features, and suggest new ideas for development. Martin and his core team are responsible for deciding what features are mature enough for official releases and where to go next. Because users are free to experiment, many people use and test new features, acting as a large quality control department.

These three advantages—open source, educational philosophy, and community—make Moodle unique in the CMS space.

In the rest of the book, we'll discuss how you can use Moodle's many features to enhance your teaching and provide your students with a powerful learning environment.

CHAPTER 2

Moodle Basics

In this chapter, we'll cover the basics of the Moodle interface and some of the options you have when setting up your course. Then we'll start adding some content to your first Moodle course.

Getting Started

As mentioned in Chapter 1, Moodle is a web-based tool you can access through a web browser. This means that in order to use Moodle, you need a computer with a web browser installed and an Internet connection. You also need to have the web address (called a Uniform Resource Locator, or URL) of a server running Moodle. If your institution supports Moodle, it will have a server with Moodle up and running. You can then get the server address from the system administrator. If you don't have access to a server with Moodle installed, and you'd like to set up your own, you can download a Moodle package from *http://moodle.org/*.

The Moodle Interface

When you first visit your Moodle site, you'll see the front page with the site news and the courses you are teaching or taking (see Figure 2-1).

Take a moment and familiarize yourself with the interface. Moodle uses a number of interface conventions throughout the system. Important information is usually presented in the middle of the screen. On the lefthand side of the screen you'll see several *blocks* that list available courses and site news. There are a number of useful blocks installed by default on a Moodle server. Your system administrator may install additional optional blocks to add different functionality.

Languages

In the upper-right corner, you may see a drop-down menu with language options. As of September 2007, Moodle has been translated into over 70 languages by the developer

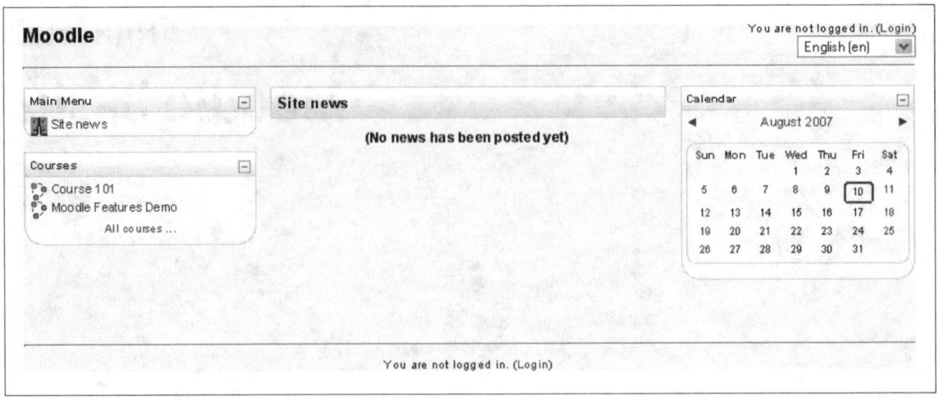

Figure 2-1. Moodle front page

community. The number of languages is now so large that Moodle only loads one language by default. Your system administrator can download additional language packs to provide support for new languages. Moodle also supports UTF-8, a standard for the display of non-Latin character sets, like Chinese or Arabic characters. The language features can be useful for learning foreign languages or supporting students from different countries.

Anyone who uses Moodle can select the language in which Moodle's labels and instructions will appear. For example, if you choose to view the site in Norwegian, the labels and help files will be translated into that language. Moodle does not translate user-generated content—such as forum posts—automatically, though it's possible to create multilanguage content (see Chapter 3).

You can choose the language settings for the front page and for each course you visit. As an instructor, you can also force students to use a given language. This is a useful feature if you're teaching a language course and want the entire course to be in that language. Or you can simply confuse the heck out of your students by choosing some really obscure language and have them guess what everything means.

The system administrator can decide not to display the language drop-down menu on the front page. If you want to change the language and find that you cannot, contact your system administrator.

Moodle's Help System and Documentation

Throughout Moodle, you will see a question mark in a yellow circle. This is a link to Moodle's very extensive help system. Although you shouldn't need it very frequently after you read this book, the community has worked hard to provide you with a help system that is tied to what you are doing at that moment.

When you click the question mark icon, a new window pops up with the help file for the item you are asking about (see Figure 2-2). After you read the help file, you can

Figure 2-2. A help file

close the window with the "Close this window" button or look at other help files by clicking on the "Index of all help files" link. You can then select any help file from anywhere in the help system.

In addition to the help system, if you are logged in as a teacher or an administrator, you'll find a "Moodle Docs for this page" link at the bottom of each page. Clicking this link will take you to the corresponding page on *http://docs.moodle.org/*. Moodle Docs is the documentation for Moodle, written by the Moodle community.

Creating an Account

Right above the language selection list, you'll find a hyperlink that says "Login." Click the link and Moodle will present you with the login to the site page, as shown in Figure 2-3. Your username and password will depend on how your system administrator set up the system. Moodle has a number of options for user authentication, including email-based self-registration, where you create your own account. If you are logging in to a server run by your university or department, check with the Moodle administrator to see if you need to create an account. As use of Moodle grows, more institutions are automatically creating accounts for all of their users, so you may already have a login.

If you need to create your own account:

1. Click the "Create new account" button.
2. Fill in the new account form by creating a username and password for yourself (see Figure 2-4).
3. Enter a valid email address. The system will send you an email to confirm your account. You won't be able to log in again until you confirm your account.
4. Click "Create my new account."
5. Within a few minutes, you should receive an email at the account you specified on the form.

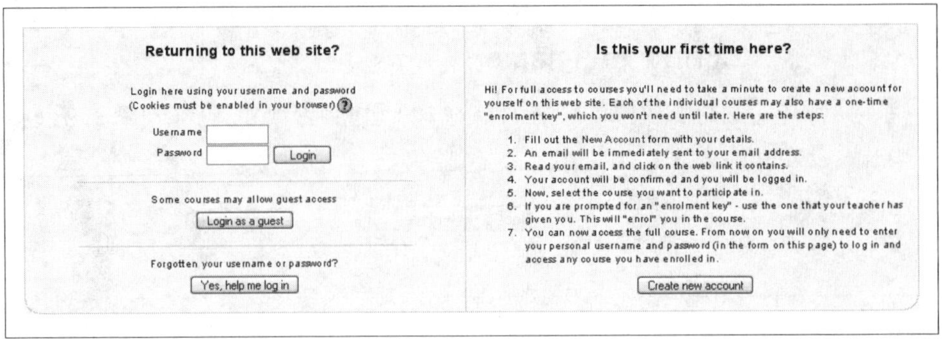

Figure 2-3. Login to the site

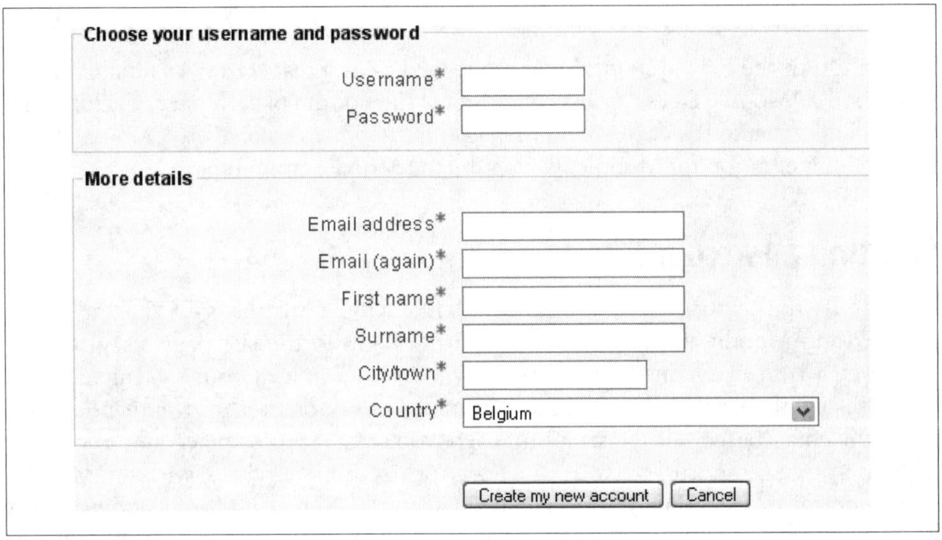

Figure 2-4. New account

6. Click the link in the email (or copy and paste it into the address window in your browser) to confirm your account.

You now have a verified account. Your account isn't automatically associated with the courses you're teaching. Most likely, your system administrator will assign you the role of teacher in the courses you're teaching.

Editing Your User Profile

This section covers the following MTC (Moodle Teacher Certificate) skills: 7.2 Profiles

Once you have successfully confirmed your account and logged in, you will find yourself back at the main page. If you look at the upper-right corner, you'll see that the

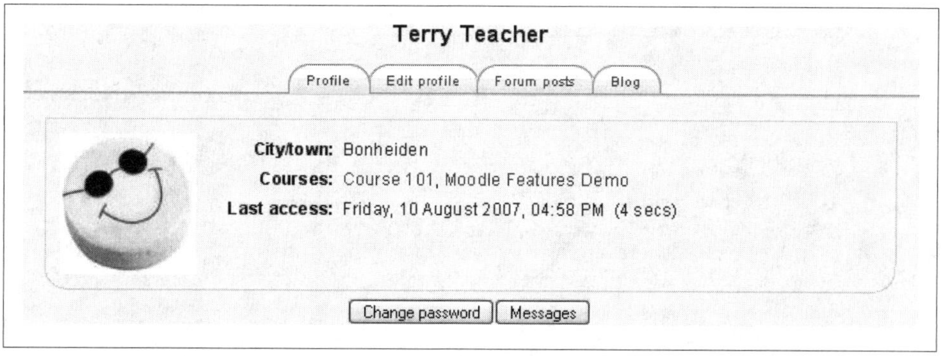

Figure 2-5. A profile

Login link has changed. It now says "You are logged in as" and whatever your name is, highlighted as a clickable word. Click on your name.

Moodle will then present you with your personal profile page, like the one shown in Figure 2-5. You'll see your profile summary and the last time you logged in. Across the top of your profile summary you will see a number of tabs. If this is a new account, you'll see three tabs: Profile, Edit profile, and Blog. As you begin to participate in forums and other activities, other tabs will appear here that will give you access to your contributions on the site.

Below your profile summary are buttons to change your password and to open the messages window. (We'll cover messaging in Chapter 5.)

Let's take a moment and edit your profile to customize the page and help other people get to know you.

To edit your profile:

1. Select the "Edit profile" tab in your personal profile page. The edit profile page will look like Figure 2-6. The profile options with a red star next to them are required fields; they must contain some data in order for you to submit the form.

   On the right side of the profile form, you'll see a Show Advanced button. There are a number of profile options that are hidden by default. These are not changed very often and can be a bit confusing for a new user. In the description of the options below, we've marked the advanced options with an asterisk.

2. If you wish, you can change the first name and surname the system has stored for you.

3. You can edit any of the following fields:

   Email address

   Make sure this is an address you check frequently and that it is correct. Moodle has a lot of important email features, and you wouldn't want to miss out because your email address has a typo or is not an address you check frequently.

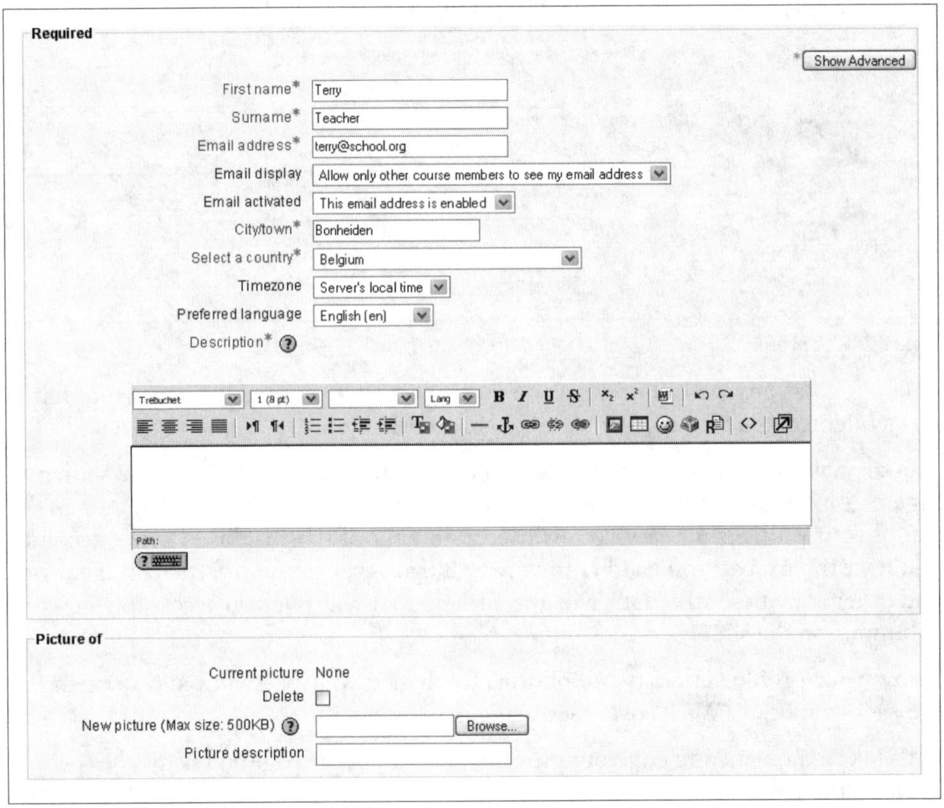

Figure 2-6. Editing a profile

Email display

You can choose who can see your email address. Your choices are to hide your email from everyone, allow only the people in your courses to see it, or display it to everyone who logs in to the site. If you choose to hide your email from other people, they will not be able to send you email directly from Moodle.

Email activated

This toggle will disable or enable Moodle's ability to send email to the address in your profile. If you never want to receive email from Moodle, disable your email address here.

Email format*

Here you can select whether mail sent from Moodle is formatted using HTML or is sent in plain text. Most modern email clients can receive and properly display HTML mail, although this may be a setting you have to enable in your email preferences. If you have a slow connection, or you simply prefer your email plain and simple, the plain-text option is probably a good choice.

Forum auto-subscribe*

Moodle forums are a powerful communication tool for classes. We will discuss forums in detail in Chapter 5. For now, it's enough just to mention that you have the option of "subscribing" to forums, which means that new forum posts will be sent to you via email. This is a great way of keeping current with your course discussions without having to log in and look at the forums every day. Of course, if your discussions really get cooking, you'll end up with a lot of email, but at least it won't be spam.

Forum tracking*

If you choose to enable forum tracking, Moodle will highlight posts added since the last time you read the forum. This is a useful way of quickly identifying new content in a forum.

When editing text*

This option lets you choose whether to use Moodle's native HTML editor to enter text or to use plain text. Moodle's HTML editor is an easy way to enter formatted text into your course site. We'll cover the specifics of how it works in Chapter 3.

Ajax and JavaScript*

Ajax is the set of programming tools that enables dynamic web interfaces. Moodle developers are beginning to experiment with new interface techniques to make Moodle easier to use. If options are not available here, your system administrator has not yet enabled the experimental Ajax interface.

Screen reader*

Selecting this option lets Moodle know you are using a screen reader. In the near future, this will change the layout of Moodle pages to make it easier for the screen reader to interact with Moodle.

Time zone

The time zone setting can be very important, especially if you're working with an international audience or if you will be traveling. Be sure to set the time zone to your local time, not the server's local time.

Jason: I almost missed a meeting because I didn't set my time zone. The Moodle server we were using was in another country and I had left my profile setting on the default server's local time. The meeting was set for 11 p.m., which seemed odd to me. Then I realized I had the wrong time zone. When I changed the setting, I realized the meeting was scheduled for 8 a.m. my time!

Preferred language

Setting your language here makes it your default language for all pages.

Description

The description box gives you a place to tell your Moodle community a little about yourself. If you don't feel comfortable writing a description, just put a space in here so you're allowed to submit the form.

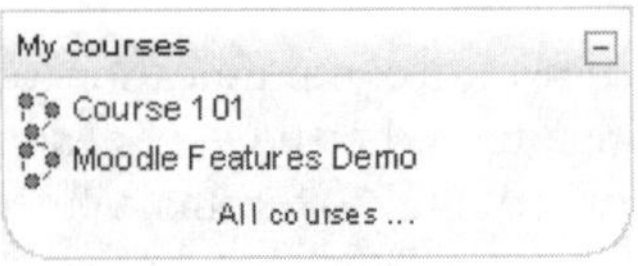

Figure 2-7. My Courses block

4. The remaining optional fields allow you to include personal details about yourself, including your photo or a representative image and contact information. Your picture will appear by your postings in the forums, in your profile, and on the Participants page.

5. When you're done, click the "Update profile" button at the bottom of the page.

To upload a new picture:

1. Prepare the picture you want to use by converting it to a JPG or PNG if you haven't already. It should be smaller than the maximum upload size.

2. Click the Browse button and locate your prepared picture. Then click Choose in the dialogue box.

3. Click the "Update profile" button at the bottom of the page. Moodle will crop your picture into a square and shrink it to 100×100 pixels.

4. Enter a description of your picture for the benefit of anyone using a screen reader.

Moodle provides you with a number of ways to personalize your experience and share information about yourself with other people. Your profile will be linked to your forum posts and other contributions around the site. The picture from your profile will be your icon, so pick something that represents who you are on the Moodle site or a shot of your good side.

Now let's take a look at a course, the main organizing feature of Moodle.

A First Look at a Course

On the left side of the front page, you'll see the My Courses block, which includes a list of all the courses you are teaching or taking as a student, as shown in Figure 2-7. You can access your courses by clicking on the course name in the block.

Let's start with the upper-left corner of the course page, as shown in Figure 2-8. There you'll see the name of your course as entered when the course was created. Your system administrator either entered your course name by hand or she got it from your institution's course database. (Read the "Course Settings" section later in this chapter if you need to change the name.)

Below the course name is a navigation bar that fills with the hyperlinked names of pages as you navigate from one page to another. Frequently, the best way to return to your

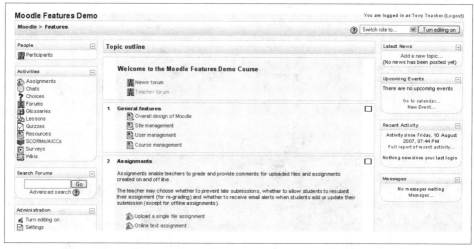

Figure 2-8. Course page

course page is to click on the course short name in the navigation bar. For example, in Figure 2-8, you would click on Features to go back to the course page from another page in the course.

Below the navigation bar are three columns. The far-left and far-right columns contain tool blocks, while the center column contains your course content and activities. The topmost tool block on the left is the People block. From here, you and your students can view the individual profiles of other participants in the course and check who is a member of student workgroups.

Beneath the People block is the Activities block. As you add forums, quizzes, assignments, and other activities to your course, the activity types will be listed here. By clicking on the activity type, students can view all activities of that type that are currently available to them. For example, if you gave a quiz every week, each content section would list a quiz, and if you clicked the Quizzes link in the Activities block, it would list all of the quizzes in the course.

Next in the left column is the Search Forums block, which we'll cover in Chapter 5. At the time of this writing, a site search is under development.

Below the Search Forums block is the Administration block. Assuming you've been assigned the role of teacher, you'll find links to set your course options, assign roles, perform backups of the course, and manage student grades in the Administration block (see Figure 2-9). In this chapter, we'll cover the first two tools, "Turn editing on" and "Settings," and we'll cover the rest in detail as they arise throughout the book.

The far-right column includes three blocks that report on activity in the course. The Latest News block lists the latest items added to the News forum, such as important news stories that pertain to the subject you're teaching. The Upcoming Events block

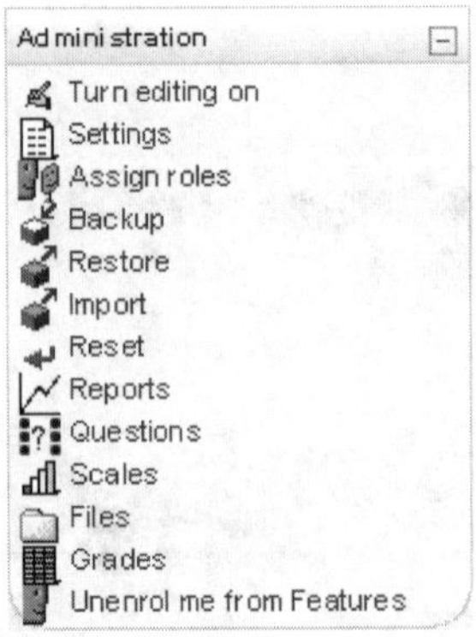

Figure 2-9. Administration block

lists events you've created in the calendar, such as exams and holidays, together with assignment and quiz deadlines. At the bottom of the block are links to view the calendar and add new events. Also, there's the Recent Activity block, which lists recent course activity, such as forum postings and uploads.

The middle column is where the action is. This is where you add all of your content and activities, such as forums, quizzes, and lessons for students to access. Before we get to that, however, you need to make a choice about the format in which to present your course.

Course Formats

This section covers the following MTC skills: 2.2 Course format

Unlike some CMSs that force you into one format, Moodle provides you with a number of options for the general format of your course. You can choose to order your course chronologically by week, conceptually by topic, or socially with a big forum as the central organizing principle.

The course formats you can choose are:

LAMS format
  The Learning Activity Management System (LAMS) is an open source Learning Management System (LMS) that allows teachers to use a Flash-based authoring environment for developing learning sequences. LAMS has been integrated with Moodle to allow teachers to develop LAMS activities within a Moodle course. This course format makes LAMS central to the course, only displaying the LAMS interface. If you are interested in using LAMS, check with your system administrator to see if he has installed and configured LAMS. Very few institutions use LAMS, as it duplicates much of the Moodle functionality.

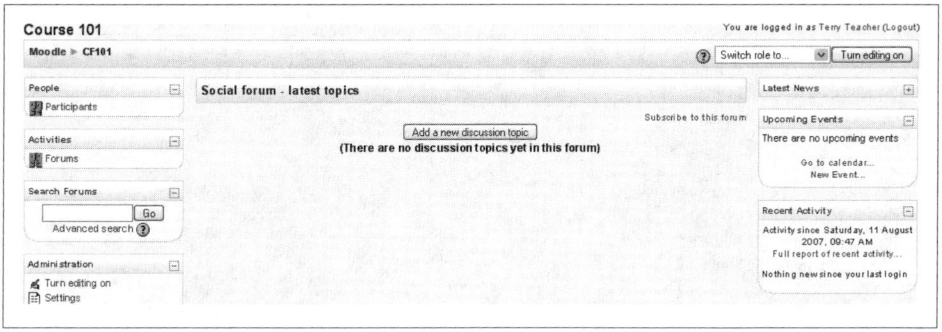

Figure 2-10. Course page in social format

SCORM format

> The Sharable Content Object Reference Model (SCORM) is a content packaging standard. SCORM packages are self-contained bundles of content and JavaScript activities that can send data to Moodle about the students' scores and current locations. Moodle can use SCORM packages as an activity type or as a course format. If you have a large SCORM object you want to use as an entire course, you can select this course format.

Social format

> The social format is based on a single forum for the whole course, as shown in Figure 2-10. It's useful for less formal courses or for noncourse uses such as maintaining departmental sites.

Topics format

> When you create a course using the topics format, you start by choosing the number of topics you will cover. Moodle creates a section for each topic, as shown previously in Figure 2-8. You can add content, forums, quizzes, and other activities to each topic section. If your course design is concept-oriented, and students will be working through a range of concepts but not necessarily according to a fixed schedule, this is a good choice.

Weekly format and CSS/no tables

> With this format, you specify a course start date and the number of weeks the course is to run. Moodle will create a section for each week of your course, as shown in Figure 2-11. The current week is highlighted. You can add content, forums, quizzes, and so on in the section for each week. If you want all your students to work on the same materials at the same time, this is a good format to choose.

> The CSS/no tables variant of the weekly format displays the weekly course format without using tables for layout. This improves the accessibility of the format, but older browsers may have trouble displaying it correctly.

To set the course format:

1. Click Settings in the Administration block.

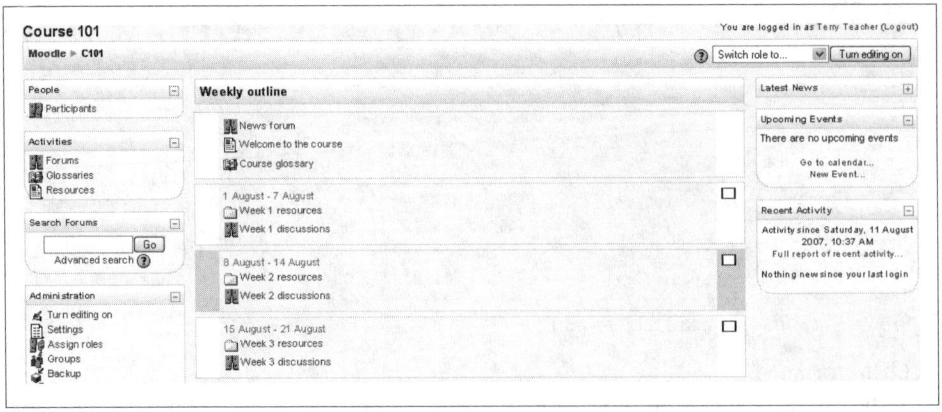

Figure 2-11. Course page in weekly format

2. Select the course format from the drop-down list just below the course summary (see Figure 2-12).

3. Enter the parameters for your course:

   - For the weekly format, set the start date and the number of weeks.

   - For the topic format, set the number of topics.

   - For the social format, set the course start date. You don't need to worry about the number of weeks or topics.

Moodle allows you to switch between formats if you find that a given format isn't working for you. Simply follow the preceding instructions and select a different format. You can also add or remove topics or weeks at any time. So you don't have to worry too much about locking yourself into a format before you really understand the system.

Course Settings

This section covers the following MTC skills: 2.1 Course settings

The settings page, as shown in Figure 2-12, where you set the course format, also gives you access to a number of important course options. You'll find it is important to take a moment to review the settings for your course to ensure that it behaves the way you want it to.

To change your course settings:

1. Click Settings in the Administration block on your course page.

2. Review each of the general options to ensure they are correct for your course:

   Category
   > Your system administrator may have created course categories, such as department or college labels, to help students and teachers find their courses.

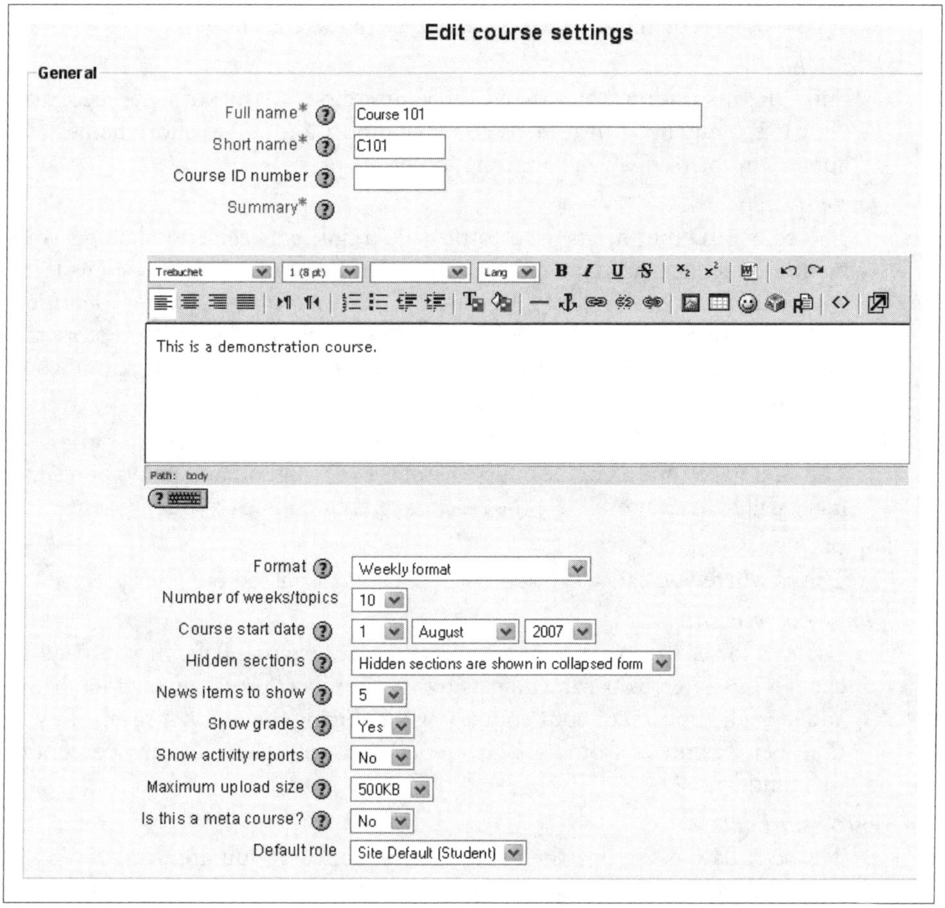

Edit course settings

General

Full name* ⑦ [Course 101]

Short name* ⑦ [C101]

Course ID number ⑦ [   ]

Summary* ⑦

| Trebuchet ▾ | 1 (8 pt) ▾ | ▾ | Lang ▾ | **B** *I* <u>U</u> S̶ | x₂ x² | ꧅ | ↶ ↷ |

≡ ≡ ≡ ≡ | ¶◀ ▶¶ | ⅛ ⅜ ⅗ ⅗ | Tᵧ ⌨ | — ⚓ ∞ ⊗ ⊗ | ☒ ☐ ☺ ☻ ▤ | ⟨⟩ ⚅

This is a demonstration course.

Path: body

⑦ ▦

Format ⑦ [Weekly format ▾]

Number of weeks/topics [10 ▾]

Course start date ⑦ [1 ▾] [August ▾] [2007 ▾]

Hidden sections ⑦ [Hidden sections are shown in collapsed form ▾]

News items to show ⑦ [5 ▾]

Show grades ⑦ [Yes ▾]

Show activity reports ⑦ [No ▾]

Maximum upload size ⑦ [500KB ▾]

Is this a meta course? ⑦ [No ▾]

Default role [Site Default (Student) ▾]

Figure 2-12. Editing the course settings

Depending on how your system is set up, you may be able to categorize your course by department, subject, or other organizational principle.

You will only have the option to change the category if you have been assigned the appropriate capability. (We'll cover roles and capabilities in Chapter 4.)

Full name

This is the name that is displayed on the top header of every page in your course and also in the course listings page. The name should be descriptive enough so students can easily identify the course in which they are working, but it shouldn't be too long. For example, use "English 400—Beowulf" and not "ENG400—Beowulf and the heroic poems of the ancient world."

Short name

Enter the institutional shorthand for your course. Many students recognize "Eng101," but not "Introduction to Composition." The short name also appears in the navigation bar at the top of the page.

Course ID number

The course ID number is used to provide a link between Moodle and your institution's backend data systems. Most Student Information Systems (SIS) have a unique identifier for each course. Moodle has its own unique identifier, which is different from the SIS ID. This field is used by Moodle to store the SIS unique ID so Moodle will know which course the SIS is talking about when synchronizing courses and enrollments.

Summary

The summary appears in the course listings page. A good one-paragraph summary will help communicate the essence of your course to your students.

Format

This is where you can set the course format as discussed previously.

Number of weeks/topics

Use this to set the number of sections your course will have. If you need to change this later, you can. Increasing the number results in sections being added to the bottom of your course page; reducing the number results in sections being removed from the bottom of your course page, and any content in them hidden.

Course start date

The start date is the day the course is first active. If you are using a weekly course format, the first week will start on the date you set here. The start date is also used in course reports as the earliest possible date for which you can obtain logs, activity, and participation reports. In general, if your course does have a real starting date, then it makes sense to set this date to that, no matter what course format you are using.

Hidden sections

When you hide an upcoming topic section to prevent your students from jumping ahead, you can choose to display the title as a collapsed section or simply hide the topic altogether. Displaying the collapsed sections gives your students a road map of the upcoming topics or weeks, so it's probably a good idea to leave this on the default setting.

News items to show

Use this setting to determine the number of course news items displayed on the course page.

Show grades

This setting allows you to select whether students can see the gradebook. If set to No, it doesn't stop instructors from recording grades, but simply prevents the students from seeing them.

Show activity reports

This setting allows students to view their activity history in your course. This is useful if you want students to reflect on their level of participation.

Maximum upload size

This setting limits the size of files you or your students upload to the course. Your system administrator sets the maximum size for the system, but you can choose to make the limit smaller than the system maximum. You can also further limit the size of files that your students upload as assignment submissions and for other activities. (We'll cover them as they come up later in the book.)

Is this a meta course?

A meta course automatically enrolls participants from other "child" courses. Meta courses take their enrollments from other courses. This feature can populate many courses from one enrollment or one course from many enrollments. For example, a course is part of a program (meta course). Each time a student enrolls in (or unenrolls from) this course, they are enrolled/unenrolled from any meta course(s) associated with it.

 You cannot designate a course as a meta course if you have already enrolled students. If you want to change a course into a meta course, you will need to unenroll all the students first, then set the course as a meta course and choose the child courses from which the meta course will draw its enrollments.

Default role

The default role is assigned to everyone who enrolls in your course, unless they are specifically granted another role. We'll cover roles in Chapter 4.

3. Select the enrollments options:

Enrollment plug-ins

Moodle has a number of methods of managing course enrollments, called enrollment plug-ins, which we'll cover in Chapter 16. This setting allows you to choose an interactive enrollment plug-in, such as internal enrollment or PayPal. Your system may well use a noninteractive enrollment plug-in, in which case this setting has no effect. We recommend you leave this setting as default and leave the choice of enrollment plug-ins to your system administrator.

Course enrollable

This setting determines whether a user can self-enroll in your course. You can also limit enrollments to a certain date range.

Enrollment duration

This setting specifies the number of days a student is enrolled in the course, starting from the day she enrolls. If set, students are automatically unenrolled after the specified time has elapsed. This setting is useful for rolling courses without a specific start or end date.

Be very careful when using the enrollment duration setting.

Jason: When I first started using Moodle, I thought the enrollment duration was how long a student had to enroll in a course, not how long she would stay enrolled. After 14 days, hundreds of students were suddenly unenrolled from their courses, causing headaches for weeks.

4. Select the enrollment expiry notification options to determine whether users are notified that their enrollment is about to expire and how much notice they should be given.

5. Select the groups options:

Group mode

Moodle can create student workgroups. We will cover groups extensively in Chapter 4. For now, you need to decide whether your students will be organized into groups and, if so, whether the groups will work independently or will be able to view each other's work.

Force groups

You can set the group mode separately for many activities or force group mode to be set at the course level. If everything in the course is done as part of a group, or you are running cohorts of students through a course at different times, you'll probably want to force group mode to make management easier. Forcing the course group mode overrides the individual activity group settings. If you have forced group mode, every activity in the course will have that group mode set.

6. Select the availability options:

Availability

Use this setting to control student access to your course. You can make a course available or unavailable to students without affecting your own access. This is a good way to hide courses that aren't ready for public consumption or hide them at the end of the semester while you calculate your final grades.

Enrollment key

A course enrollment key is a code each student must enter in order to self-enroll in a course. The key prevents students who aren't in your class from accessing your Moodle course. Create the key here and give it to your students

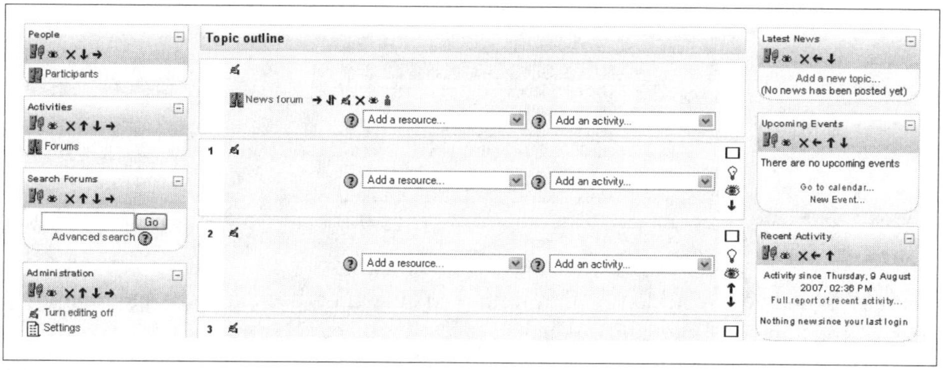

Figure 2-13. Course page with editing turned on

when you want them to enroll in your Moodle course. They will need to use the key only once when they enroll.

Guest access

You can choose to allow guests to access your course, either with an enrollment key or without it. Guests can only view your course and course materials; they can't post to the forums, take quizzes, or submit assignments.

Cost

If you are using an interactive enrollment method such as PayPal, you can enter a course cost. Students will then be required to make a payment before enrolling in the course.

7. Choose whether to force the language. If you do so, your students cannot change languages within the course.

8. Once you've made all your selections, click the "Save changes" button.

Editing Mode

This section covers the following MTC skills: 3.1 Managing blocks

Now that you've decided on a format and settings for your course, we'll look at how to add content. To start the process, you'll first need to turn editing on (see Figure 2-13), which will allow you to add resources and activities to your course. At the top right of the page of any course you are teaching, you'll see a button labeled, surprisingly enough, "Turn editing on." Clicking on this button will present you with a new array of options.

Starting at the top of the screen, let's look at what turning editing on enables you to do. At the top of each section, you'll see an icon of a hand holding a pencil. When you click it, you are presented with a Summary text area. You can use this to label and summarize each topic or weekly section in your course. You should keep the summary to a sentence or two for each block to avoid making the main page too long. Click "Save

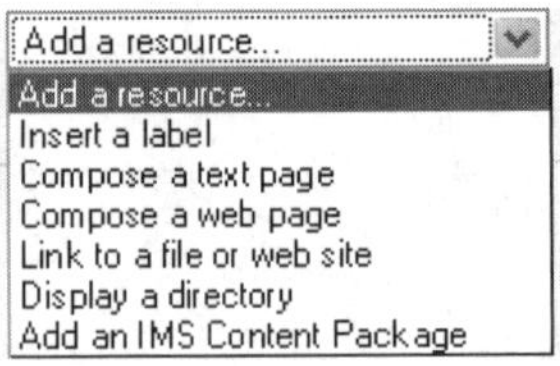

Figure 2-14. "Add a resource" menu

changes" when you've added your summary. You can go back and change it later by clicking the hand-and-pencil icon again.

Underneath each block title and adjacent to the News Forum link you'll see the icons described in Table 2-1.

Table 2-1. Icons

Icon	Function
 👁 ✁	Show or hide item. If you want to keep an item in your course, but don't want your students to see it, you can use this to hide it from them.
✗	Delete item. Removes the item or block from your course. Resources and activities will be permanently removed; blocks can be added again using the Blocks menu.
⬍	Move item. Clicking this will allow you to move an item to another section in the middle column.
← →	Move right or left. You can move blocks to the left- or righthand columns. You can also use this to indent items in the middle column.
↑↓	Move up or down. Moves items up or down in their respective columns.

Use these icons throughout Moodle to customize the interface for your needs.

In addition to the icons for manipulating blocks and activities, each section in the middle column has two drop-down menus. On the left, the menu labeled "Add a resource" gives you tools for adding content such as web pages and links to web sites. On the right, the "Add an activity" menu gives you tools to add activities such as forums, quizzes, lessons, and assignments.

The "Add a resource" menu, as shown in Figure 2-14, gives you access to tools for adding content. There are a number of ways you can create content directly within Moodle or link to content you've uploaded. We'll describe each of these tools briefly now, and cover them in depth in the next chapter:

Insert a label
> You can use labels to organize the sections in your course page. The only thing they do is provide a label within the topic or weekly section.

Compose a text page
> From here, you can create a simple page of text. It doesn't have many formatting options, but it is the simplest tool.

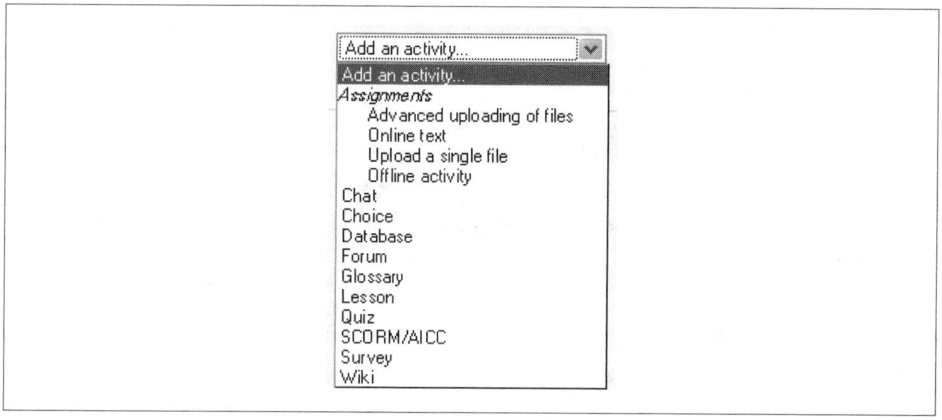

Figure 2-15. "Add an activity" menu

Compose a web page

If you want more formatting options, you can compose a web page. If you elected to use the HTML editor in your personal profile, you can simply create a page as you would using a word processor. Otherwise, you'll need to know some HTML for most formatting.

Link to a file or web site

If you want to upload your course documents in another format, you can save them in Moodle and provide easy access for your students. You can also easily create links to other web sites outside your Moodle course.

Display a directory

If you upload a lot of content, you may want to organize it in directories. Then you can display the contents of the entire folder instead of creating individual links to each item.

Add an IMS Content Package

IMS Content Packages are resources packaged to an agreed specification, often with internal navigation.

The "Add an activity" menu, as shown in Figure 2-15, allows you to add interactive tools to your course. The bulk of this book is dedicated to describing how each of these tools works and how to apply them in your course.

Table 2-2 explains each tool very briefly. We'll learn more about these tools as they come up later in the book.

Table 2-2. Activity types

Activity type	Description
Assignments	A tool for collecting student work, either uploaded files or assignments created on- and offline
Chat	A chat room where people can meet at the same time and send text messages
Choice	A simple poll

Activity type	Description
Database	A tool for creating shared collections of data
Forum	Threaded discussion boards—a powerful communication tool
Glossary	Dictionaries of terms that you can create for each week, topic, or course
Lesson	A set of ordered materials that uses questions to determine what content the student sees next
Quiz	A web-based quiz with a variety of question types, such as multiple choice, true/false, short answer, and matching
SCORM/AICC	A tool for enabling SCORM or AICC (Aviation Industry Computer-Based Training Committee) packages to be included in the course
Survey	Gathers feedback from students using prepackaged questionnaires
Wiki	A collaboratively edited web page

Adding Content to a Course

By now, you're probably wondering, "When the heck do I get to add stuff to my course?" We've provided a lot of background so you'll understand some of the available options. But now's the time to start building your course.

Let's start with a news item to announce to everyone that your online materials are coming soon. The News Forum is a special type of forum (for a full description of forums, see Chapter 5). It is automatically created when the course is first generated. Everyone in the course can read the postings and the news is automatically emailed to them. It's a good tool for making general announcements and sending reminders to students about upcoming assignments.

To add a news item:

1. Click the News Forum link near the top of your course page.
2. Click the "Add a new topic" button. You'll see the page to add a new topic, as shown in Figure 2-16.
3. Type your new message to your class.
4. Click the "Save changes" button. You will be returned to the News Forum page.
5. Click on your course name in the navigation bar at the top to return to your course page.

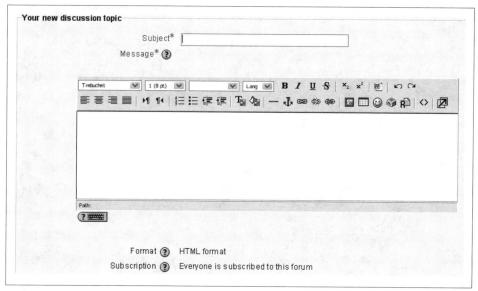

Figure 2-16. Add a new discussion topic

Summary

In this chapter, we've looked at how to create an account and personalize your profile. We've become acquainted with Moodle's user interface and tools, and we've chosen a course format. In the next chapter, we'll start adding different types of content to your new Moodle course.

CHAPTER 3

Creating and Managing Content

Adding Content to Moodle

This section covers the following MTC skills: 4.1 Resources

The first thing most people want to do when they create a course in Moodle is add some content, such as a syllabus or a course outline. As we explained in Chapter 2, you can add content to your course using the "Add a resource" drop-down menu in the center sections of your course (see Figure 2-14). In this chapter, we'll use all of the tools in the resource menu. Future chapters will cover the tools in the "Add an activity" menu.

 Remember that you need to turn editing on to see the "Add a resource" and "Add an activity" menus.

The first tool, "Insert a label," creates a label directly on your course page. The next two tools, "Compose a text page" and "Compose a web page," can be used to develop content directly in Moodle. The following two, "Link to a file or web site" and "Display a directory," are used to manage content developed in other programs, such as Word or PowerPoint. You can also add content from other web sites and take advantage of the rich library of information available on the Web. Finally, "Add an IMS Content Package" enables you to add prepackaged content from sites around the Web.

Let's begin by creating a simple label for your course.

Adding a Label

This section covers the following MTC skills: 4.6.1 Labels

Labels enable you to add additional text or graphics to your course page. Labels can be used to add banners to courses, label sections of resources and activities, or provide quick instructions on the front page of your course. To add a label:

1. Click the "Turn editing on" button.

2. Select "Insert a label" from the "Add a resource" menu.

3. Create your label using the HTML editor (see the following section "Composing a Web Page" for more details on this).

4. Select whether to make your label visible by selecting Show or Hide from the Visible menu.

5. After you have created your label, click the "Save changes" button.

Once you have created a label, the full text of the label will appear in the section where you created it.

 You can use a hidden label to provide information only for other teachers on your course, since students are unable to see hidden items.

 If you want to use a label to identify a grouping of resources and activities within a section, you can indent the links under the label using the arrows adjacent to each resource or activity link. This will give your grouping some visual separation from the rest of the content.

Composing a Text Page

This section covers the following MTC skills: 4.2 Compose a text page

A text page is a simple plain-text page with little formatting. You can add paragraphs and whitespace, but that's about it.

Text pages are very easy to create:

1. Click the "Turn editing on" button.

2. From the "Add a resource" menu select "Compose a text page." Moodle will then display the page to compose a text page like the one in Figure 3-1.

3. Enter a name for the text page.

 The name you give the page will be displayed in the content section on your course page. Students will access your page by clicking on the name. Be sure to give the page a descriptive name so students will know what they are accessing.

4. Write a summary of the page in the Summary field.

5. Add your text in the Full Text field.

6. Scroll down to the bottom of the page and click the "Save changes" button.

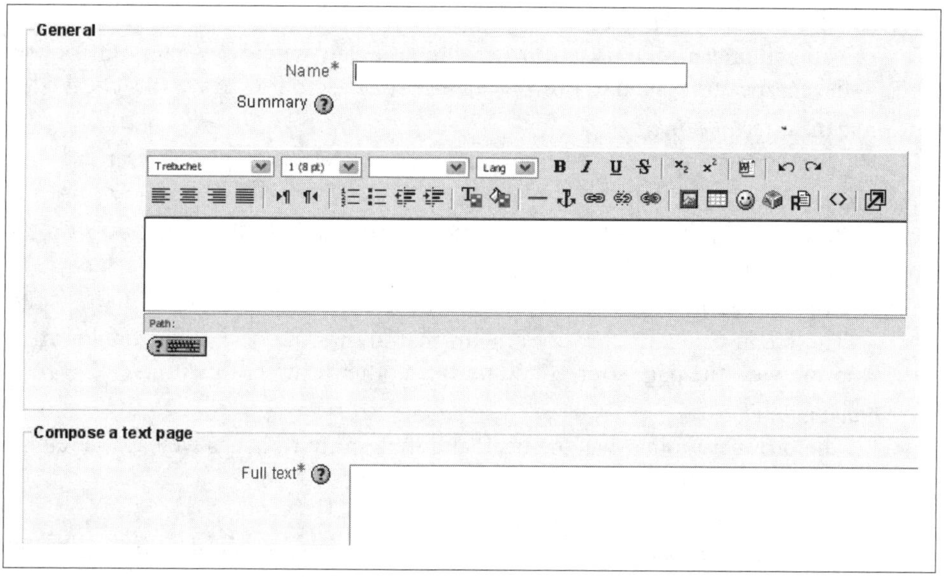

Figure 3-1. Compose a text page

That's all there is to it.

Window options

You can choose whether text pages and web pages that you create are displayed in the same window or in a new window.

To display a resource in the same window:

1. Click the Show Advanced button in the Window area.
2. Select "Same window" from the Window drop-down menu.
3. Select the option:

   Show the course blocks
   > This will display the blocks from your course page on either side of the resource you have created.

To display a resource in a new window:

1. Click the Show Advanced button in the Window area.
2. Select "New window" from the Window drop-down menu.
3. Select the options for the window:

   Allow the window to be resized
   > Checking this will allow the user to change the size of the window after it has opened. Unless you have a specific reason for not allowing the user to resize, you should leave this checked.

Allow the window to be scrolled
> You can prevent the user from scrolling the new window. Again, unless you have a specific reason to prevent the user from scrolling, leave this checked.

Show the directory links
> This will display the user's bookmark or favorites bar in his browser.

Show the location bar
> You can hide the address bar, and thus the site's URL, in the pop up by unchecking this box.

Show the menu bar
> The menu bar is the browser menu that allows the user to set bookmarks, print, view the page source, and perform other browser functions.

Show the toolbar
> The browser toolbar has the back and forward buttons, as well as the reload and stop buttons.

Show the status bar
> The status bar is the lower area of the browser that shows how much of the page has loaded and the target of a link.

Default window width and height
> You can set the size of the new window to match the size of the linked page.

Common module settings

Any resource may be hidden by selecting Hide from the Visible drop-down menu. This has the same effect as clicking on the Hide icon (an eye) adjacent to the resource link on the course page. Other teachers on your course can always view hidden items, whereas students cannot.

 You can hide particular resources, then allow students to see them after your lesson. Teacher resources can be kept hidden permanently.

Composing a Web Page

This section covers the following MTC skills: 2.3 Editor; 4.3 Compose a web page

Adding a plain-text page to Moodle isn't the only way to add content. With Moodle, you can easily use the HTML editor to create sophisticated pages that can be displayed in any web browser. The HTML editor works like a word-processing application right in your browser, as you can see in Figure 3-2. Simply type directly into the text area and use the formatting tools to customize it.

To compose a web page:

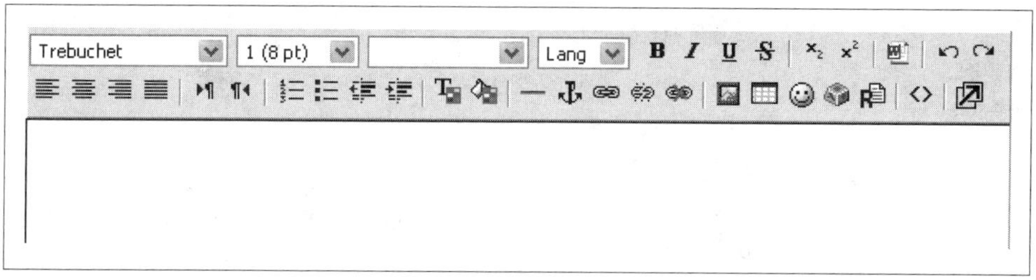

Figure 3-2. HTML editor

1. Click the "Turn editing on" button.
2. From the "Add a resource" menu select "Compose a web page."
3. Enter a name for the web page and write a summary.
4. Create your web page using the HTML editor.
5. Scroll down to the bottom of the page and click the "Save changes" button.

Using the HTML editor

 The HTML editor doesn't work in all browsers.

The HTML editor provides the tools displayed in Table 3-1.

Table 3-1. HTML editor icons

Icon	Function
 Trebuchet	Font
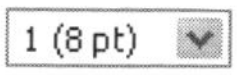 1 (8 pt)	Font size
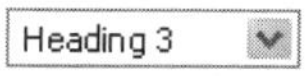 Heading 3	Style
 **B** *I* U S	Bold, italic, underline, strikethrough
 x₂ x²	Subscript or superscript
	Clean Word HTML
	Undo or redo your last action
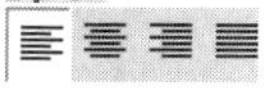	Left, center, right, or full justify
	Direction from left to right or from right to left
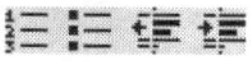	Numbered or bullet list, decrease or increase indent
	Change font or background color
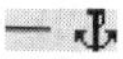	Horizontal rule, create anchor
	Insert web link, remove link, prevent automatic linking
	Insert image, table, or smiley

Icon	Function
🎲 📄	Insert special character, search and replace
<> | 🖾	Toggle text and WYSIWYG mode, enlarge editor

 The Clean Word HTML tool is useful when copying and pasting content from a Word document, as it removes unnecessary HTML tags.

Linking to a File or Web Site

This section covers the following MTC skills: 4.4 Link to a file or web site

You don't have to create all of your content directly in Moodle. You can also upload and store any digital content that you have created in other applications. Documents you create in a word processor or presentation package can be shared with students in your course. You can also easily add links to other web sites to give your students access to important web resources.

Uploading files

Although it's easy to generate content directly in Moodle, you can also upload any type of electronic file you like. All you need to do is make sure your students can access it with the appropriate software on their computers.

Once you've added a file to your files area, you can add it as a resource for your students in two ways—by creating a link to a file, or by creating a link to a directory within the files area.

To add a link to a file:

1. Click the "Turn editing on" button.

2. From the "Add a resource" menu select "Link to a file or web site."

3. On the Edit page (see Figure 3-3), enter a name for the resource and write a summary.

4. Click the "Choose or upload a file" button. A new window will pop up with the files area directory structure.

5. Find the file you want to add in the files area. Alternatively, you can upload a new file here.

6. On the right of each file listed, you will see a Choose link in bold (see Figure 3-4). Click the link opposite the file you want to add. The files window will close and the location of the file will be entered automatically into the page.

7. Scroll down to the bottom of the page and click the "Save changes" button. The name of the resource will now be a link in the course section.

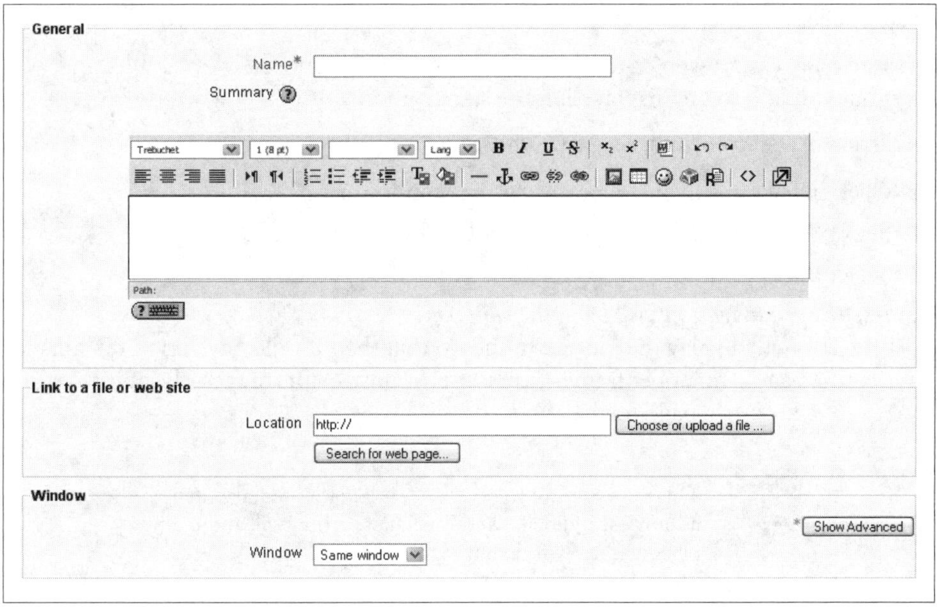

Figure 3-3. Link to a file or web site

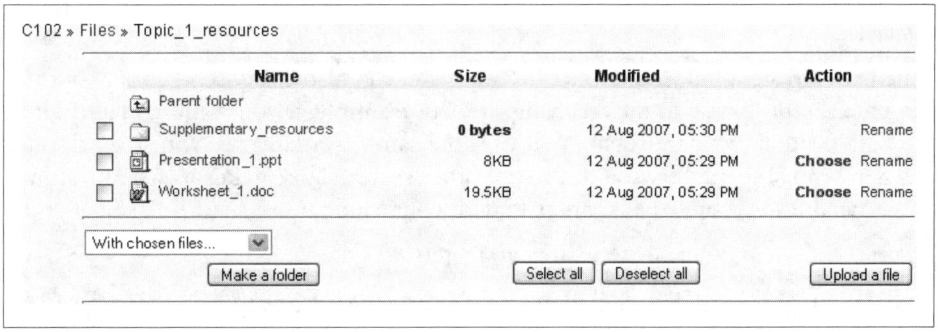

Figure 3-4. Choose a file

Creating links to other web sites

To add a link to another web site:

1. Click the "Turn editing on" button.
2. From the "Add a resource" menu select "Link to a file or web site."
3. Enter a name for the link and write a summary (see Figure 3-3).
4. In the location field, enter the address of the page you want to link to. If you need to look for the address, click the "Search for web page" button, and Moodle will open a new window containing Google.
5. Scroll down to the bottom of the page and click the "Save changes" button.

Window options

As for text pages and web pages that you create, you can choose whether files and web sites that you link to are displayed in the same window or in a new window.

To display a resource in the same window:

1. Click the Show Advanced button in the Window area.
2. Select "Same window" from the Window drop-down menu.
3. Select the option:

    Keep page navigation visible on the same page
    This will display the file in a frame, so that the Moodle navigation remains on the page in an upper frame. Otherwise, your students may not be able to return to the course page easily.

 This option is not normally necessary for media content such as movies, audio files and Flash files, as they will automatically be embedded within a navigable page.

The options for displaying a resource in a new window are the same as for text pages and web pages.

Parameters

When you create a link to another web site, you can also easily send data about the student and the course to the receiving site. For example, if you want to create a link to another site in your university that uses the same usernames as your Moodle site, you can send students' usernames to the other server. This makes it easier to utilize other dynamic web sites that share data with your Moodle site.

To send data to another server using parameters:

1. Click the "Show Advanced" button in the parameters area.
2. Select the data you want to send from the drop-down list shown in Figure 3-5.
3. The variable name is the name of the variable that the receiving server is expecting. For example, if you're sending the student's username and the server wants a variable called userID, select username in the parameter list and put userID in the "Variable name" field.

Displaying a Directory

This section covers the following MTC skills: 4.5 Displaying directories

The other option for displaying files is to create a link to a directory within the files area. To display a directory:

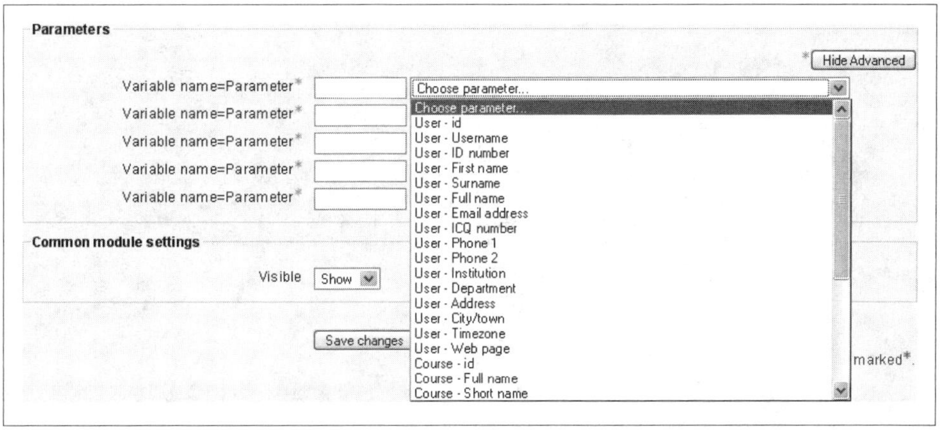

Figure 3-5. Parameter list

1. In editing mode, select "Display a directory" from the "Add a resource" menu in the course section where you want to add the directory.

2. On the Edit page (see Figure 3-6), enter a name for the resource and write a summary.

3. Select the folder you want the students to be able to browse from the "Display a directory" drop-down. If you leave the default—Main files directory—selected, students will be able to browse the entire course files area.

4. Click the "Save changes" button.

5. When a student clicks on the resulting directory link, she will see a list of all the files in that folder. If the folder contains subfolders, she will also be able to browse these.

Adding an IMS Content Package

IMS Content Packages are resources packaged to an agreed specification, making it possible for a package to be reused in different systems without needing to convert it to a different format. Content-authoring software often provides the option of packaging as an IMS Content Package. You may have IMS Content Packages from a different CMS system or have purchased some IMS Content Packages as course content.

To add an IMS Content Package:

1. In editing mode, select "Add an IMS Content Package" from the "Add a resource" menu in the course section where you want to add the package.

2. On the Edit page (see Figure 3-7), enter a name for the resource and write a summary.

3. Click the "Choose or upload a file" button. A new window will pop up with the files area directory structure.

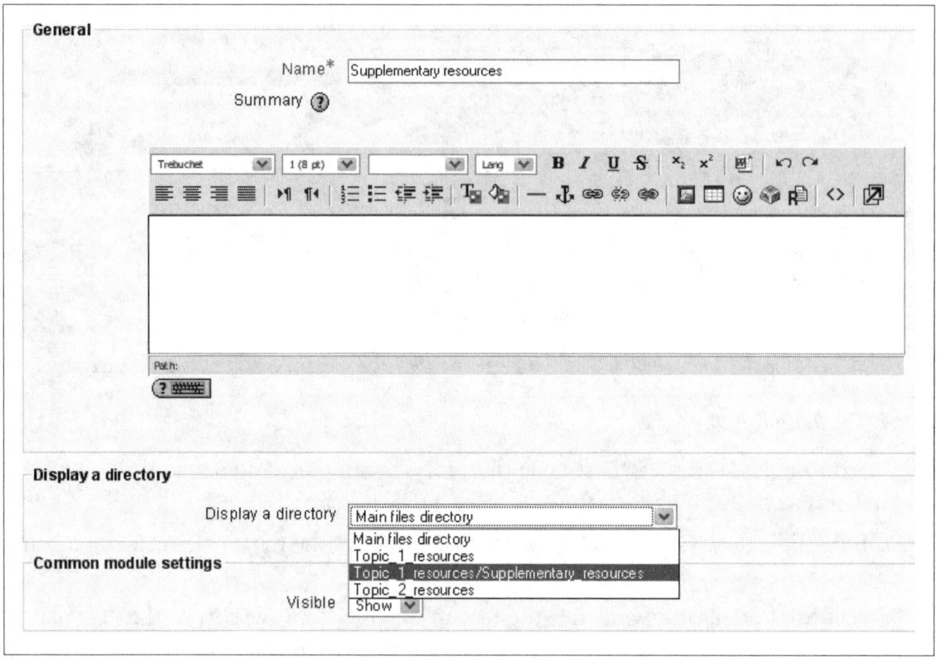

Figure 3-6. Display a directory

4. Upload the zipped IMS Content Package and click the Choose link opposite to it.

5. Select appropriate display parameters, depending upon the package navigation structure. If you're not sure, leave the parameters as default.

6. Click the "Save changes" button.

7. Click the Deploy button. (This unzips the package and loads it for viewing.)

8. The name of the IMS Content Package will now be a link in the course section.

Adding Media Content

This section covers the following MTC skills: 6.4.1 Embedding .swf files; 6.7.1 Linking to external resources on CD

Adding media content can help you communicate some ideas and processes more easily than text alone. Imagine trying to teach a language if the students aren't able to hear it spoken. Or how much easier it would be to learn how volcanoes work if you could see a video or an animation. Fortunately, Moodle makes it easy to add rich media content to your course. The Moodle media filters automatically recognize your media type and put the right sort of link into your web page so students can access it easily.

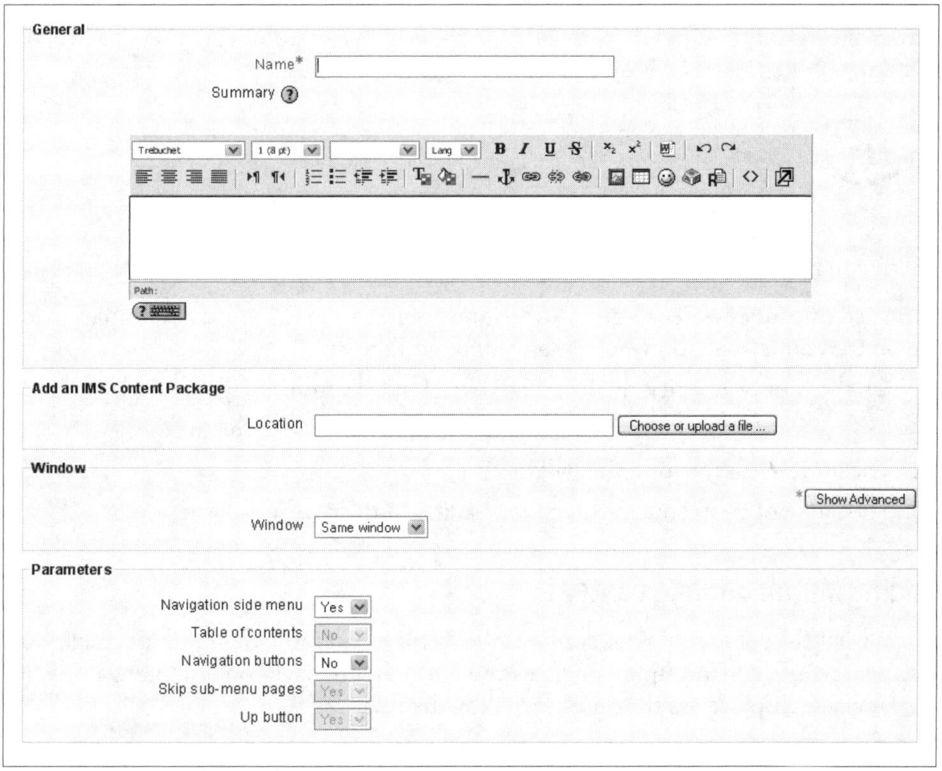

General

Name*

Summary

Add an IMS Content Package

Location [   ] [Choose or upload a file ...]

Window

* [Show Advanced]

Window [Same window ▼]

Parameters

Navigation side menu [Yes ▼]
Table of contents [No ▼]
Navigation buttons [No ▼]
Skip sub-menu pages [Yes ▼]
Up button [Yes ▼]

Figure 3-7. Add an IMS Content Package

If these instructions don't work, contact your system administrator and ask if the multimedia plug-ins are enabled in the filters settings.

Media content may be added using the same steps as for the earlier section "Uploading files":

1. In editing mode, select "Link to a file or web site" from the "Add a resource" menu in the course section where you want to add the link to the media file.

2. Enter a name for the resource and write a summary.

3. Click the "Choose or upload a file" button. A new window will pop up with the files area directory structure.

4. Either upload the media file or, if you uploaded it previously, find the file you want to add in the files area.

5. Click the Choose link opposite the media file. The files window will close and the location of the file will be entered automatically into the page.

6. The name of the resource will now be an active link in the content block.

MP3 files are automatically embedded in a streaming player made with Flash.

If your media content files are very large, an alternative to uploading them to Moodle is linking to them on CD or on a particular network drive.

 If these instructions don't work, contact your system administrator and ask if local files are allowed in the Resource module. Using this feature may require changes to your browser's security settings.

Linking to resources on CD is very similar to linking to a file:

1. In editing mode, select "Link to a file or web site" from the "Add a resource" menu in the content section where you want to add the link.
2. On the Edit page, click the "Choose a local file" button.
3. Browse for the local file, then click the "Choose this file path" button.
4. The location of the local file will be entered.
5. The name of the resource will now be a link in the course section.

Adding Multilanguage Content

If you want the content of your course to be displayed in more than one language, you can create content in multiple languages and the multilanguage content filter will ensure the language displayed is the one selected by the user.

 Your system administrator needs to enable the multilanguage content filter for these instructions to work.

To add multilanguage content:

1. Create your content in multiple languages.
2. Click [<>] in the HTML editor to change to code-editing mode.
3. Enclose each language block in the following tags, where xx and yy are two-letter language codes (as shown in the languages drop-down menu on the front page of your Moodle site):

```
<span lang="xx" class="multilang">your content in lang xx here</span>

<span lang="yy" class="multilang">your content in lang yy here</span>
```

Managing and Updating Your Content

Uploading content is only half the battle of content management in Moodle. You'll need to ensure that your uploaded content is current, and you'll occasionally want to

Figure 3-8. Course Administration block

replace or delete files. Fortunately, Moodle has some useful features to help you manage your content once it's on the server.

File Area Tools

This section covers the following MTC skills: 8.4 Files

Once you've uploaded your files, they are stored in the files area. When you create a link to a file, you store the file in the files area and create a link for your students to access it.

To access the files area, click the Files link in the course Administration block, as shown in Figure 3-8.

The files area, as shown in Figure 3-9, has a checkbox beside each uploaded file and folder. You can select one or more files and then move or archive them using the tools in the "With chosen files" drop-down menu on the lower-left side of the file list. If you click on the menu, you'll see three things you can do with your chosen files:

Move to another folder
    To move uploaded content to another folder in the files area:

1. Select the file(s) you want to move.
2. Select "Move to another folder."
3. Navigate to the folder where you want to move the selected files.
4. You'll see a new button at the bottom of the screen that says "Move files to here." Click the button, and the files will move to the new location.

Delete completely
    This option removes all trace of the file from your Moodle site.

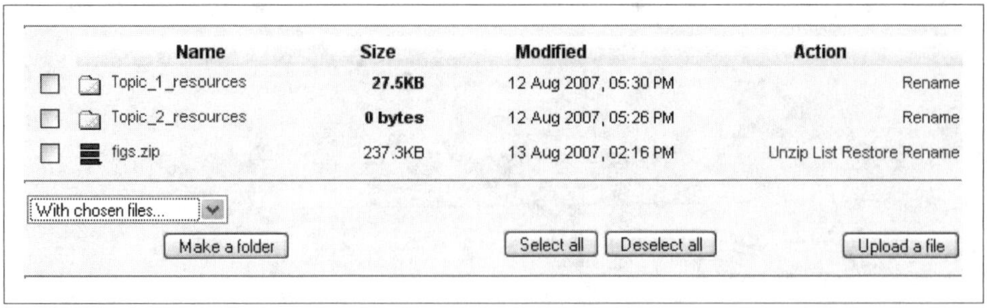

Name	Size	Modified	Action
☐ 🗀 Topic_1_resources	**27.5KB**	12 Aug 2007, 05:30 PM	Rename
☐ 🗀 Topic_2_resources	**0 bytes**	12 Aug 2007, 05:26 PM	Rename
☐ ▤ figs.zip	237.3KB	13 Aug 2007, 02:16 PM	Unzip List Restore Rename

With chosen files... ⌄

[Make a folder] [Select all] [Deselect all] [Upload a file]

Figure 3-9. Files area

Create ZIP archive

A ZIP archive is a compressed file that holds the files you've selected. It's an easy way to create an archive of older files or an easy-to-download collection of documents, such as all of the images for a lecture. Once the archive has been created and moved to the target computer, you'll need to unzip it to access the content inside. If you want students to download the archive, they will need an unzipping utility such as WinZip, MacZip, or StuffIt Expander to unpack the archive. Modern versions of Windows and Macintosh have built-in ZIP utilities. Moodle has a built-in ZIP utility as well that will allow you to unzip the archive directly into your files area. As Figure 3-9 shows, there are a few new options that come with a ZIP archive. These include:

Unzip

Unpacks your archive into your files area.

List

Clicking this displays a list of files stored in the archive. You cannot access files through this list.

Restore

If you've backed up your Moodle class and uploaded the ZIP archive of the backup, you can restore your content using this link. We'll cover this in more detail in Chapter 4.

Tracking Versions

One of the biggest challenges you will face in keeping your content organized is dealing with versioning. As the semester progresses, you may have multiple versions of your syllabus that reflect changes to the calendar. Or you may have multiple versions of a presentation that has evolved over the years. There are a couple of strategies you can use to track versions and ensure that your students are accessing the correct version.

The easiest way is to develop a naming scheme for your files. While many people will attach a version number, we recommend using a *date stamp*. A date stamp lets people know just how recent the version is, and you don't have to track the current version number. To add a date stamp, simply add the date on which you saved the version to the end of the filename. For example, the first version of a syllabus for your fall course may be called *Syllabus_8_30.rtf*. Later in the semester, you may post a revised version named *Syllabus_9_21.rtf*. Date versioning helps you keep track of the version on the server and the latest version on your computer.

There are also a number of tools in Moodle to help you deal with versioning. We recommend creating a folder in your course to archive older versions of documents. To create an archive folder:

1. Click on the Files link.
2. Click the "Make a folder" button.
3. Name the folder "Course archives" and click the "Save changes" button.

Later, you can use the file tools to move old versions of a file into the archives area, which enables you to keep a record of older versions while keeping only the latest version in the active area.

Effective Content Practices

There are a few effective practices that can make life easier for you and your students. First, there are file format tricks to ensure your students can download and use your content. Second, make sure the bit size of your files is as small as it can be, so your students won't grow old waiting to download tomorrow's lecture notes. Third, there are creative ways to use static content in your courses to help you and your students succeed.

File Formats

This section covers the following MTC skills: 6.2 Audio and video; 6.3 Documents and resources; 6.6 Other multimedia formats

Every file you create and save on your computer has a specific file format. For example, Word files are saved in Word format, and can be opened only in a compatible version of Word. However, this can cause problems if your students don't have the same version of Word you do. A solution is to continue to create your documents in Word but save them as Rich Text Format, or RTF, a format that a wide variety of word-processing programs can open. In most versions of Word, you can save a file as RTF by following these steps:

1. Select "Save As" from the file menu.
2. Choose RTF from the file type drop-down.
3. Save the RTF copy of your document.

There are a number of file formats for displaying text and images that almost everyone can open, regardless of their computing platform, and you should strive to use these whenever possible. These formats include RTF, Hypertext Markup Language (HTML), Portable Display Format (PDF), and picture formats, including PICT, TIFF, JPEG, GIF, and PNG.

Table 3-2 describes some common file formats.

Table 3-2. File types

File type	Description	Software needed to use the file
RTF	A word-processor format that is readable by a wide range of applications. You can save Word and PowerPoint documents as RTF.	Most modern word processors will read RTF, including OpenOffice.org Writer.
HTML	The language of the Web. Every web page displayed in a browser is created in HTML. Moodle has a built-in HTML editor you can use to create documents directly in Moodle.	Any web browser. Some word processors will also read HTML documents.
PDF	PDF is a file format created by Adobe Systems for document exchange. PDF files may be created with Acrobat (not the reader but the professional package) or the OpenOffice.org suite.	Acrobat Reader is a free download from Adobe.
PowerPoint (ppt)	As the most widely used presentation-creation software, PowerPoint files are natural candidates for upload. The presentations are easy to share, but be careful about file size and access.	PowerPoint, PowerPoint viewer, or OpenOffice.org Impress.
Pictures (PICT, TIFF, JPEG, GIF, PNG)	There are a lot of graphic file formats. Generally, only GIF, JPEG, and PNG are viewable directly in a browser.	GIF, JPEG, and PNG require a browser. Other formats require appropriate external viewers.
Audio files (WAV, MP3, RAM, MOV)	Audio files can be large, depending on your bit rate and compression format. Be sure the file size is smaller than the maximum file upload size for Moodle. Check with your system administrator.	Your students will need media player software. Many students will be able to play audio in MP3 format.
Video files (MOV, WMV, RV)	Your Moodle server may not accept a large video file. Before you attempt to upload a large video file, ask your system administrator about file size limits. Your students will need to download the entire video, which may be a problem with a slow dial-up connection.	To view a video, your students will need a media player that can play the appropriate format. Know whether your movies can play in Quicktime, Windows Media Player, or RealPlayer.

Reducing File Sizes

As important as creating files your students can open is making sure those files are a manageable size. Graphics are usually the biggest offenders, and they crop up in some unlikely places. There are three strategies that will give you the best results for the effort.

Strategy 1: Save your PowerPoint presentations as PDF

Big PowerPoint files are often the worst file-size offenders. It's too easy to add cool transitions, clip art, and images that expand a simple hour-long presentation into a multimegabyte behemoth that takes an hour to download. Not a good use of time for something that students will simply print out and bring to class.

We recommend exporting your presentation as PDF using OpenOffice.org. Students will get the benefits of the outline of the lecture, including graphics, and be able to print copies of the presentation slides, and the file will be quick and easy to download.

Strategy 2: Scan articles as text, not images

There are many good articles that just aren't available in electronic format. If you want to avoid printing an entire reader, scanning articles is an easy way to give your students access to important resources. Many libraries now have electronic reserve services that will scan them for you.

Scanning articles can result in very large files because most scanner software, by default, scans everything as a graphic. So when you scan a page, you're really creating a picture of the page that is much larger than a text version. The computer has to store information about every dot on the page, not just information about the characters and their placement.

The solution is to use a software tool called Optical Character Recognition, or OCR. This great tool recognizes the shape of the letters and gives you a text version of the article. You can then manipulate the text version in the same way you'd edit any other text document. It has the added advantage of being accessible to screen readers for students with visual disabilities.

OCR software is probably available somewhere on your campus. OmniPage Pro is currently the most popular OCR package. It's come a long way in the last few years and is now very powerful. If you have a relatively clean photocopy of the articles you want to share, scanning them will be a very fast process.

Strategy 3: Reduce your image size and use compression

Finally, if you have digital images, it's very important to optimize their size and resolution for sharing over the Web. Modern digital cameras and scanners can produce amazing, crystal-clear images, but at a price of very large file sizes. A full-resolution photograph in a modern camera can be 4 megabytes, which will take more than 5 minutes to download on a 56k modem.

Most cameras and scanners come with free utilities that enable you to manipulate images. Other programs such as Photoshop are fully featured, professional packages with lots of tools. To reduce your file size, you only need some very simple tools, provided by most image-manipulation software.

The key to getting manageable images is to first reduce the size of the image. If your image will be primarily viewed on the screen, you can make it 72 dpi and it will still be viewable. If you plan to have your students print the image, then it will need to be higher resolution. Experiment with some different sizes and resolutions to get a result you're happy with.

When your image is the right size, save it at the minimum quality as a web-compatible format such as JPG or GIF. These formats make your file size even smaller by eliminating unnecessary and redundant data.

By reducing the size of your files, you'll make life easier for yourself and your students. But the smallest, most portable files in the world don't mean much if your students can't use them successfully in your class. Next, we'll discuss some interesting ways you can use content to make your Moodle class a valuable resource for your students.

Creative Content

Moodle allows you to upload just about any file that resides on your computer. However, the key to a successful content strategy is knowing what content helps your students be successful and what is unnecessary or confusing. Below are two best practices for adding content to your course. These practices work well in a range of course designs, but there are others that might work just as well for your particular course.

Uploading lecture notes

One of the easiest ways to use Moodle to increase student learning is to upload your lecture notes before the lecture. Providing access to your lecture outlines *before* a class meeting gives your students a tool to help prepare for class and structure their class notes. If students know which topics you consider important enough to include in your lecture, they are more likely to pay attention to those areas in any assigned readings. During class, they can use the lecture notes as a basic outline and concentrate on elaborating the main ideas with examples. Lecture notes are also a useful tool for students whose first language is different from that of the speaker. If they get lost during a lecture, they can refer to the notes to get back on track.

If you use PowerPoint in your lectures, a simple way to create and upload lecture notes is to save your slides as an RTF file. The RTF file eliminates graphics and other extras and provides the students with a plain-text outline. It will be easy to download and print for class.

External web sites

Effectively using the Web means you don't have to create or photocopy everything you want to use in your class. There is a lot of quality content available on the Web, if you know where to look and how to evaluate it. A full discussion about vetting online resources is beyond the scope of this book, but your institution's librarian can recommend some sources to get you started.

Most newspapers and news magazines have online versions you can bring into your class for discussions of current events. Universities, schools, and nonprofit organizations publish huge amounts of content available for you to use free of charge. In addition, there is a growing open content movement, which publishes content available for anyone to use.

Most open content is published under a Creative Commons license, which allows users to choose the type of public license they want to use (*http://creativecommons.org*). Authors can use the CC licenses to license their work for use through any combination of attribution (their name stays attached), with a share-alike license (you can share any derivative works as long as you use the same license), or noncommercial use (you can't use the materials for commercial purposes). The Creative Commons site also has a search engine for content that has been licensed using a CC license.

This book has been licensed for use under the Creative Commons attribution and share-alike license. You are free to make and distribute copies or works based on this book as long as you attribute the content to us, and allow other people to do the same with your works.

In addition to the general content released by people under the Creative Commons licenses, some universities have begun publishing course materials for use by the general public. These collections are known as OpenCourseWare (OCW) repositories. MIT has the most well-known collection, but other universities are following suit. Some of the bigger collections are:

MIT (http://ocw.mit.edu)
MIT offers a comprehensive collection of courses from accounting to zoology. Some of their courses have video lectures available in addition to the syllabus, lecture notes, and problem sets.

Utah State University (http://ocw.usu.edu)
Utah State offers a good collection of basic courses with an emphasis on biological and irrigation engineering and instructional technology.

Johns Hopkins Bloomberg School of Public Health (http://ocw.jhsph.edu)
This is a collection of public health courses from one of the world's leading medical schools.

UK Open University (http://openlearn.open.ac.uk)
The OU offers full-text versions of their content, instead of just course outlines and notes.

In addition to the institutional collections, there are a growing number of user-created content sites available on the Web. These sites allow anyone to create, change, remix, and catalog content. While the quality of the content can vary wildly, there is a large and growing body of excellent content available for you to use.

Some of these sites are:

Wikipedia (http://www.wikipedia.org)
> An online encyclopedia developed by thousands of volunteers. Anyone can create and edit documents.

Wikibooks (http://en.wikibooks.org)
> A sister project of Wikipedia. It aims to create open textbooks that are freely available to the whole world.

This list is by no means exhaustive. Simply using Google as a tool in your class vastly expands the amount and variety of content available to your students.

Summary

Ultimately, the content you develop and share in your Moodle course is up to you. Static Moodle content provides resources for students as they engage in the learning process. In this chapter, we've looked at how to upload and create content for your Moodle course. In the following chapters, we'll discuss some of the dynamic activities you can add to your class to make it truly compelling.

CHAPTER 4

Managing Your Class

Now that we have covered the basics of setting up a course and adding content, we need to take a look at some of Moodle's underlying capabilities. At first glance, this may seem like administrivia, but understanding roles and groups is one of the keys to unlocking Moodle's full potential as a learning environment. A person's role in a course determines what he can do—in other words, what capabilities he has. It's a very powerful system, but it does have a bit of underlying complexity. You can use groups to create student workgroups, recitation sections, or any other arbitrary grouping you need to realize your learning design.

We will start by discussing roles, since anyone who wants to do something in your course needs to be assigned a role.

Understanding and Using Roles

This section covers the following MTC skills: 7.1 Enrolling participants; 7.5 Roles

The new roles and permissions system in Moodle provides you with a huge amount of flexibility for managing how students and other people interact with your course. In older versions of Moodle (prior to 1.7), there were only six roles possible: guest, student, non-editing teacher, editing teacher, course creator, and administrator. Whilst the new system supports these roles out of the box, it also allows you to create and customize roles, and to change what a given role can do in each activity. For example, you can now create permissions in individual forums, which allows you to let students act as moderators in one forum while you retain the moderator role in all of the other forums in your course.

If it seems a bit daunting, don't worry. Using roles and permissions is something you can take slowly. You can start the usual way, assigning people as students, teachers, and other roles specified by your institution. Later, when your course design grows more elaborate, you can begin to experiment with overrides and assigning specific roles in specific contexts.

We'll start simply, by assigning users to predefined roles in your course. Then we'll take a look at the roles and capabilities system and later discuss how to use the advanced features.

Assigning Roles in Your Course

Most of the time, students will enroll themselves or be added automatically by your university's enrollment system, so there shouldn't be much need for you to manually enroll students. However, if you need to add a teaching assistant, an outside guest, or a student who is having a problem with financial aid, you must manually enroll them, i.e., assign them a role in your Moodle course.

 By default, teachers are only allowed to assign the roles of non-editing teacher, student, and guest. If you want to assign the role of teacher, you will need to ask your system administrator for this to be allowed.

To assign a user the role of student:

1. Click "Assign roles" in the Administration block.
2. Choose the type of role you wish to assign, e.g., student
3. On the "Assign roles" page, there are two columns, as shown in Figure 4-1. The left column lists users who currently have that role, and the right column lists users who don't.

 Users must have an account on your Moodle site before you can assign them a role in your course. If they don't appear in either the existing or potential users list, they will need to create an account before they can be assigned a role.

Between the two columns is a hidden assignment checkbox next to an eye icon, for hiding which role a user is assigned to so that the user doesn't appear in the list of course participants. Click the checkbox before assigning a role if required.

 Role assignments are not hidden from admins or teachers. They can always see who is assigned a role in a course.

 Hidden assignments are also useful if you don't want everyone with teacher rights to be listed in the course description on the front page of your Moodle site.

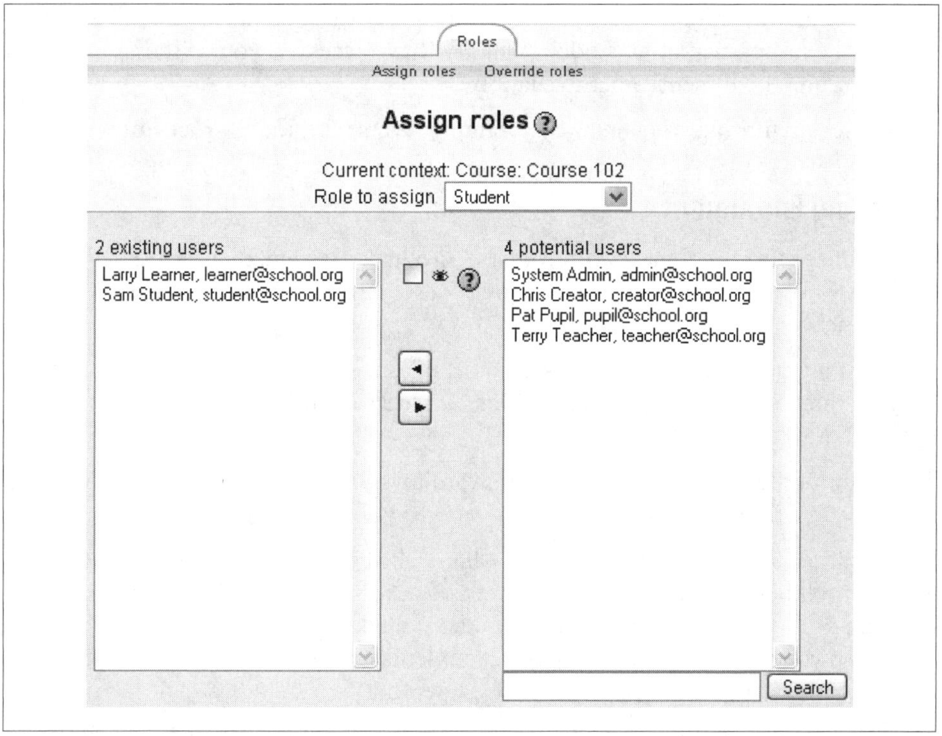

Figure 4-1. Assigning a role

4. Find the student you want to add to your course in the righthand column. You can limit the list by searching for the student's name or email in the Search box below the righthand column.

5. Select the student's name from the list and use the left-facing arrow button to add the student to the list in the lefthand column.

> You can add multiple students by holding down the Shift key to select a number of students in a row. If you want to select multiple students who aren't listed next to each other, hold down the Ctrl key (or Apple key on a Mac) and click each name you want to add.

Students will have access to your course as soon as you assign them a role. They won't need to have an enrollment key or to confirm the enrollment.

Removing Students

If a student drops your class, you'll want to remove the student from your Moodle course as well. Leaving a student enrolled in your Moodle course when she is not on the official roster makes grading and class management much more difficult. When you record grades or look for student assignments, extra students on the roll gets confusing. The nonparticipating student will also have access to your discussion boards and other potentially sensitive information.

Fortunately, removing students is easy. Simply reverse the above procedure.

Managing Enrollment

If your university doesn't have an automatic enrollment system, then ensuring that only students who are officially enrolled in your course have access to your Moodle course can be tricky.

Jason: At my university, students used to be able to drop and add courses at will for the first three weeks of the semester. Many instructors found it difficult to track the constant movement in the roster.

To minimize the amount of work you need to invest in this administrative detail, we recommend a three-pronged strategy.

First, use the course enrollment settings to limit who can enroll in the course and when. Set an enrollment period for the length of your drop/add time. Be sure to set an enrollment key as well. Only students who know the key will be able to enroll in your course, so you won't need to worry about students enrolling without permission. For more information on these settings, see Chapter 2.

Second, closely monitor your official course roster during the drop/add period. Be consistent about dropping and adding students on a regular basis so you don't have a big mess at the end of registration.

Third, encourage students who are enrolled to create an account and join your Moodle course as quickly as possible. Many instructors make logging in and joining their Moodle course a small, mandatory assignment. This helps students by forcing them to access your online resources early in the semester, and it makes enrollment management easier for you, since you won't have to add as many students manually.

Capabilities and Permissions

The new roles system introduces some new terminology that is important to understand before you dive in.

This may be confusing at first, but it's worth taking some time to understand the power of the new system.

Jason: I was part of the design team for this system and even I had to look up a few details!

There are four primary concepts to understand:

Role

A role is an identifier of the user's status in some context (e.g., teacher, student, forum moderator).

Capability

A capability is a description of a particular Moodle feature (e.g., moodle/blog:create). Capabilities are associated with roles. There are over 150 capabilities within Moodle.

Permission

A permission is a value that is assigned to a capability for a particular role.

Context

A context is the scope within which a role assignment is valid. Contexts are organized in a hierarchy, where lower (more specific) contexts inherit capabilities from higher (less specific) contexts. The contexts in Moodle in order of inheritance are:

System

All contexts in the site, including site settings and user administration

Site

The site front page course and its activities

Course category

All courses in a category

Course

A single Moodle course

Module

A module instance within a course (a specific forum, quiz, wiki, etc.)

Block

A specific block instance within a course (at the time of this writing this feature is not fully implemented)

User

A user's profile or personal activities

Roles are made up of a matrix of capabilities and permissions that determine what a user can do within a given context. For example, a user may have course creator privileges at the site level but be unable to post to a particular forum in a certain course.

The permissions determine whether someone can use a capability. Permissions may be set to one of four values:

Inherit

The default setting. If a capability is set to inherit, the user's permissions remain the same as they are in a less specific context, or another role where the capability is defined. For example, if a student is allowed to attempt quiz questions at the course level, his role in a specific quiz will inherit this setting.

Allow

> This enables a user to use a capability in a given context. This permission applies for the context that the role gets assigned plus all lower contexts. For example, if a user is assigned the role of student in a course, she will be able to start new discussions in all forums in that course (unless a forum contains an override with a prevent or prohibit value for the capability).

Prevent

> Prevent disables a capability for a user in a given context but does not disallow it in a more specific context. You can prevent students from adding attachments to forum posts in your course, but allow them to do so in one particular forum.

Prohibit

> Prohibit is rarely needed, but occasionally you might want to completely deny permissions to a role in a way that *cannot* be overridden in any lower context.

Keep in mind that permissions are set within a role, and then people are assigned to roles in a given context. A person can be assigned to more than one role, depending on the context, or even multiple roles within the same context.

Role Overrides

The capabilities within a given role can also be overridden within a specific context. Let's say you want to create a forum in which students can rate each other's forum posts. (By default, only teachers can rate forum posts.)

The way to achieve this is through a role override. As long as the capabilities you want to allow your students to have in your course (or within a module in your course) aren't prohibited at a higher level, you can override the permissions. Within your course, for example, you can override roles at the course level or in a particular activity. If you want to change what students can do anywhere in your course, override the role at the course level. If you want to create a different set of permissions for a given activity, override the role in the activity itself.

 Overriding roles is itself a permission. By default, teachers are unable to override roles so this ability must first be granted by your system administrator for the course or site as appropriate. They must also set which roles can be overridden by the teacher role. If you don't see the "Override roles" link in the Roles tab, ask your system administrator.

The override interface will only show you the capabilities for the context you are overriding. So if you want to allow students to rate forum posts, you can override the student role in a particular forum. You will only see the forum capabilities in the interface, as shown in Figure 4-2.

To set a role override for an activity:

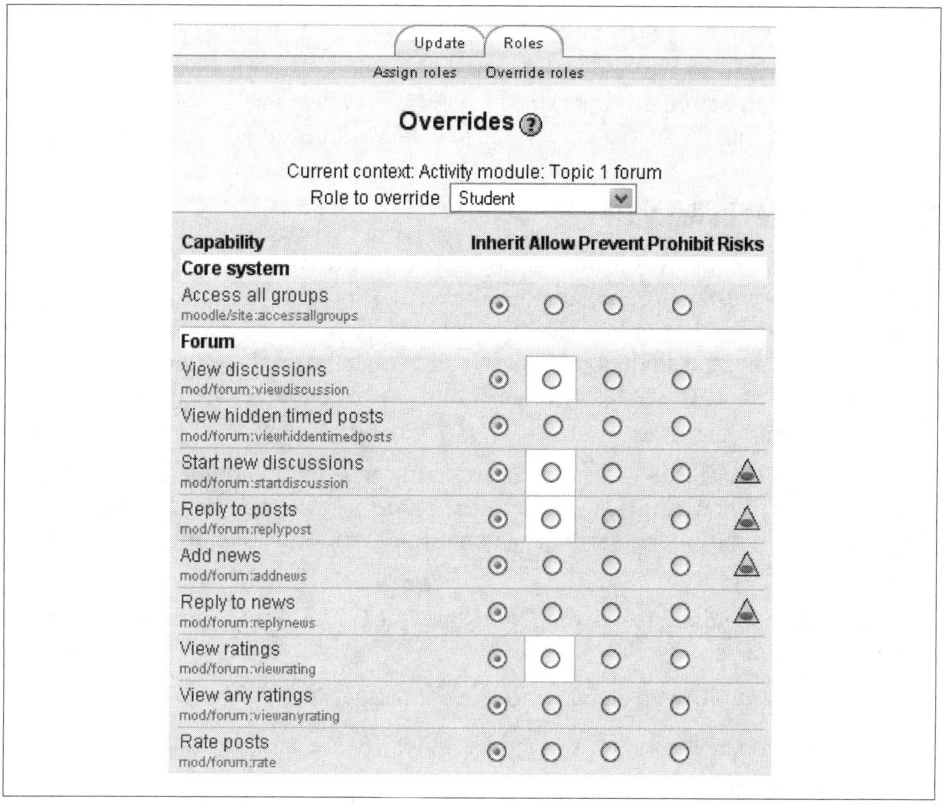

Figure 4-2. A role override

1. Click the Update button for the activity for which you want to create the override.
2. Click the Roles tab and then click the "Override roles" link just below the tabs.
3. Choose the role you want to override, e.g., student.
4. Modify the permissions for the override on this activity. (The permissions the role currently has are highlighted in white.)

> Be sure to read the security risks (indicated by the yellow triangle on the right side of the permissions list) for each capability. Some capabilities can present severe risks to student data if you are not careful.

5. Click the "Save changes" button. Anyone with the role you have just overridden will now have those capabilities in this activity when they next log in to Moodle.

To set a role override at course level:

1. Click "Assign roles" in the Administration block.
2. Click the "Override roles" link.

The remaining steps are the same as for setting a role override for an activity.

Overrides allow you to create a lot of variation in the way students interact with an activity. However, before digging into the overrides system itself, be sure you have a clear understanding of what you are trying to achieve educationally with the override.

Assigning Roles in Activities

In addition to assigning roles in your course, you can also assign roles in activities. Let's say you want to create a forum and allow particular students to moderate the discussions. To moderate, they will need to be able to delete posts, edit posts, and move threads. But the normal student role doesn't allow them to do these things, nor do you want them to be able to moderate other forums in your course, or all students to be able to moderate.

The way to achieve this is by assigning a role in the activity module context. If you assign the role of non-editing teacher to the students you want to moderate forum discussions, then the students will have non-editing teacher capabilities in that forum only.

The method of assigning a role in the activity module context is very similar to assigning a role in your course.

To assign a user a role in an activity module context:

1. Click the Update button for the activity in which you want to assign a role.
2. Click the Roles tab.
3. Choose the role you want to assign, e.g., non-editing teacher.
4. On the "Assign roles" page, find the user you want to assign the role to in the righthand column.
5. Select the user's name from the list and use the left-facing arrow button to add the user to the list in the lefthand column. The user will now have the role you have just assigned in the activity when he next logs in to Moodle.

 Depending on the capabilities you want to allow, there may not be a suitable role you can assign. You may need to contact your system administrator and ask for a new role to be created.

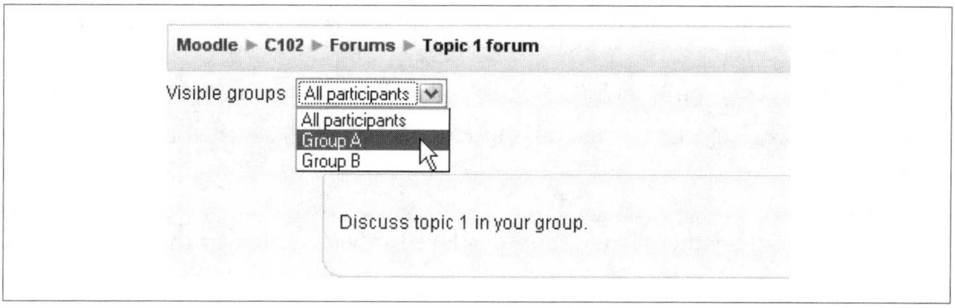

Figure 4-3. Visible groups in a forum

Student Groups

This section covers the following MTC skills: 8.1 Using and managing groups

Moodle has an unusual but effective way of managing small student workgroups within your course. You can define groups at the course level, then set each activity to a group mode or leave it available to everyone. The group mode you choose may also determine the behavior of the module. Think of groups as a filter. If you are a member of a group within a course, and an activity is set to group mode, Moodle will filter out any work from anyone who is not part of your group. You are all looking at the same activity, but you can't interact with anyone who is not in your group.

There are three group mode options:

No groups
Everyone participates as part of the class. Groups are not used.

Separate groups
Each group can see only their own work. They can't see the work of other groups.

Visible groups
Each group does their own work, but they can see the work of the other groups as well, as shown in Figure 4-3.

Once the group mode is set for the course or activity, students will interact with your Moodle course as they normally would. The only difference will be the people they meet in certain activities, such as forums. For example, if you set the group mode of a forum to separate groups, Moodle will create a forum for each group. Each student will see the same link to the forum, but she will be able to access only the discussions for her particular group. You need to create the forum only once; Moodle takes care of creating the individual group forums.

To utilize the group mode, you first need to create the student groups:

1. Click Groups in the Administration block.
2. On the Groups page, there are two columns, as shown in Figure 4-4. The left column lists the groups you have created. Initially, this list is empty, as there are

no groups created by default. The right column lists the students assigned to the selected group.

3. To create a new group, click the "Create group" button at the bottom of the page.

4. On the "Create groups" page, as shown in Figure 4-5, set the options for your group:

Group name

This is the name of the group displayed in various places throughout your course.

Group description

Write a brief description of the group and its purpose. The description is displayed above the list of group members on the Participants page.

Enrollment key

Enrollment keys allow users to enroll themselves in a course. You can set an enrollment key in your course settings, as we covered in Chapter 2. If you set a group enrollment key too, then anyone who enrolls in the course using that key will also automatically be made a member of the group.

 You need to set an enrollment key in your course settings, as well as set a group enrollment key, otherwise students will not be prompted to enter a key when they attempt to enroll. Students only need to enter the group enrollment key and do not need to know the course settings enrollment key.

 Make sure that the first letter for each group enrollment key is the same as the course settings enrollment key. If a student makes a mistake typing in the enrollment key, he is provided with the first letter of the course settings enrollment key as a hint.

Hide picture

Hiding the picture for the group prevents the group picture from being displayed in various activities throughout your course.

New picture

You can upload a profile picture for the group or replace an old picture with a new one.

5. Click the "Create group" button.

6. The name of the group will now appear in the groups list. Select the group you just created.

7. On the "Add/remove users" page, there are two columns, as shown in Figure 4-6. The left column lists the existing members of the group, and the right column lists the potential members. To add a student to the group, select the

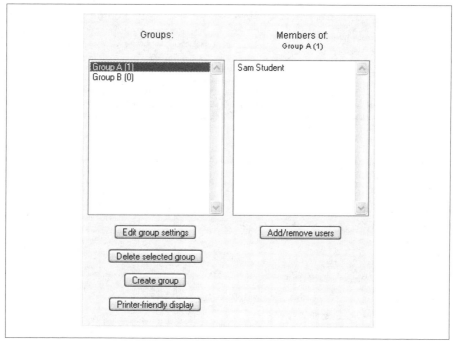

Figure 4-4. Groups

student's name from the potential members list and use the left-facing arrow button to add the student to the list in the lefthand column.

 As for assigning users the role of student in your course, you can add multiple students by holding down the Shift key to select a number of students in a row. If you want to select multiple students who aren't listed next to each other, hold down the Control key (or Apple key on a Mac) and click each name you want to add.

8. Repeat steps 3 to 7 for each group you need.

 It's possible to assign students to more than one group. If you do so, it can be confusing for both you and the students. You will need to carefully watch the number of students assigned to each group to make sure you haven't left someone out. Students will need to be careful about interacting with the right group in the right place. If you have set a module to separate groups mode, students will need to select between the groups where they are members.

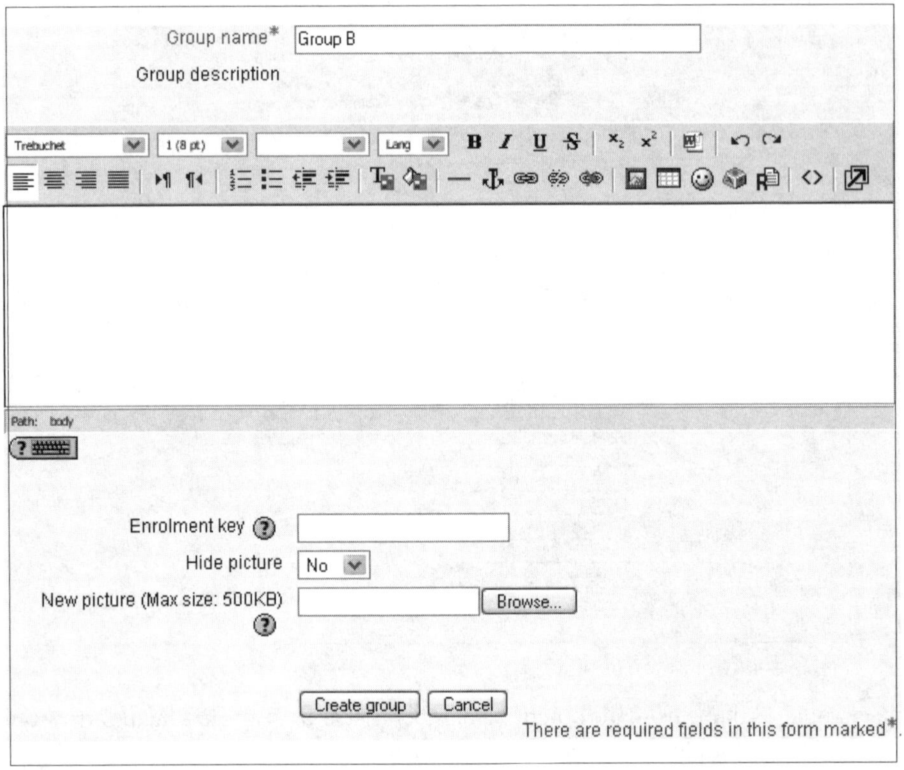

Figure 4-5. Creating a group

 If you have a lot of students to organize into groups, you might like to try the "batch upload of groups" facility. Click "Import" in the Administration block, then follow the instructions in the "upload groups" help file.

If you've not forced the group mode in your course settings, you can set it for each activity, either when adding the activity (in the common module settings), or by clicking the group mode icon opposite the activity name when editing is turned on for your course page. The group mode icon toggles between the three possible group modes shown in Table 4-1.

Table 4-1. Group mode icons

Icon	Group mode
♟	No groups mode
♟♟	Visible groups mode
♟♟	Separate groups mode

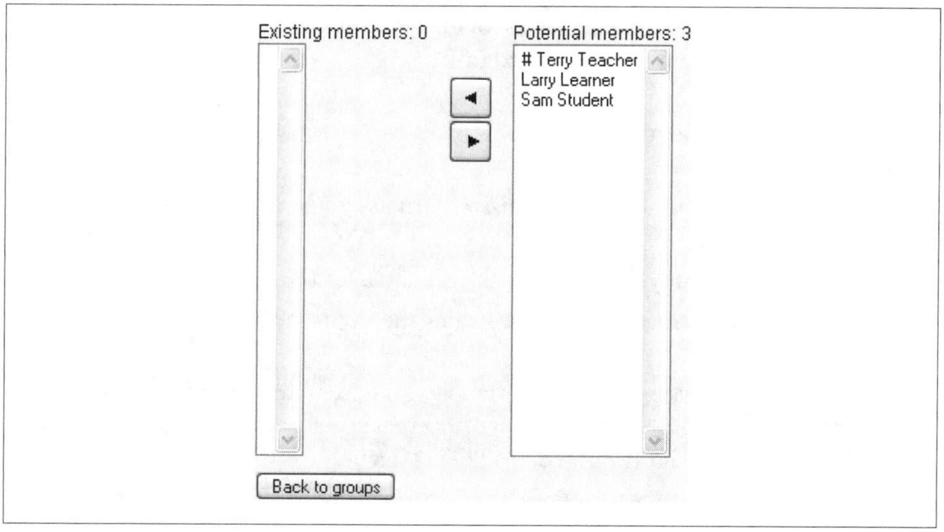

Existing members: 0   Potential members: 3

    # Terry Teacher
    Larry Learner
    Sam Student

◄
►

Back to groups

Figure 4-6. Adding/removing users

If you've forced the group mode in your course settings, then you will not be able to toggle between group modes on your course page.

Backups

This section covers the following MTC skills: 8.6.1 Backup

After spending a lot of time setting up your course and delivering it to your students, you'll want to make sure you don't lose your work. Fortunately, Moodle gives you a backup tool to create archives of your courses. Backups can also be used to copy course resources and activities from one course to another.

To make a backup:

1. Click Backup in the Administration block.
2. The "Course backup" page, as shown in Figure 4-7, lists all the modules and activities in your course.

   Choose which activities you want to include in the backup, and whether to include user data, by using the Include All/None links at the top of the page and/or by selecting the checkboxes next to each module or activity name. User data consists of all student files, submissions, forum postings, glossary entries, etc.
3. Select the following backup options:

   Meta course
   If your course is a meta course, this option will preserve the setting in the restored course.

Users
> This backs up the user accounts for everyone in the course. If you select None, then no user data will be backed up.

Logs
> This backs up all course activity logs.

User files
> This backs up all student submissions for assignments and other file uploads.

Course files
> This backs up any file stored in the files area for the course.

4. When you have selected your options, click the Continue button to start the backup process.

5. On the next page, you can preview the files and users that Moodle will include in the backup and, if you wish, change the suggested backup filename, which is *backup-COURSESHORTNAME-DATE-TIME.zip*.

 If you change your mind about what to include in the backup, you can use your browser's back button to return to the previous page.

6. Click the Continue button.

7. On the next page, the progress of the backup is displayed together with a report if it was successful. You should see the message "Backup completed successfully" at the bottom of the page. Click the Continue button.

8. You will then be taken to the backupdata directory in the files area for your course, as shown in Figure 4-8. Click the filename of the backup file to download it to your desktop.

 Some browsers or operating systems will automatically try to decompress a ZIP archive. If the browser or operating system unpacks the archive, you can simply delete the decompressed file. If you need to upload a backup to restore or copy a course, be sure to use the ZIP archive file.

Restoring and Copying Courses

This section covers the following MTC skills: 8.7.1 Restore

Your backup ZIP file can be restored to create a new course or to copy activities into an existing course.

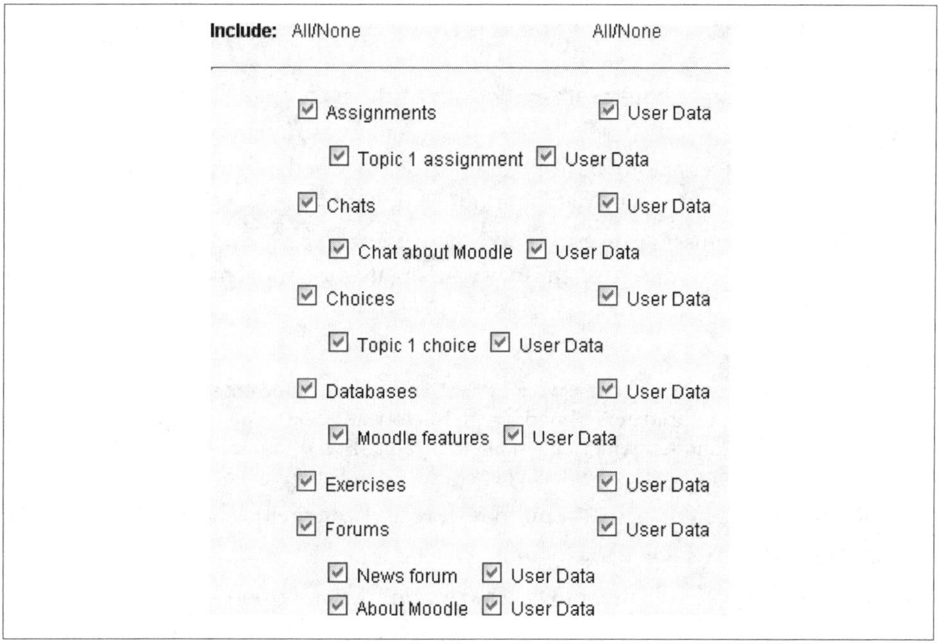

Include: All/None   All/None

- ☑ Assignments   ☑ User Data
  - ☑ Topic 1 assignment ☑ User Data
- ☑ Chats   ☑ User Data
  - ☑ Chat about Moodle ☑ User Data
- ☑ Choices   ☑ User Data
  - ☑ Topic 1 choice ☑ User Data
- ☑ Databases   ☑ User Data
  - ☑ Moodle features ☑ User Data
- ☑ Exercises   ☑ User Data
- ☑ Forums   ☑ User Data
  - ☑ News forum ☑ User Data
  - ☑ About Moodle ☑ User Data

Figure 4-7. Backing up a course

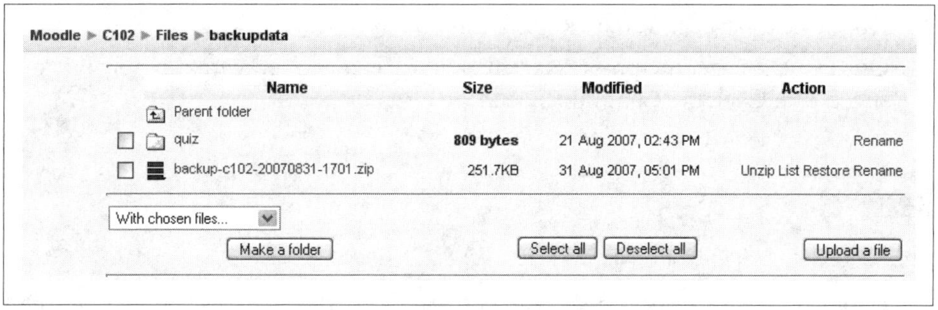

Moodle ► C102 ► Files ► **backupdata**

	Name	Size	Modified	Action
	Parent folder			
☐	quiz	**809 bytes**	21 Aug 2007, 02:43 PM	Rename
☐	backup-c102-20070831-1701 .zip	251.7KB	31 Aug 2007, 05:01 PM	Unzip List Restore Rename

With chosen files... ▼

[Make a folder]   [Select all] [Deselect all]   [Upload a file]

Figure 4-8. The backupdata directory

You will only be allowed to restore to a new course if you have been given appropriate permission at the course category or site level. Contact your system administrator if necessary.

To restore a course:

1. Either upload a backup ZIP file to your course files area (as covered in Chapter 3) or click Restore in the Administration block to access the backupdata directory, as shown in Figure 4-8.

2. Click the Restore link opposite the file you want to restore.

3. On the next page, click Yes to the question "Do you want to continue?" to start the restore process.

4. Click the Continue button at the bottom of the next page, listing details of the backup.

5. On the next page, as shown in Figure 4-9, select whether you want to restore to the existing course, adding data to it or deleting it first.

   If you have permission to restore to a new course, the restore page will contain additional options for setting the new course category, short name, full name, and start date.

 Restoring a course without user data and changing the short name and start date is a good way to roll forward a class you want to use in another semester. An alternative method is to reset the course using the Reset link in your course Administration block.

6. Choose which activities you want to restore and whether to include user data.

7. Select course users if you are including user data.

8. Select appropriate role mappings. The options depend upon the roles you are allowed to assign. By default, teachers are only allowed to assign the roles of non-editing teacher, student, and guest.

9. Click the Continue button.

10. On the next page, click the "Restore this course now!" button.

11. On the next page, the progress of the restore is displayed with a report if it was successful. Click the Continue button.

Reports

This section covers the following MTC skills: 8.3.1 Logs

Once your course is up and students are working, Moodle provides you with detailed logs and participation reports of student activity.

To access course reports:

1. Click Reports in the Administration block.

2. On the Reports page, choose from the following:

   Logs
   Select any combination of group, student, date, activity, and actions, then click the "Get these logs" button.

   You can see what pages the student accessed, the time and date she accessed it, the IP address she came from, and her actions (view, add, update, delete), as shown in Figure 4-10.

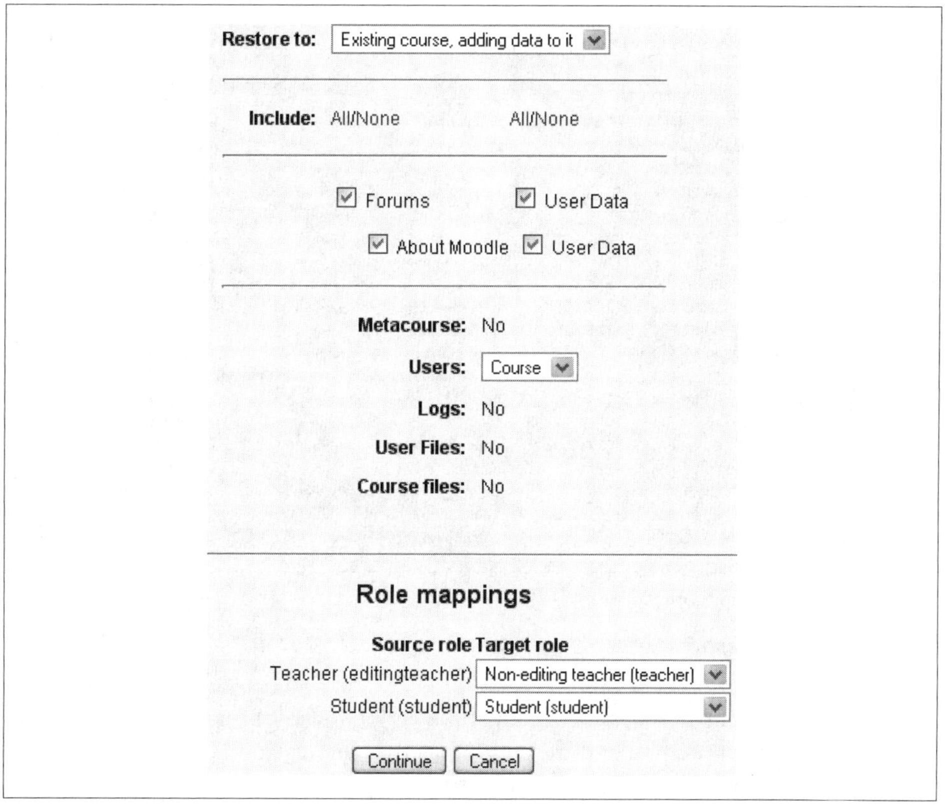

| Restore to: | Existing course, adding data to it ▼ |

Include: All/None   All/None

☑ Forums   ☑ User Data

☑ About Moodle ☑ User Data

Metacourse: No
Users: Course ▼
Logs: No
User Files: No
Course files: No

Role mappings

Source role Target role
Teacher (editingteacher) | Non-editing teacher (teacher) ▼
Student (student) | Student (student) ▼

Continue   Cancel

Figure 4-9. Restoring a course

You can choose to display the logs on a page (as shown in Figure 4-10) or download them in text, ODS, or Excel format.

 The Logs page contains active links enabling you to access the student's profile page or a particular page that the student was viewing. The IP address link provides an estimate of the student's location.

Current activity

The "Live logs from the past hour" link in the middle of the Reports page opens a pop-up window listing all course activity in the past hour, which refreshes every minute.

Activity report

This lists how many times each course activity has been viewed and the last time it was viewed.

| Course 102 ▾ | Group B ▾ | Larry Learner ▾ | All days ▾ | All activities ▾ |

Displaying 18 records

Time	IP Address	Full name	Action	Information
Tue 28 August 2007, 04:26 PM	127.0.0.1	Larry Learner	choice choose	Topic 1 choice
Tue 28 August 2007, 04:26 PM	127.0.0.1	Larry Learner	choice view	Topic 1 choice
Tue 28 August 2007, 04:26 PM	127.0.0.1	Larry Learner	choice view	Topic 1 choice
Tue 28 August 2007, 04:26 PM	127.0.0.1	Larry Learner	course view	Course 102
Tue 21 August 2007, 05:56 PM	127.0.0.1	Larry Learner	quiz view	Topic 1 quiz
Tue 21 August 2007, 05:56 PM	127.0.0.1	Larry Learner	quiz review	Topic 1 quiz
Tue 21 August 2007, 05:56 PM	127.0.0.1	Larry Learner	quiz close attempt	Topic 1 quiz
Tue 21 August 2007, 05:55 PM	127.0.0.1	Larry Learner	quiz attempt	Topic 1 quiz
Tue 21 August 2007, 05:55 PM	127.0.0.1	Larry Learner	quiz view	Topic 1 quiz
Tue 21 August 2007, 05:55 PM	127.0.0.1	Larry Learner	quiz review	Topic 1 quiz
Tue 21 August 2007, 05:54 PM	127.0.0.1	Larry Learner	quiz close attempt	Topic 1 quiz
Tue 21 August 2007, 05:54 PM	127.0.0.1	Larry Learner	quiz attempt	Topic 1 quiz
Tue 21 August 2007, 05:54 PM	127.0.0.1	Larry Learner	quiz view	Topic 1 quiz
Tue 21 August 2007, 05:54 PM	127.0.0.1	Larry Learner	course view	Course 102
Sat 18 August 2007, 06:07 PM	127.0.0.1	Larry Learner	upload upload	C:\xampp\htdocs\moodle\m
Sat 18 August 2007, 06:07 PM	127.0.0.1	Larry Learner	assignment upload	Topic 1 assignment
Sat 18 August 2007, 06:06 PM	127.0.0.1	Larry Learner	assignment view	Topic 1 assignment
Sat 18 August 2007, 06:06 PM	127.0.0.1	Larry Learner	course view	Course 102

Figure 4-10. Viewing logs of student activity

Participation reports

To generate a participation report:

a. Select an activity module, the time period to look back over, to show only student reports, and the actions you are interested in (views, posts, or all actions), then click the Go button.

b. A list of all instances of the selected activity module in the course will be generated. Select one, then click the Go button.

The participation report, as shown in Figure 4-11, lists the number of times each student has done the action selected.

If you wish, you can select particular users and send them a message. Select "Add/send message" from the drop-down menu and click the OK button.

Statistics

If your system administrator has enabled site statistics, you can also get more detailed summary reports from the statistics menu.

The logs and participation reports are useful for tracking students' activity in a class. If a student doesn't spend time with the material, he will have difficulty succeeding in the course. Frequently, students who don't do well simply haven't spent the time working with the material.

If you analyze your course reports on a regular basis, you can monitor when your students engage with the course material. You won't be able to tell exactly how long they spent with a certain activity or resource because the logs report only the time of access.

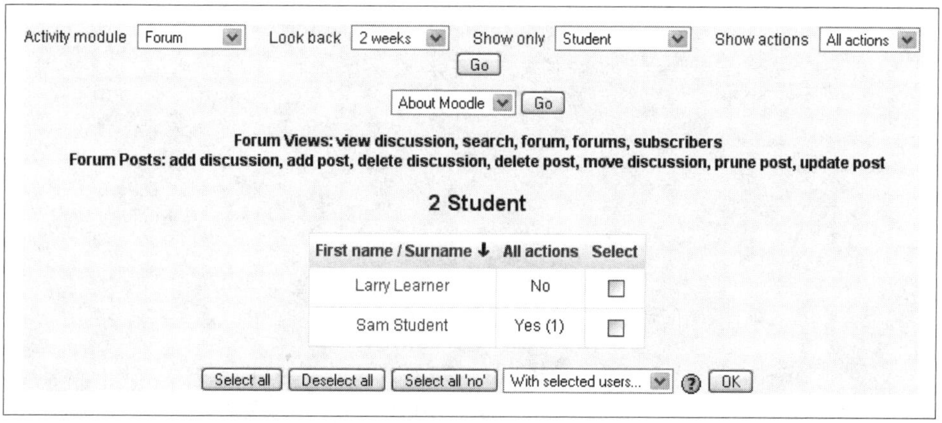

Figure 4-11. Viewing a participation report

Of course, you can guess how long a student spent with a resource by noting the time when the student began the next activity.

Logs and participation reports can also tell you which resources and activities students find most valuable. For example, if you upload all your PowerPoint slides for students to take notes on in class, but no one accesses them, you might want to find out why.

CHAPTER 5

Forums, Chats, and Messaging

Forums

This section covers the following MTC skills: 5.4 Forums

Forums are a powerful communication tool within a Moodle course. Think of them as online message boards where you and your students can post messages to each other while easily keeping track of individual conversations. Forums are the primary tool for online discussion and are the central organizing feature in the social course format. You've already posted your first message to a forum back in Chapter 2. When you posted your news item, you were posting to a special forum used in every course for announcements and news.

Forums allow you and your students to communicate with each other at any time, from anywhere with an Internet connection. Students don't have to be logged in at the same time you are to communicate with you or their classmates. Figure 5-1 demonstrates how conversations are tracked through time, and readers can review the history of a conversation simply by reading the page. The technical term for this type of communication is *asynchronous*, meaning "not at the same time." Asynchronous communications are contrasted with synchronous forms such as chat rooms, instant messaging, or face-to-face conversations.

Because forums are asynchronous, students can take their time composing replies. They can draft and rewrite until they are happy with the results instead of feeling under pressure to respond immediately. A lot of research indicates that more students are willing to participate in an asynchronous forum than are willing to speak up in class. For students whose primary language is not that of the course, people with communicative disabilities, and the just plain shy, forums offer a chance to take as much time as they need to formulate a reasonable reply. Other students, who might be afraid of embarrassing themselves by making a mistake when they speak up in class, can double-check their responses before they send them in.

The asynchronous nature of the forums creates many opportunities for you not only to replicate the conversations you have in class, but also to create entirely new activities that are difficult in a classroom setting.

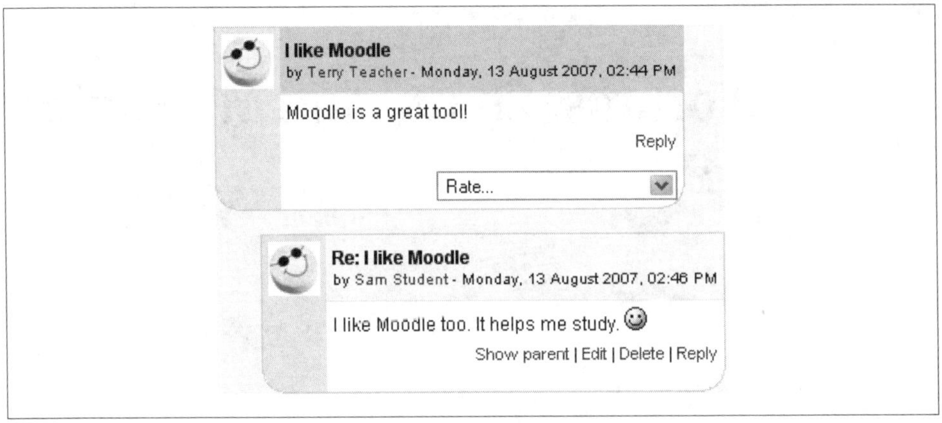

Figure 5-1. A forum discussion

Before we start creating a forum, it is important to make sure we're using the same vocabulary. It might be useful to think of the forum module as a party. Each forum is a room at the party: there's a living room, a kitchen, and a dining room. In each room, there are groups of people having discussions. Each discussion has a thread with everyone replying to each other about the topic. Without people having discussions, a forum is an empty, quiet space. Each forum can contain one or more discussions, which are comprised of one or more posts and replies.

Moodle forums also allow subscriptions. When a user subscribes to a forum, all new posts are automatically sent to the email address stored in the user's profile. This makes it easy to keep track of what's happening in the forums without constantly logging in.

Creating a Forum

Creating a forum is relatively easy. The key to success is choosing the right options for the type of forum you want to create. In addition to the news forum, Moodle has four basic forum types:

A single, simple discussion
> You can create only one discussion in this forum. This will keep the conversation focused on one particular topic.

Each person posts one discussion
> Each person on the class can start only one discussion. This would be useful when each person needs to post an assignment or a question. Each discussion can then have multiple replies.

Q & A forum
> This forum requires students to post their perspectives before viewing other students' postings. After the initial posting, students can view and respond to others' postings.

Standard forum for general use
> There can be one or more discussions in this forum, and anyone with permission can post multiple discussions.

To add a forum to your class:

1. Click the "Turn editing on" button.
2. Select Forum from the activity menu in the course section where you would like to add the forum.
3. On the "Adding a new forum" page, as shown in Figure 5-2, give the forum a descriptive name.
4. Select the forum type you want to use.
5. Write a descriptive forum introduction.
6. Select the general options:

   Force everyone to be subscribed?
   > If you select Yes, everyone in your course will automatically receive emails of new posts. Otherwise, people can choose whether to subscribe.

   Read tracking for this forum?
   > Read tracking highlights unread forum posts.

   Maximum attachment size
   > When students attach files to their posts, you'll want to limit the maximum size of their posts so you don't use up all your server space. This is especially important if you are paying a commercial hosting company for your Moodle site.

7. Select the grade options:

   Allow posts to be rated
   > Forum posts can be rated using either a numerical scale or a scale made up of words. By default, only teachers can rate forum posts, though you can use a role override to allow students to rate each others' posts. This is a useful tool for giving students participation grades. Any ratings given in the forum are recorded in the gradebook (which we'll cover in Chapter 13).

   Grade
   > If you allow posts to be rated, you can choose a scale rating using the Grade drop-down menu. You can create your own scale (which we'll cover in Chapter 13), but for now, just pick the default "Separate and Connected ways of knowing" scale or a number between 1 and 100. The points you choose are the total for the entire forum.

   Restrict ratings to posts with dates in this range
   > You can allow only posts within a certain date range to be rated. This is useful if you want to keep students focused on the most recent content.

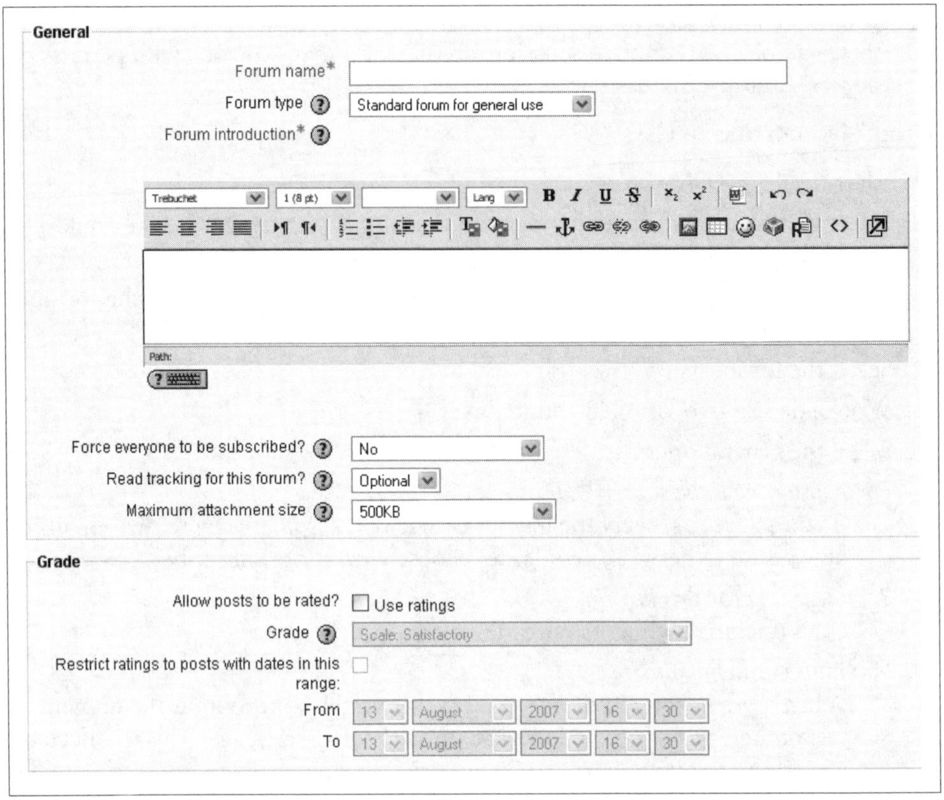

Figure 5-2. Adding a new forum

8. Select the post threshold for blocking options, if appropriate. Students can be blocked from posting a certain number of times in a given period and warned when they are approaching the threshold.

9. Select the common module options:

Group mode

This is another location in which to set the group mode for the activity. If group mode is forced in the course settings, then this setting will be ignored.

Visible

This determines whether students may view the activity or not.

10. Click the "Save changes" button. The forum name will now be a link in the course section where you added it. If you want to go back to change any of the options, you can click on the hand icon to return to the editing forum page.

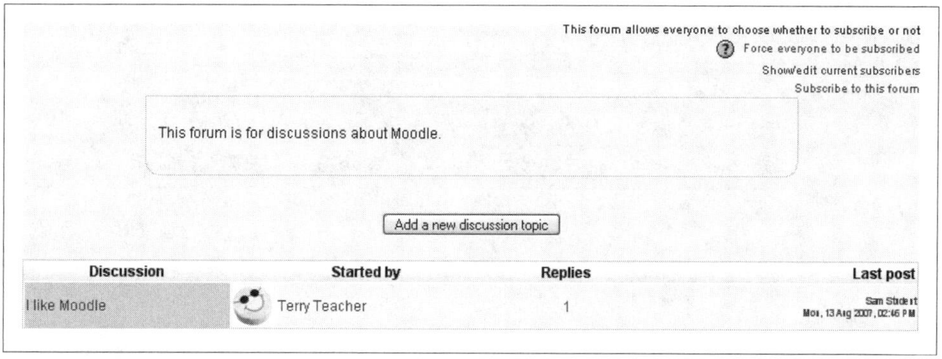

Figure 5-3. Viewing a forum

Using Forums

If you click on the forum name on the course page, you'll see the main forum page, as shown in Figure 5-3.

There are some interesting features on this page. At the top right of the page is the text "This forum allows everyone to choose whether to subscribe or not" or "This forum forces everyone to be subscribed," depending on whether you are forcing everyone to subscribe or not. Subscribing to a forum will send the user an email when there are new postings in the forum. The users can choose how they receive their emails in their profile. An alternative way of receiving forum posts is via an RSS feed. RSS feeds need to be enabled across the site and for the forum module by a system administrator.

If you click on the "Force everyone to be subscribed" link, you can flip back and forth between forcing subscription or not. If you aren't forcing users to subscribe, the next link will read "Show/edit current subscribers," which will give you an interface for seeing who's subscribed and changing who is and isn't receiving email. The last link will read "Subscribe to this forum," which will subscribe you when you click it.

Below the subscription links, you'll find the forum introduction you wrote when you created the forum. Below the introduction, you'll see a button labeled "Add a new discussion topic." You can use this to create the first discussion in the forum. If you've prohibited students from creating discussions, you'll need to create one to allow anyone to use the forum.

To create a new discussion:

1. Click the "Add a new discussion topic" button.
2. On the new discussion topic page, shown in Figure 5-4, give your new discussion a subject.
3. Write your message in the space provided. If you don't have the HTML editor enabled, you can choose the formatting type you used in your message. Most of

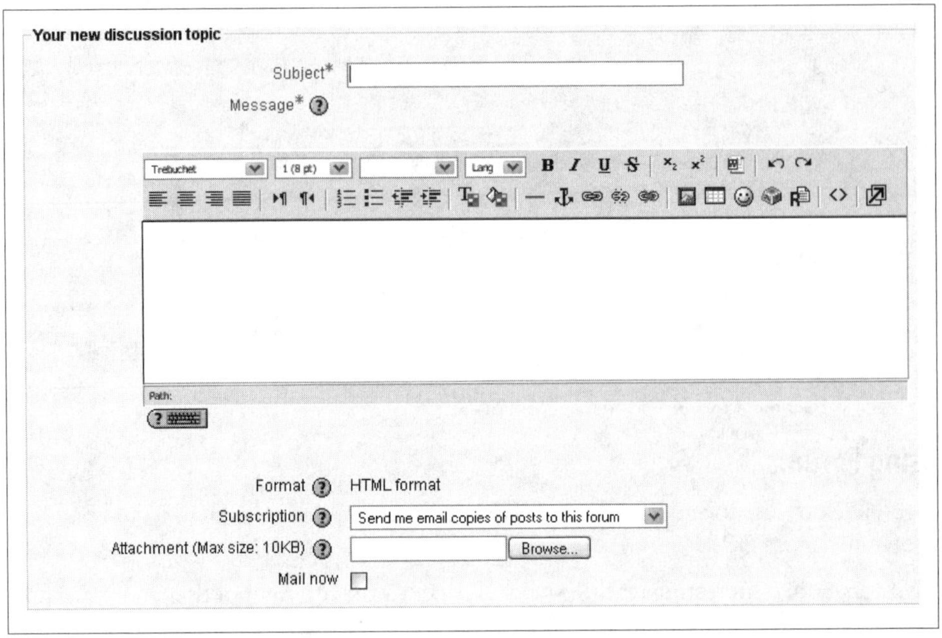

Your new discussion topic

Subject*

Message* ⑦

| Trebuchet ∨ | 1 (8 pt) ∨ | ∨ | Lang ∨ | **B** *I* <u>U</u> S | x₂ x² | ▦ | ↩ ↻ |

≡ ≡ ≡ ▤ | ¶ı ı¶ | ≔ ≔ ⇥ ⇤ | Tₐ ⬧ | — ⬚ ⊕ ⬀ ⊕ | ▣ ▥ ☺ ◈ ▣ | ‹› | ⬚

Path:

⑦ ⌨

Format ⑦   HTML format

Subscription ⑦   [Send me email copies of posts to this forum ∨]

Attachment (Max size: 10KB) ⑦   [   ] [Browse...]

Mail now ☐

Figure 5-4. Adding a new discussion topic

the time, you'll want to leave it on Moodle Auto-Format, which will try to automatically recognize the format you used in the post.

4. You can choose to subscribe to the forum if subscriptions were enabled when the forum was created.

5. If you want to attach a file, such as an RTF document or a picture, click the Browse button, find the file on your computer, and click Open. Be sure your document is smaller than the maximum attachment size for the forum.

6. Click the "Save changes" button.

Once you submit your discussion topic, you'll see a screen telling you the post was successfully saved and how long you have to make changes to your post. The time you have to make changes is set by your system administrator for everyone on the Moodle site. The default is 30 minutes, so most of the time you'll have half an hour to go back and edit your post before it's mailed to the subscribers. After it's been sent, you can't edit it unless you have the privilege set for your role.

Unless you have checked the "Mail now" box, your post won't be mailed to subscribers until the editing time has passed. Unless your system administrator has changed the default, your forum posts won't be sent out for at least 30 minutes.

Figure 5-5. An emailed forum post

The success screen should automatically send you back to the main forum page. You'll see the discussion you just created. If you click on the discussion name, you'll see the post you wrote with any attachments in the upper-right corner of the message body.

If you can still edit the post, you'll see an Edit link at the bottom of the message body.

After the editing time has passed, your post will be emailed to all subscribers. If a student or instructor has opted to receive HTML-formatted email, she will receive an email that looks just like the posting in the browser. Otherwise, she will receive the plain-text version. As Figure 5-5 illustrates, the email will have links labeled Reply and "See this post in context," which will bring the user right to the forum post so she can post a reply.

If you've enabled ratings, you'll also see a drop-down menu at the lower-right side of other users' posts with the scale you've chosen. At the bottom of the page, below all the posts in the discussion, you'll see a button labeled "Send in my latest ratings." If you select a rating for the post and click the button, you'll submit your scores for the posts. The scores are then stored in the gradebook.

Once you've submitted a rating, it will appear next to the rating menu. If you click on the rating, you'll see everyone's ratings for that post.

Searching Forums

This section covers the following MTC skills: 3.14 Search Forums

All of the forums within a course are searchable as well as browsable. Performing a forum search can find useful information easily. All forums within the course are searched simultaneously.

The Search Forums block on your course page enables you to quickly search for a particular word within a forum post. If you obtain more than one page of results, you may wish to try an advanced search.

An advanced search enables you to refine your search in any/all of the following ways:

These words can appear anywhere in the post
> One or more words you type in here will be found in all the places in the post they appear.

This exact phrase must appear in the post
> The phrase you enter must appear exactly as you enter it.

These words should NOT be included
> Identifying words you don't want can help narrow down the resulting list of messages.

These words should appear as whole words
> The search engine will return posts that contain your words as part of a larger word. For example, if you search for "cat," posts with the word "catalog" will be returned. Selecting whole words will look for a space before and after the words you have entered.

Posts must be newer/older than this
> This narrows down the number of posts according to time limits.

Choose which forums to search
> This enables searching within one forum only.

These words should be in the subject
> If you know the subject line of the posts you want, you can limit your searches by the subject line.

This name should match the author
> If you only want posts from certain authors, enter their names here.

Managing Forums

Once you've created forums for your students, you will need to manage them during your course. As we discussed earlier, forums are great tools for getting people who don't usually talk in class to participate. If you make your discussions an important part of your class, you can really get people talking.

Of course, a lot of people talking in a forum means there's more to manage. Forums can quickly sprout and spread like an unruly weed, unless you do some management and pruning.

Managing expectations

The first key to managing a forum is managing student expectations. In your syllabus, let students know how often you intend to respond to questions and posts. Let them know if you will be checking in once a day or once a week. If you don't set expectations, some students will expect you to be on call 24 hours a day.

Jason: A professor I used to work with received a series of emails starting at 1:30 in the morning. The student wrote a question at 1:30 a.m., asked again at 2:00 a.m., and sent an annoyed message at 2:30 a.m.. Finally, at 3:00 a.m., the student sent an email saying he was going to bed and was very upset the instructor had not answered his question in time to complete the assignment. Needless to say, the professor was very surprised to find the entire series of emails when she awoke the next morning.

Behavior issues

Dealing with rude and unruly students is another challenge of online discussions. Some students may say things in an online discussion they would never say in person. Rude or hurtful remarks can shut down a discussion or completely divert the thread of the conversation.

To avoid these situations, make your expectations for student conduct clear in your syllabus and elsewhere in the site. The use of rating scales can also moderate students' behavior if their grade depends on getting good ratings from you or their peers. Of course, if the situation gets out of control, your ultimate recourse is to simply delete the students' posts from the forum and then deal with it as you would any other disciplinary issue.

Archiving forums

When forum threads get very long, you may want to archive them and start up the conversation again with a good summary. Discussions can be archived one by one or by backing up the complete forum with user data, then restoring it.

To archive a discussion:

1. Create a forum named "Archive forum" somewhere in your course (the first or last course section is a good idea).
2. Go to the forum containing the discussions you want to archive.
3. Enter the discussion by clicking on the discussion name. At the top-right corner of the screen, you'll see a drop-down menu labeled "Move this discussion to" (see Figure 5-6).
4. Select "Archive forum" from the list.
5. You'll now see the discussion in the archive forum. Click the Forums link in the navigation bar and select the original forum from the list.
6. Post a summary of the archived discussion in the original forum to restart the discussion.

Using an archive forum allows you to keep the discussions manageable, while retaining all of the detail of the original. It's also an easy way to move good discussions from class to class or semester to semester.

Managing discussions is also easier with some help. A number of studies have reported the benefits of assigning groups of students to moderate duties for discussions around given topics. If a group of students knows they are responsible for being able to discuss

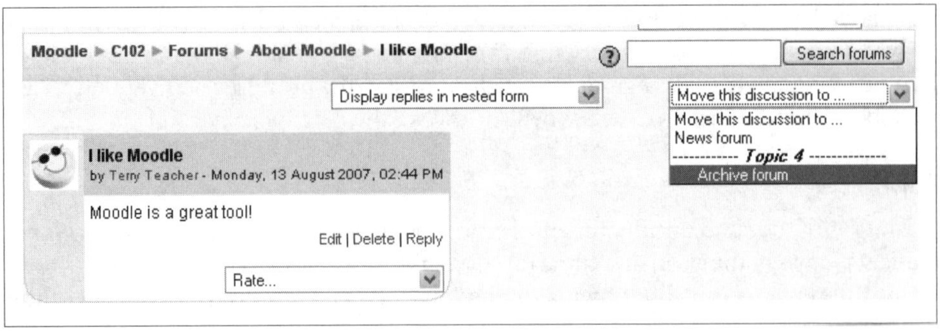

Figure 5-6. Moving a discussion

an issue intelligently with their classmates, they are much more likely to be sure they've done the reading and really understand the topic. They can be responsible for moving the conversation along, answering basic questions, and archiving and summarizing a discussion.

To create student moderator groups, assign a small team of students to each forum or discussion. Be sure to enable ratings for everyone, in order to allow the student group to use ratings.

Forum Capabilities

Forum capabilities are more fine-grained than any other module, giving you the ability to create a wide range of roles:

View discussions
> The basic capability allows a user to view forum discussions but not reply or start new ones.

View hidden timed posts
> This allows a user to set a display start and end date for new discussions.

> Timed posts need to be enabled by your system administrator in order to make use of this capability.

Start new discussions
> This allows a user to create a new discussion if the forum allows multiple discussions.

Reply to posts
> This allows a user to reply to posts within a discussion. You'll probably want to override this capability, as well as the capability to start new discussions, for an archive forum.

Add news
> A user with this capability can post news to the course news forum. By default, only teachers can add news.

Reply to news
> This allows a user to reply to news postings in the news forum. By default, only teachers can reply to news postings.

View ratings
> This allows a user to view his own forum ratings.

View any ratings
> This allows a user to see forum ratings of other users.

Rate posts
> This allows a user to rate forum posts if rating is allowed in the forum. By default, only teachers can rate forum posts.

Create attachments
> This allows a user to attach a file to her forum post.

Delete own posts (within deadline)
> This allows a user to delete his own forum posts within a certain time, usually 30 minutes.

Delete any posts (anytime)
> This allows a user to delete any forum post at any time.

Split discussions
> This allows a user to split discussions to create new discussions. By default, only teachers can split discussions.

Move discussions
> A user with this capability can move discussions to other forums in the course.

Edit any post
> This very powerful capability allows a user to edit any forum post at any time. By default, only teachers can edit any post.

Always see Q & A posts
> This allows a user to view Q & A forum posts without first posting.

View subscribers
> This allows a user to view the list of subscribers to a forum.

Manage subscriptions
> This allows a user to edit and delete forum subscriptions.

Initial subscription
> This allows a user to be subscribed initially to forums. By default, all roles have this capability, apart from administrators and course creators, so they don't receive a lot of forum subscription emails.

Throttling applies
> This allows a user to be blocked from posting in a forum, according to the blocking options in the forum.

Effective Forum Practices

Forums are an important tool in your Moodle toolbox. They are the primary method for students to communicate with you and each other. Social constructivism is all about discussion and negotiated meaning.

Jason: I would argue that good moderation and intelligent deployment of discussion opportunities are more important to the success of a course than the static content.

 MIT has said the same thing. It is posting many of its course syllabi, problem sets, and lecture notes through its OpenCourseWare initiative (*http://ocw.mit.edu*). Anyone can download course materials from over 700 courses for free. MIT does this because the value of an MIT education is not in the content, but in the interaction between students and the instructor. Moodle's forums are a key tool for you to add the same value to your course.

Getting students to participate in online forums can be a challenge. If you simply create a forum and expect students to communicate online, you will be sadly disappointed. Many times instructors create a forum, give some vague instructions, and then complain that the students aren't spontaneously communicating with each other.

Starting the discussion

For many students and instructors, starting the discussion is the hardest part. Once people start talking, at least a few will probably continue the discussion. As you start your class, it would be useful to have some icebreakers to help students get to know one another and to get used to discussing issues online.

The most effective icebreakers have a strong prompt to get people started. Ask specific questions like, "If you could speak to any person, living or dead, who would it be and what three questions would you ask them?" or, "What is your favorite comfort food and why?" You could also prompt people to tell stories about themselves. For example, you could ask students to tell a story starting with "On my last trip the funniest thing I saw or did was..." or "My favorite story about an animal is...." Whatever you use, make it concrete, compelling, and open-ended.

Encouraging participation

The primary key to student participation in online forums is tight integration with your course goals. Your forums should give students a chance to practice a skill, to collaborate on a project, or to act as resources for each other. Of course, it is important to distinguish between the types of forums and the reasons for using them in your class.

Let's take an example to help make this clearer. Suppose you have a weekly reading you want students to discuss online before meeting face-to-face. There are two possibilities for this forum. If you want students to use the forum as a practice exercise, you'll want to create a place where students can practice applying the new ideas they encountered in the reading. So you may want to make each week a discussion of a case study. If you want the forum to be a resource, you may want each student to post a question about the reading. You can then use the questions as a basis for discussion in class.

The final strategy for encouraging participation is to engage with the forums yourself. If your class meets face-to-face, bring up important postings and discussions in class. By merging the online environment with the face-to-face environment, you show your students that you value their participation. One of the best examples of merging online discussions with a course happened in a management course of 400+ students. The instructor assigned groups of students to small discussion groups. She and her teaching assistants randomly read a subset of the discussions each week for assessment. The instructor would also bring the best questions and discussions to class, frequently devoting half of her lecture to talking about what was happening online.

Grading forums

Of course, being clear about the goal of the forum is only one step. As we discussed earlier, your goals for the class may be very different from your students' goals. You may want them to engage with the material because of its intrinsic value. Most students, however, are overworked, concerned about their grades, and doing only what is required in a large majority of their classes.

To help encourage alignment between your goals and your students' goals, you will need to have a grading strategy for student participation. Moodle has some great tools to help you create and manage graded forums. To be successful, you must clearly define your grading criteria. You will need to grade on quality, not just quantity. A student logging in to say "I agree" once a day is not adding to the discussion. Someone who posts a thoughtful reply once a week is adding more to the course. Of course, you will need to balance between grading for quality and allowing a discussion where everyone is trying to be more clever to get a grade.

Many students need scaffolding to be able to participate effectively in an academic discussion. A quick glance at the discussion forums on MySpace reveals a great many posts that would not be acceptable in an academic environment. Help your students understand the difference between social forums and academic forums. Do you want them to support their argument with citations? Do you want them to acknowledge the other person's point of view and then offer a critique? Do they need to support their own arguments with facts, figures, or appeals to a higher authority?

Once you have established expectations, you can begin to score according to the quality of their interactions. It is good practice to give students some credit just for participating, but full points can only be achieved with a high-quality answer.

Creative Forum Uses

There are many creative uses of forums, so we can only present a few of the most common here. Moodle forums are so flexible, there's really no limit to the types of activities you can develop to take advantage of the technology.

Peer assessment

Forums are an often-overlooked tool for peer assessment. Andy Diament, from West Cornwall in the UK, has used forums for peer assessment. His students were learning database design by developing a project over multiple weeks. Each week they would work in pairs to complete a lesson on a new topic. They would then use their new skills to complete a little more of their project and upload it to the forums for review. Each pair had their work critiqued and the best work of the week was used as a starting point for the next section of the project. Not only did the students learn from the peer review process, but they were able to develop their own project using the best work of the class.

Q & A forums for problem solving

John Rodgers, from Ontario, Canada, uses the Q & A forum type to good effect in teaching mathematics. The Q & A forum allows a single question post that the students must answer before they can see other responses. A lesson starts with the instructor asking the students to solve a math problem, identify and correct a misconception, decode the meaning of symbols from context, or engage in some other sort of exercise. The students usually spend 20–40 minutes working together in small groups to formulate a response. After the students post their answers, the Q & A forum allows them to see how others in the class have solved the problem. When that is complete, the students usually are given a series of questions to answer (using the quiz module) to see if their approach to solving the problem is robust enough. John reports, "Students are more engaged both in terms of depth (the problems force them to generate a deep understanding) and breadth within the class (the bottom of the class now engages the content at a far higher level). The time I can spend as an instructor providing quality mentoring has increased by an order of magnitude and the use of time has dramatically improved."

This is a great example not only of using the forums but of using the power of technology to shift the role of the instructor from delivering information to mentoring students.

Interviews

Bringing outside experts into your class can be difficult. You have to coordinate schedules, tear them away from their busy lives, and then hope your students are prepared enough to ask interesting questions. You can eliminate many of these problems by using the forums for communication between students and experts. The easiest strategy is to invite the expert into your forums as a regular participant. Simply give her an account and enroll her in your class. She can then participate in the forum and elsewhere in the course.

However, some people will be reluctant to participate in such an open-ended discussion. As an alternative strategy, create a forum in which students can submit questions for an interview with an expert. They can then vote on the best questions. You select the top 10 questions and send them via email to the interviewee. Your expert can then respond, via email, when it is convenient for her. If you post her responses to a new forum, your students can respond to her answers and even prepare a second round of questions, if your expert is up for it.

Debates

While many instructors frequently hope some level of debate will spontaneously break out between students around controversial issues or new concepts, it's sometimes difficult to get the ball rolling. Try assigning your students to groups on different sides of an issue. Each post must be a reasoned argument for their side of the issue, supported by evidence. They can be graded on how well they reason and support their argument.

Role-playing and storytelling

Tisha Bender, in her book *Discussion-Based Online Teaching*, discusses the advantages of using asynchronous discussions for role-playing and storytelling. In one course, she has students adopt a character from a story or novel and then play out a scene in character using the forum. The rest of the class watches the new drama unfold in front of them. Students have time to think about their responses and refine their contributions to better reflect the voice of the character rather than their own voices. Students are also less reluctant to fully respond as the character in an online forum, as they avoid the embarrassment of a face-to-face encounter.

Frequently asked questions

How many times do you answer the same question from three different students? Frequently, many students have the same questions about assignments, difficult concepts, or grades. If everyone is meeting face-to-face, you can answer the question out loud, but other students may not be listening to the answer. A fully online environment is harder to manage when the questions from students arrive via email. Many teachers of fully online courses complain about the constant barrage of repetitious questions. We recommend you create a forum in which students can ask questions about the administration of the course, and separate forums for questions about the subject matter. Have them consult the forums and the responses before sending you yet another email about the date of the final exam.

This feature is also useful in a business environment.

Reading study groups

A strategy to encourage students to do their assigned reading is to create reading study group forums. This strategy works well with groups of three to five students who are collectively responsible for discussing a reading before class. Each student asks one question about the reading, and the group must answer all the questions before the start of the class session. This encourages students not only to read the assignment but to think more deeply about it through the question-and-answer process.

This strategy of having groups of students asking each other questions about course material supposedly originated with a group of engineers who were taking a class together. They were all transferred as a group midway through the semester but didn't want to drop the class. The instructor agreed to videotape the lectures and mail them to the students. Very quickly, the instructor noticed the engineers' performance in the class was getting worse, so he insisted they watch the videotape together. He told them they had to stop the tape every 15 minutes, and each person was to ask a question about what they had just seen. They couldn't continue until every question was answered. By the end of the class, the remote group of engineers performed a third of a letter grade higher than the rest of the class.

Social forum

Although the majority of your forums will focus on the course material, it's important for your students to have an informal way to get to know each other, especially if the course is completely online. A social forum gives people a place to talk without worrying about being graded or having to appear really smart. It's a good idea to start your social forum with some fun questions. Ask everyone to post an introduction telling the class where they are from; what they hope to get out of the class; and their favorite food, favorite movie, or something interesting. The more interesting the introductory post, the more likely people will respond to it and get a real discussion going.

Chats

This section covers the following MTC skills: 5.2 Chat

The Moodle chat module is a simple synchronous communication tool allowing you and your students to communicate in real time. If you've ever used an instant messaging system like AOL, MSN, or iChat, you've used a system similar to the Moodle chat. In the forums, you and your students don't have to be logged in at the same time. In a chat, everyone needs to be logged in at the same time in order to communicate.

Creating a Chat

To use the chat tool, you will need to create a chat room for you and your students and set a time when everyone will log in and meet. You can create one session for the entire course or set up repeating sessions for multiple meetings.

To create a chat session:

1. Click the "Turn editing on" button.
2. Select Chat from the "Add an activity" drop-down menu in the course section where you would like to add the chat.
3. In the resulting page, shown in Figure 5-7, give the chat room a name and provide directions on how to use the room in "Introduction text."
4. Set the time for the first chat session in "Next chat time."
5. Select the general options for the chat room:

    Repeat sessions
    There are four options here:

    Don't publish any chat times
    Creates a chat room that is always open and has no specified meeting times

    No repeats
    Creates a one-time chat room that will meet only during the time specified in step 4

    At the same time every day
    Creates an entry in the course calendar for a daily chat at the time specified in step 4

    At the same time every week
    Creates a weekly entry in the course calendar

    Save past sessions
    When a chat is complete, the transcript will be available for the amount of time specified here.

    Everyone can view past sessions
    This determines whether transcripts are available to students or just the teacher.

6. Select the common module options:

    Group mode
    This is another location in which to set the group mode for the activity. If group mode is forced in the course settings, then this setting will be ignored.

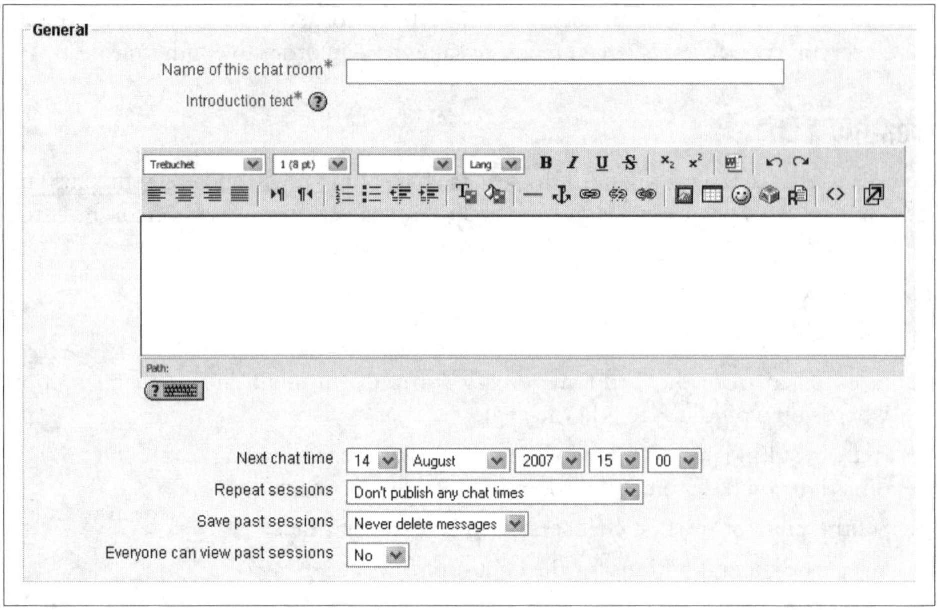

Figure 5-7. Adding a new chat

> *Visible*
>> This determines whether students may view the activity or not.

7. Click the "Save changes" button. The name of the chat room will now be a link in the course section where you added it.

Using Chats

Even if you've set chat times, the chat is always open to students. Moodle does not restrict access to the chat based on the times you set when you created it. Instead, it creates entries in the course calendar that remind people to log in for the chat at certain times. If a student wants to wander into the chat at another time, he could talk to himself or anyone else who wanders by.

There are two versions of the chat room, an ordinary one and a version without frames and JavaScript, as shown in Figure 5-8.

In the ordinary version you can type messages in the text field at the bottom of the screen and/or beep other users. You may want to remind students to keep the beeping to a minimum, as it can be annoying.

Once you type a message in the text area, hit Enter and your message will be broadcast to everyone logged in to the chat. The Moodle chat works by refreshing the screen every five seconds, so you may not see your message right away.

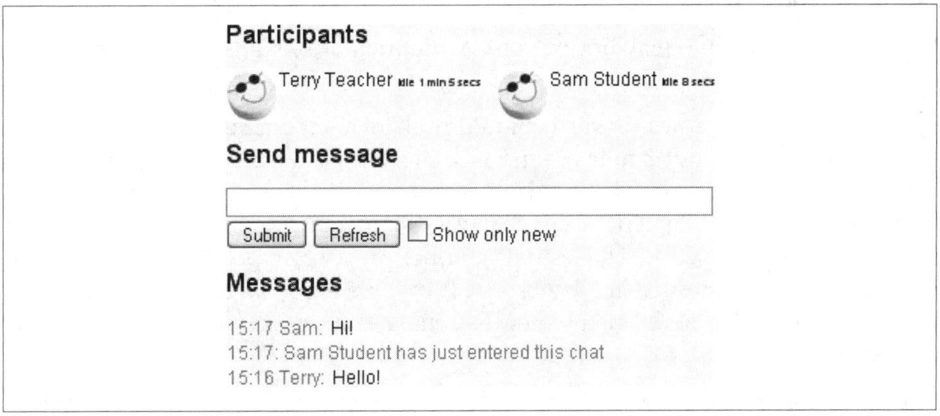

Participants

Terry Teacher Idle 1 min 5 secs   Sam Student Idle 8 secs

Send message

[   ]
[Submit] [Refresh] ☐ Show only new

Messages

15:17 Sam: Hi!
15:17: Sam Student has just entered this chat
15:16 Terry: Hello!

Figure 5-8. An ongoing chat

On the right side of the screen, Moodle lists the chat participants and how long they have been idle.

In the version without frames and JavaScript, you can send messages by typing in the text field and then clicking the Submit button. Clicking the Refresh button displays all recent messages.

 A few larger sites have learned from hard experience that the current chat room in Moodle is not scalable to large numbers of simultaneous conversations. In fact, most servers can't handle more than three or four simultaneous chats. If you want to use chat a lot, your system administrator should consider using a chat server daemon to reduce server load.

Chat Capabilities

When compared to the forum capabilities, chat capabilities are very constrained. The three capabilities available in the chat module are:

Talk in a chat
    This allows a user to chat.

Read chat logs
    This allows a user to read the logs of a chat and review what was said by whom.

Delete chat logs
    This allows a user to delete the logs of a chat. By default, only teachers can delete chat logs.

Effective Chat Practices

While the chat module may not be very feature-rich at this point, it can still be an effective learning tool.

Jason: I know of one professor who couldn't speak for a semester due to throat surgery. He posted his lecture notes to his course web site, and held class meetings in the chat room instead of on campus. The students were expected to come to the chat meeting having already read the materials. The chat was set up as a question-and-answer session in which students typed their questions and the professor typed his responses. The entire process was recorded in the archives. I was able to review the archives and was amazed at the quality of the interaction. The chat room was an ideal tool for this type of discussion.

The key to a successful chat is good moderation. The nature of the chat room makes it difficult to track different conversations. If everyone in the class is talking at the same time, the conversation will go by too quickly. It's important to set some ground rules to make the chat useful for everyone. Try to keep everyone on the same track of the conversation. If the conversation starts to get out of control, gently try to bring people back to the main flow.

Creative Chat Practices

Online office hours

Many students may not be able to come to your office hours, particularly working students, who have arranged their schedules to make it to class. The chat room is an easy way to allow your students to contact you during a scheduled time to ask a quick question about an assignment or a lecture.

Group chats

If you've set up student groups, each group can have its own chat. Set up a chat room and set the group mode to separate or visible groups. Each group can then use its chat room for communication between group members.

Last-minute exam preparation

You could set up a chat room a week or even a night before an examination for students to discuss any study questions. Students who are working at the last minute will appreciate the opportunity to ask each other questions about the material.

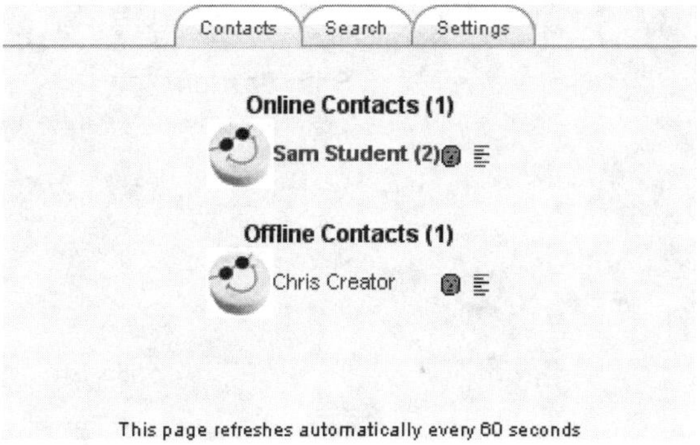

Figure 5-9. Messages window

Figure 5-10. Messages block

Messaging

This section covers the following MTC skills: 3.7 Messages

Messaging is a private communication tool between student and teacher or between two students.

Using Messaging

> If these instructions don't work, contact your system administrator and ask if messaging between site users is enabled.

Unlike forums and chats, messaging is not course-specific; users may send messages to each other regardless of whether they are enrolled in the same course. Your profile page contains a Messages button for opening the Messages window (see Figure 5-9).

To encourage the use of messaging in your course, you may wish to add a Messages block (see Figure 5-10) and/or an Online Users block to your course page.

To add a Messages block to your course page:

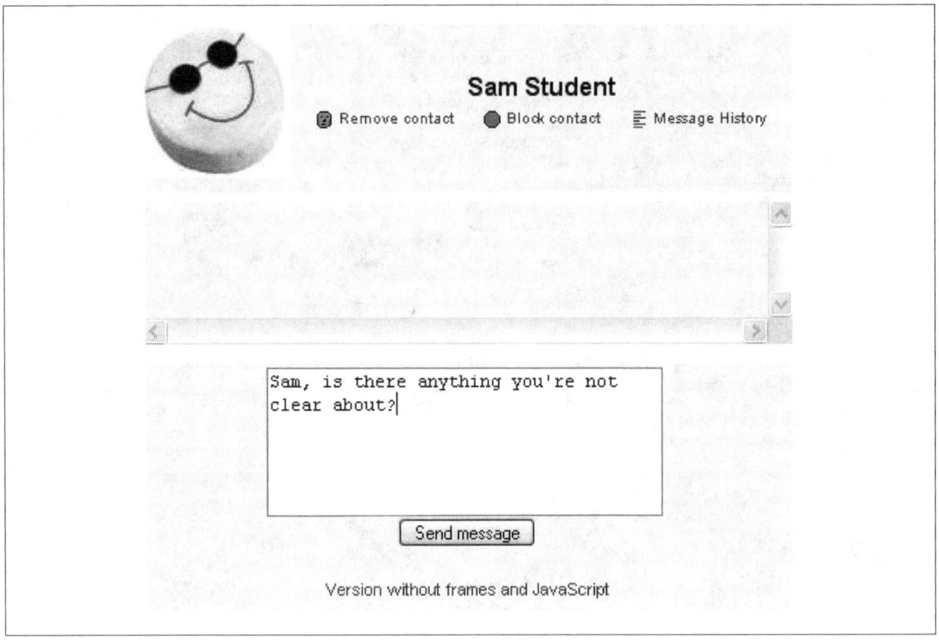

Figure 5-11. Sending a message

1. Click the "Turn editing on" button.
2. Select Messages from the "Add blocks" menu.
3. If appropriate, move the Messages block up and/or left, using the arrow icons under the block title.

The Messages link in the Messages block provides another way of opening the Messages window.

Sending messages

To send a message:

1. Open the Messages window, either using the button in your profile page or via the link in the Messages block.
2. In the Messages window, click on the Search tab to search for the person. If appropriate, check the box "Only in my courses," then click on the person's name.
3. Type the message in the text field in the pop-up box (see Figure 5-11), then click the "Send message" button. A copy of your message will appear above the text field.

Reading and replying to messages

When you are sent a message, the Messages window will pop up. Also, the Messages block will display the name of the person sending the message with a link to read the message. If you have chosen to receive copies of messages via email (see "Message settings), you will get a copy of the message in your email after the time you have specified if you are not logged in.

After reading a message, you may type a reply, then click on the "Send message" button.

Searching messages

In addition to searching for people, the Search tab in the Messages window provides the option to search for keywords, for only messages to or from you, and to include in the search people you have previously blocked from contacting you.

Managing contacts

You can add people to your list of contacts by clicking the "Add contact" icon (a face) opposite their names in the Messages window. Similarly, you can block or remove contacts added previously.

Message history

You can obtain a record of messages sent to/from a person by clicking the "Message history" icon (a few lines) opposite her name in the Messages window.

Message settings

You can change the message settings via the Settings tab in the Messages window.

Message settings include:

Automatically show Message window when I get new messages
Your browser needs to be set so that it doesn't block pop ups for your Moodle site.

Block all new messages from people who are not on my contact list
This is a way of preventing unwanted messages.

Use HTML editor
This feature is only for browsers that support the HTML editor.

Version without frames and JavaScript
This is a more accessible version for screen reader users.

Email messages when I am offline
You can receive copies of messages via email without the need to log in to your Moodle site. It's possible to set a different email address than the one in your profile.

Messaging Capabilities

Unlike forums and chat, messaging capabilities can only be set at the course or site level. These are:

Read all messages
> This allows a user to read all messages in the given context.

Send a message to many people
> This allows a user to send messages to selected users via the Participants list. By default, only teachers can send messages to many people.

> To allow a user to send a message to many people, you must also allow the user to read all messages.

Effective Messaging Practices

Messaging aids private communication with students. It is a useful alternative to email because you can track all correspondence in one place and avoid clogging your email inbox.

> *Jason*: Whilst it's true the messaging system can be set not to clog your inbox, I find email forwarding to be very useful. I'm logged in to my email more than I am logged in to all of the Moodle sites where I have an account. (At last count, I have accounts on six Moodle installations.) So I use email forwarding to make sure I get messages from people on various sites (especially *Moodle.org*).

Add contacts

The best way to manage your messages is to add as contacts people with whom you will communicate on a regular basis. The only way to access a message history with a person is through the contacts list, or by searching for the person in the search tab. It is much more convenient to have regular communication with people who are in your contacts list than to search for them constantly.

Use the participants list

One of the little-known additions to Moodle 1.6 was the ability to send messages to multiple students directly from the participants list.

To send a message to selected students:

1. Click on the Participants link in the People bock on the course page.
2. Select participants from the list or use the "Select all" button at the bottom of the list.
3. Choose "Add/send message" from the "With selected users..." drop-down menu at the bottom of the page.
4. Type the message, then click the Preview button.

---

5. When you're satisfied with the message, click the Send button.

Creative Messaging Practices

Tutorial support

Students frequently find the messaging system a useful way of sending private questions to their tutors. There are times when a student doesn't want to ask a question in a public forum. Messaging provides students with a private communication channel.

Tutors can also use the messaging system to send messages to one or more of their students. If the students for each tutor are in a group, the tutor can use the Groups filter on the participants list to find all of his students and send them a private message.

Encouraging participation

The message system, combined with the participants list, is a great tool for encouraging students to stay engaged with your course. On the participants list you can easily filter students based on how long they have been inactive. At the top of the page, one of the options is to select students who have been inactive for any length of time from a day to five months. In a normal class of 10–15 weeks, if once a week you send a message to students who have been inactive for a week, you can remind them to participate in the course. This will keep them more engaged and improve their performance and retention.

Summary

Moodle provides various channels of communication for you and your students. Forums are an asynchronous, public method for sharing ideas. Chats are a great way to have simultaneous conversations online with a group of people. Messaging provides a private channel for you to communicate directly with your students. Communication is key to success for any class, and it's even more important in an online environment.

CHAPTER 6

Quizzes

This chapter covers the following MTC skills: 5.7 Quiz

Feedback on performance is a critical part of a learning environment, and assessment is one of the most important activities in education. As educators, we can't tell what's going on inside students' heads, so we need a way for them to demonstrate what they understand and what they don't. A well-designed test, even a multiple-choice test, can give you valuable information about students' misconceptions. If the feedback is rapid enough, it can also be a critical tool for students to gauge their own performance and help them become more successful.

Moodle's quiz module is one of the most complex pieces of the system. The community has added a large number of options and tools to the quiz engine, making it extremely flexible. You can create quizzes with different question types, randomly generate quizzes from pools of questions, allow students to re-take quizzes multiple times, and have the computer score everything.

These features open up a number of strategies that usually aren't practical with paper-based testing. It's hard enough to score one batch of quizzes, and nearly impossible to score it 10 times for each student. When the computer does the work for you, it's easy to give students a chance to practice taking a test or give frequent small quizzes. We'll explore how to apply these advantages later in the chapter. For now, let's get started building your first Moodle quiz.

How to Create a Quiz

Moodle quizzes have two major components: the quiz body and the question pools. Think of the quiz bodies as containers for various types of questions from the question pools. The body is what students see when they take the assessment. It also defines how the students interact with the quiz. The questions in a quiz body can be of any type, chosen manually or at random, and displayed in a set or random order. The question pools can contain questions arranged in a manner that makes sense to you. You can create pools based on chapters in the textbook, weeks in the semester, important concepts, or any other organizational scheme. Pools can be reused in multiple quizzes, shared between classes and courses, and even moved between systems.

To start, we need to create a body for our first quiz.

Creating the Quiz Body

When you create the quiz body, you are creating a container for the questions and setting the rules for interacting with the quiz.

To create a quiz body:

1. Click "Turn editing on."

2. Select Quiz from the "Add an activity" drop-down menu in the course section where you would like to add the quiz.

3. In the "Adding a new quiz" page, as shown in Figure 6-1, give the quiz a descriptive name.

4. Write an introduction for the quiz. Be sure to include any special instructions for taking the quiz, such as the number of attempts allowed or scoring rules.

5. Select the timing options:

    Open the quiz; Quiz closes
        Choose opening and closing dates for the quiz.

    Time limit
        Determine how long students have to complete the quiz. At the end of the allotted time, the quiz is automatically submitted with the current answers.

    Time delay between attempts
        You can force a delay between multiple attempts of a quiz in order to prevent students from gaming the system by immediately answering the same questions.

6. Select the display options:

    Questions per page
        This sets the number of questions the students will see at once. If you have more questions than the number of questions per page, the students will see a navigation button at the bottom of the page where they can view the questions on other pages.

    Shuffle questions
        Set this to Yes to randomly order the quiz questions when they are displayed to the students.

    Shuffle within questions
        Set this to Yes to randomly order the parts making up individual multiple-choice or matching questions.

7. Select the attempts options:

Attempts allowed

Use this option to set the number of times a student can take a quiz. You can set it to unlimited times or to a number from 1 to 6.

Each attempt builds on the last

If you allow multiple attempts, you can choose to let students build their answers over time. If you set this to Yes, the student's responses from the last attempt will be visible the next time she tries to take the quiz.

Adaptive mode

In adaptive mode an additional Submit button is shown for each question. If the student presses this button, then the response to that particular question is submitted to be scored and the mark achieved is displayed to the student. The quiz will then allow the student to try again immediately, but a penalty will be applied to the score. The penalty is set in the Apply Penalties option.

8. Select the grades options:

Grading method

If you allow multiple attempts, you can choose which score is recorded. Your choices are highest grade, average grade, first attempt, and last attempt.

Apply penalties

This only applies if the quiz is run in adaptive mode.

Decimal digits in grades

Use this to set the number of decimal places in the grade for the quiz.

9. Select the options for students to review the quiz. You may choose whether to show students their responses together with their scores, the correct answers, and general and/or specific feedback:

Feedback

This is question response-specific text.

General feedback

This is text shown after attempting a question regardless of response given. It may be used to provide background information or perhaps a link to further information.

10. Select the security options:

Show quiz in a secure window

Selecting this option will open the quiz in a new window without the forward and back buttons, address bar, or other navigational features. This will prevent students from navigating to other sites during the quiz.

Require password

You can set a password for the quiz that students will need to enter before they can take the quiz. You can use this to restrict who takes a quiz and when they take it.

Require network address

This option restricts access to the test to certain IP address ranges. If you want to require students to take a test from a certain lab on campus, set the network address range to cover the networks in the lab. For example, if you want to require access from computers with an IP range of `10.10.10.0` to `10.10.10.50`, you would enter `10.10.10.0/50`. To allow access from all computers in a subnet (say, on the campus), enter the partial address you want to use.

11. Select the common module options:

Group mode

This is another location in which to set the group mode for the activity. If group mode is forced in the course settings then this setting will be ignored.

Visible

This determines whether students may view the activity or not.

12. Add overall feedback, i.e., text that is shown to a student after he has completed an attempt at the quiz. The text varies depending upon the quiz grade.

13. Click the "Save changes" button.

 If you can't find some of the above options, try clicking the Show Advanced button. Your system administrator may have hidden certain options in order to simplify the page.

Once you have saved your changes, you'll see the second editing screen where you will write and select questions to include in the quiz body.

Creating Questions for a Quiz

You can create your quiz questions on the "Editing quiz" page. Here, you'll also categorize your quiz questions and add them to the quiz body you just created.

On the left of the page, as shown in Figure 6-2, you'll see a block displaying the questions you've added to the current quiz. Since this is a new quiz, there are no questions there, and Moodle tells us this.

On the right of the page you'll see a category selection menu labeled Category and a button labeled "Edit categories." Categories are used to organize your quiz questions for your course, and they can be containers for sharing questions between courses. By default, there is one category, called Default. If you click on the category menu, you'll see it as an option.

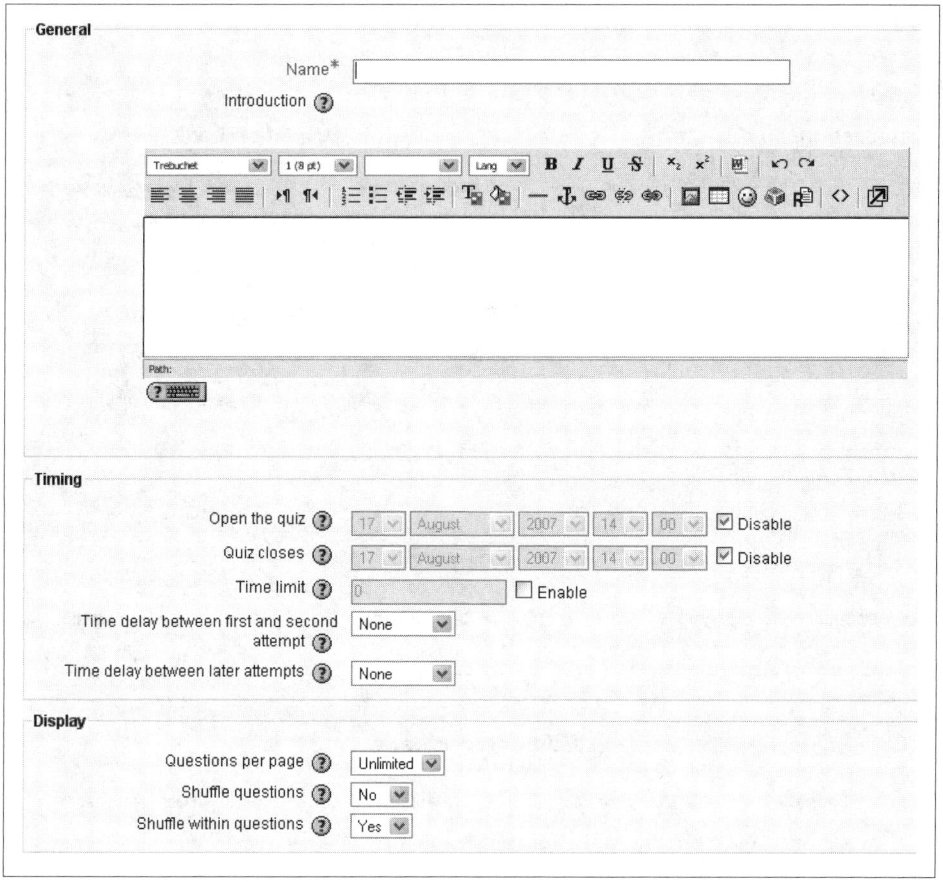

Figure 6-1. Adding a new quiz

It's good practice to create categories to organize your questions.

Jason: The level of detail in the categories is up to you, but I tend to lean toward more detailed categories that I can combine into larger groups later if I want to. For example, I'll break down questions related to a reading into a couple of concepts. It's easier to clump questions together later than it is to pull them apart.

Let's start out by making a category to hold the questions for our quiz:

1. From the "Editing quiz" page, click on the "Edit categories" button.

2. Above the list of current categories, as shown in Figure 6-3, you will see a space to add a new category.

3. Choose which category to place your new category in. If no other categories have been created, only Top will be available.

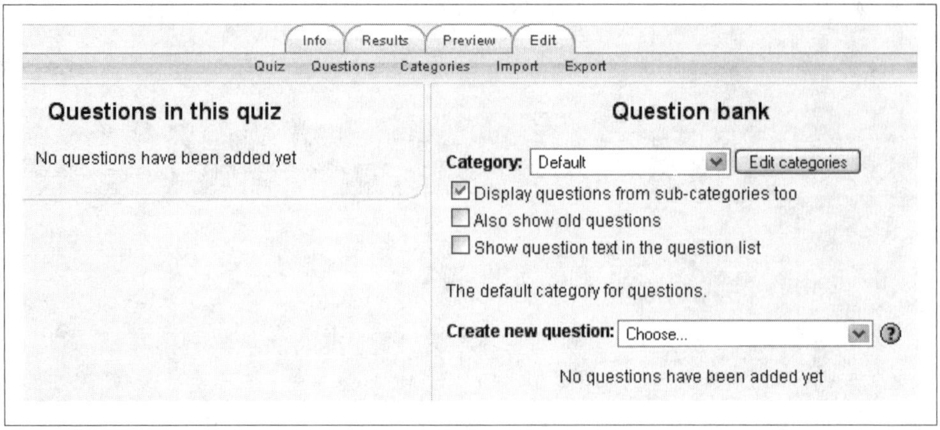

Figure 6-2. Adding questions

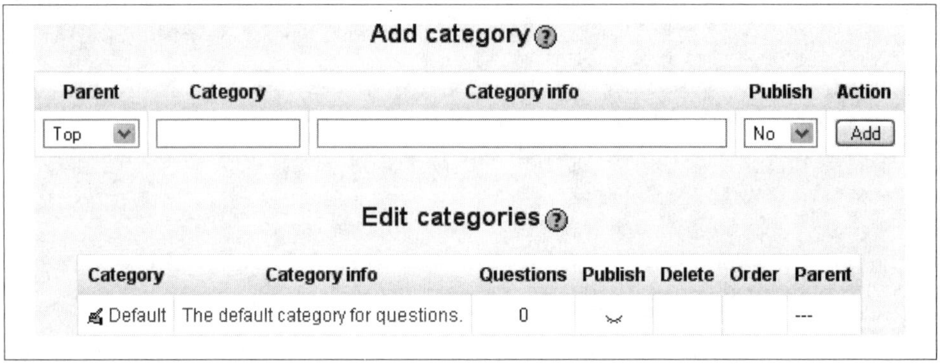

Figure 6-3. Edit categories

4. Type the name of your new question category in the text box.

5. Add a meaningful description in the "Category info" area.

6. If you'd like to share your question with teachers of other courses on your Moodle site, select Yes in the Publish column.

7. Click the Add button. Your new question category will appear in the list of current categories.

8. When you are done adding categories, click on the Quiz link below the tabs to return to the "Editing quiz" page.

Once you've created your categories, it's time to add some questions:

1. From the "Editing quiz" page, select a category to which you want to add a question. The area below the category will display the question-creation block.

2. Select the question type you want to create from the "Create new question" drop-down menu:

Multiple choice
> Both single- and multiple-answer multiple-choice questions are possible.

True/false
> This is a simple multiple-choice question with only two possible answers.

Short answer
> Students answer this question by typing a word or phrase. You need to provide a list of acceptable answers.

Numerical
> This is a short-answer question that accepts a numerical value instead of a word.

Matching
> This is a standard two-column matching question.

Random short-answer matching
> The subquestions for the matching exercise are randomly drawn from short-answer questions in the category.

Description
> This is for embedding some text in the quiz. (It's not a question type.) It can be used to give mid-quiz instructions.

Calculated
> This is a mathematical equation with placeholders for values that will be pulled randomly from a dataset when a student takes the quiz.

Essay
> This is a question requiring a paragraph or two of text. Students are not assigned a grade until you have reviewed and manually graded the question.

Embedded answers (Cloze)
> This is a question with multiple question types embedded within it, such as multiple choice, short answers, and numerical.

3. Fill in the form for the question type you are creating.
4. Click the "Save changes" button at the bottom of the form.

Each question type has its own form and options. We'll spend the next few pages detailing the options for each question type.

Multiple-choice questions

Moodle provides you with a lot of flexibility when creating this common question type. Figure 6-4 shows an example question. You can create single- and multiple-answer questions, display pictures in the question, and give relative grading weights to individual answers.

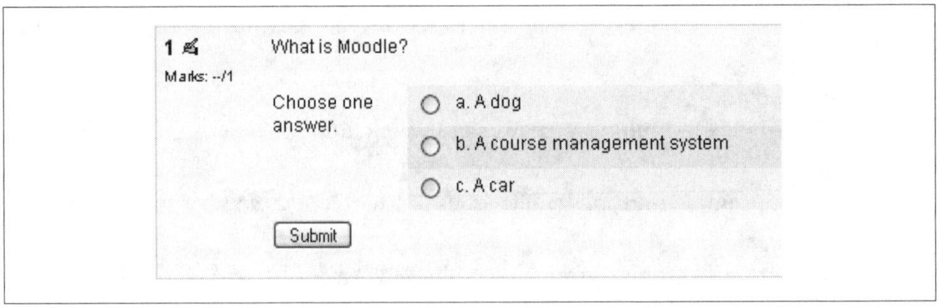

Figure 6-4. A multiple-choice question

To create a multiple-choice question:

1. Select "Multiple choice" from the "Create new question" drop-down menu.

2. On the multiple-choice question-editing page, start by giving the question a descriptive name. You'll use the name to track your questions later, so "Question 1" isn't a good idea.

3. Create the question text. If you're using the HTML editor, you can format the question just like a word-processing document.

   If you want to add an image to the question, you have two options:

   • If you've already uploaded an image to your files area (see Chapter 3 for details), it will be available to add to the question stem in a drop-down menu under the Question text area.

   • If you're using the HTML editor, you can click the image icon. This will pop up the Insert Image window. You can choose to upload an image into your files area from this window or add the URL of an image on the Web. If you add a file to your files area, click the name of the file after you upload it to insert the link into the URL text entry at the top of the screen. Then click OK.

4. Set the default question grade.

5. If you are intending to run the quiz in adaptive mode, set the penalty factor for each wrong response. The penalty factor should be a number between 0 and 1. A penalty factor of 1 means that the student has to get the answer right in her first response to get any credit for it at all. A penalty factor of 0 means the student can try as often as she likes and still get the full marks.

6. If you wish, add general feedback, i.e., text shown after attempting a question regardless of response given. General feedback will be displayed only if selected in the options for students to review the quiz.

7. Choose whether students can select only one answer or multiple answers.

8. Choose whether answers should be shuffled.

9. Write your first response in the Choice 1 answer field, as shown in Figure 6-5.

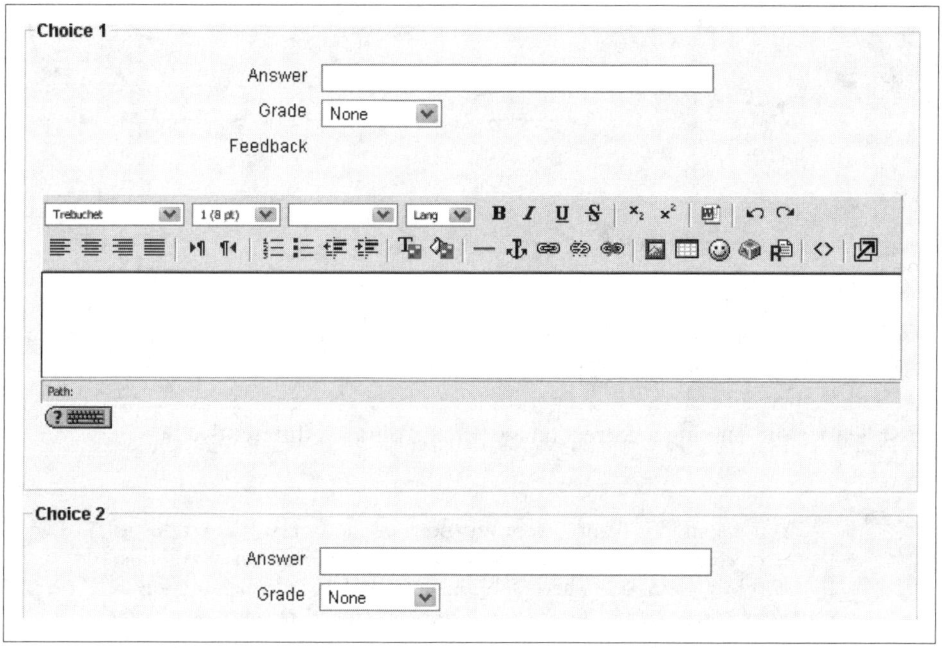

Choice 1

Answer [   ]

Grade [None ▾]

Feedback

[toolbar: Trebuchet ▾ | 1 (8 pt) ▾ | ▾ | Lang ▾ | **B** *I* <u>U</u> S̶ | x₂ x² | 🖼 | ↺ ↻]

[toolbar: ≡ ≡ ≡ ≡ | ¶ ¶ | ≝ ≝ ⇥ ⇤ | T₂ ⧆ | — ⚓ ⊜ ⊜ ⊜ | 🖼 ⊞ ☺ 🌐 🗐 <> 🗷]

Path:

[? ⌨]

Choice 2

Answer [   ]

Grade [None ▾]

Figure 6-5. A choice answer field

10. Select a grade percentage for the answer. This is the percentage of the total points possible for the question, selecting a given answer is worth. You can select negative percentages as well as positive percentages. So if a question is worth 10 points, selecting one correct response out of two in a multiple-choice question may give you 50 percent of the possible points (i.e., 5 points). Selecting a wrong answer may take away 10 percent (i.e., 2.5 points).

11. If you wish, you can add feedback for each response. Feedback will be displayed only if selected in the options for students to review the quiz.

> It may be a bit more work, but it's good practice to tell the students why each answer is right or wrong using the feedback area. If students know why an answer is right or wrong, they can analyze their own thinking and begin to understand the question.

12. Fill in the response choices in the rest of the form. Any unused areas will be ignored.

13. If you wish, you can add overall feedback for any correct/partially correct/incorrect answer. This is especially useful for multiple-answer questions where it is difficult to control what feedback students receive just using the answer-specific feedback.

14. Click the "Save changes" button to add the question to the category.

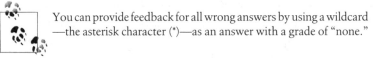

> **2** What is Moodle?
>
> Marks: --/1
>
> Answer: _____
>
> [Submit]

Figure 6-6. A short-answer question

Short-answer questions

Short-answer questions require the student to type an answer to a question, as shown in Figure 6-6. The answer could be a word or a phrase, but it must match one of your acceptable answers exactly. It's a good idea to keep the required answer as short as possible to avoid missing a correct answer that's phrased differently.

 You may find it helpful to prototype your short-answer questions to catch common acceptable answers you hadn't thought of. To do this, start by creating a few acceptable answers and include the question in a quiz for no points. Be sure to tell students you are testing a new question. Once the quiz is over, review students' answers and add their acceptable answers to the list.

To create a short-answer question:

1. Select "Short answer" from the "Create new question" drop-down menu.
2. Give your question a descriptive name.
3. Create the question text. If you want students to fill in a blank, use the underscore to indicate where the blank is.
4. Select an image to display if you want to add a picture to the question (see step 4 in the previous section for more details).
5. If you wish, add general feedback.
6. Choose whether capitalization is important. Case-sensitivity can be tricky. Will you accept "george Washington" as well as "George Washington" as an answer?
7. Fill in the answers you will accept. Give each answer a percentage of the grade if required. You could give common misspellings partial credit with this option.
8. Add feedback for each acceptable answer.

> You can provide feedback for all wrong answers by using a wildcard —the asterisk character (*)—as an answer with a grade of "none."

9. Click the "Save changes" button to add the question to the category.

3 What is 2 + 2?

Marks: --/1

Answer: [   ]

[Submit]

Figure 6-7. A numerical question

Numerical questions

Numerical questions are a lot like short-answer questions for equations, such as the one shown in Figure 6-7. You can create a question with an equation, and your students type in a numerical answer. Students will get credit for answers within the range of answers you specify.

To create a numerical question:

1. Select Numerical from the "Create new question" drop-down menu.
2. Give the question a descriptive name.
3. Type the equation or numerical question for your students to solve. Moodle has a couple of text filters, called Algebra and TeX, that allow you to type an equation and have it properly typeset when displayed. You may need to ask your system administrator to enable the filters.
4. Select an image to display if you want to add a picture to the question (see step 4 in the section "Multiple-choice questions" for more details).
5. If you wish, add general feedback.
6. Enter the correct answer and grade. You may choose to add a number of correct answers with different levels of accuracy and corresponding different levels of credit.
7. Enter the accepted error, i.e., the range above or below the correct answer. For example, if the correct answer is 5, but you will accept 4 or 6 as answers, your accepted error is 1.
8. Add feedback for each acceptable answer.

 As for short-answer questions, wrong-answer feedback may be provided using a wildcard.

9. If you want to accept answers in multiple units (e.g., metric or imperial units), specify the unit multiplier and the unit label in the areas.
10. Click the "Save changes" button to add the question to the category.

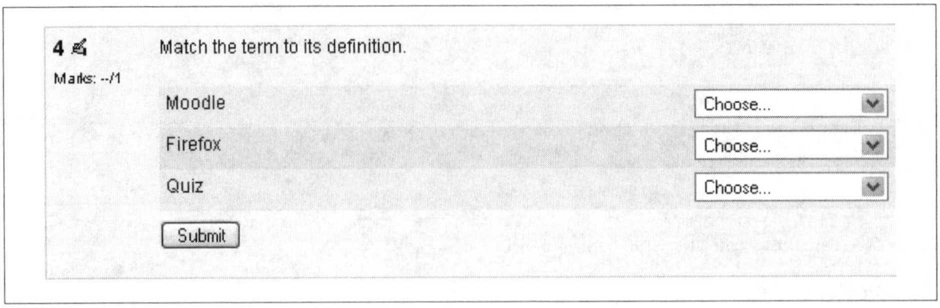

4 ☝ Match the term to its definition.

Marks: --/1

Moodle	Choose... ▼
Firefox	Choose... ▼
Quiz	Choose... ▼

[Submit]

Figure 6-8. A matching question

Matching questions

Matching questions ask students to match multiple question stems to multiple possible answers (see Figure 6-8). They are useful for testing students' understanding of vocabulary and their ability to match examples to concepts. Setting up a matching question in Moodle is a bit different from setting up other types of questions.

To create a matching question:

1. Select Matching from the "Create new question" drop-down menu.
2. Give the question a descriptive name.
3. Enter the question text to tell the students what they are matching.
4. Select an image to display if you want to add a picture to the question (see step 4 in the section "Multiple-choice questions" for more details).
5. If you wish, add general feedback.
6. For the first matching item, enter the question and a matching answer.
7. Fill in at least three questions and answers. You can enter as many as 10 items. You can provide extra wrong answers by giving an answer with a blank question.
8. Click the "Save changes" button to add the question to the category.

Moodle will display the question in two columns. The first will contain the questions. The second will display a drop-down menu for each question with all possible matching answers as options.

 Matching questions look better on screen if you put the longer piece of text in the question rather than the matching answer. For example, when vocabulary-matching, put the single word in the answer and the definition sentence in the question. Otherwise, the drop-down menu for long questions will be awkward to use and difficult to read.

Random short-answer matching questions

This is an interesting question type. You take random multiple short-answer questions and their correct answers and create a matching question out of them. It's an interesting way to reuse your short-answer questions in a new format.

To create a random short-answer matching question:

1. Select "Random short-answer matching" from the "Create new question" drop-down menu.
2. Give the question a descriptive name.
3. Enter the question text to tell the students what they are matching, or use the default text.
4. If you wish, add general feedback.
5. Select the number of questions you want to add to the matching question.
6. Click the "Save changes" button to add the question to the category.

Calculated questions

A calculated question is a mathematical equation with placeholders for values that will be pulled randomly from a dataset when a student takes the quiz. For example, if you wanted to create a large number of multiplication problems to drill your students, you could create a question with two placeholders and a multiplication sign such as {a} * {b}. When a student takes the test, Moodle will randomly select values for a and b. The test will very rarely appear the same way twice.

To create a calculated question:

1. Select Calculated from the "Create new question" drop-down menu.
2. Give the question a descriptive name.
3. Enter your question into the question field. All variables you want Moodle to replace with generated values must be placed in curly braces.
4. If you wish, add general feedback.
5. Enter the formula for the answer (see Figure 6-9). Be sure to use the same placeholders so Moodle can substitute the same values.
6. Determine the tolerance for error that you will accept in the answer. The tolerance and tolerance type combine to give a range of acceptable scores.
7. Select the number of significant figures or decimal places you want in the correct answer.
8. Add correct answer feedback.
9. Enter the units for the answer (e.g., meters, kg, etc.). Moodle will look for the correct units. If you want to enter other acceptable units, such as metric versus imperial distances, enter them along with a conversion factor.

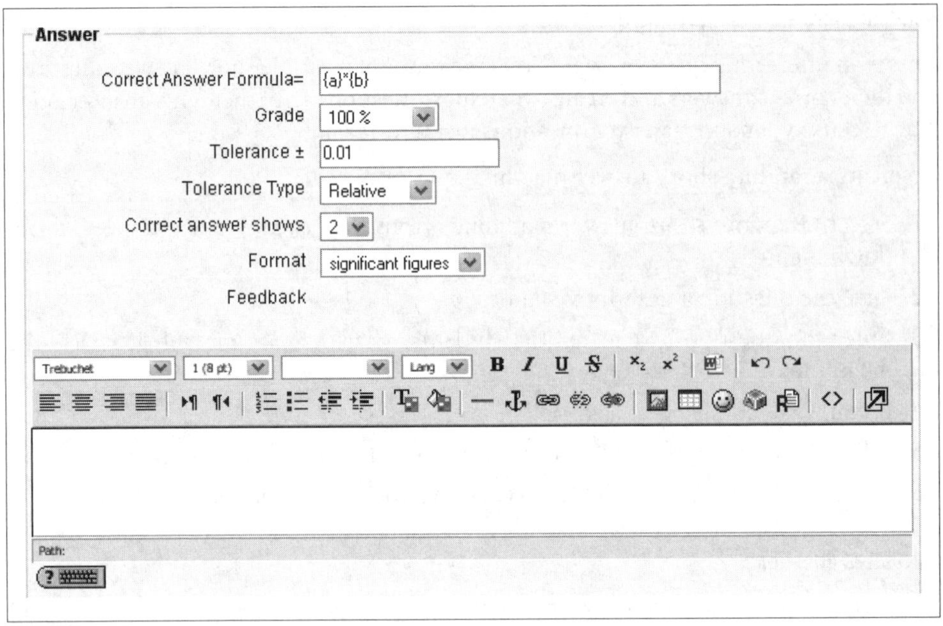

Figure 6-9. A calculated question answer field

10. Click the "Next page" button.

11. On the next page, choose whether to create substitution values for each placeholder only for this question, or for other questions in the same category.

12. Click the "Next page" button.

13. Create a dataset for the question or questions in the category. For each placeholder, generate a series of acceptable values. The more values you generate, the more a question can be used without repeating values. Figure 6-10 illustrates the interface for datasets for calculated questions.

14. Click the "Save changes" button.

Calculated questions can use more than simple arithmetic operators. The full list of operators includes abs, acos, acosh, asin, asinh, atan, atanh, ceil, cos, cosh, deg2rad, exp, expm1, floor, log, log10, log1p, rad2deg, round, sin, sinh, sprt, tan, tanh, atan2, pow, min, max, and pi. Each function's placeholders and other arguments are in parentheses. For example, if you want students to calculate the sine of one angle and two times the cosine of another, you would enter sin({a}) + cos({b}*2).

Essay questions

An essay question is a free-response text area where students can enter larger blocks of text in response to your question, as shown in Figure 6-11. These questions are not scored by the computer, and you will need to grade each answer manually.

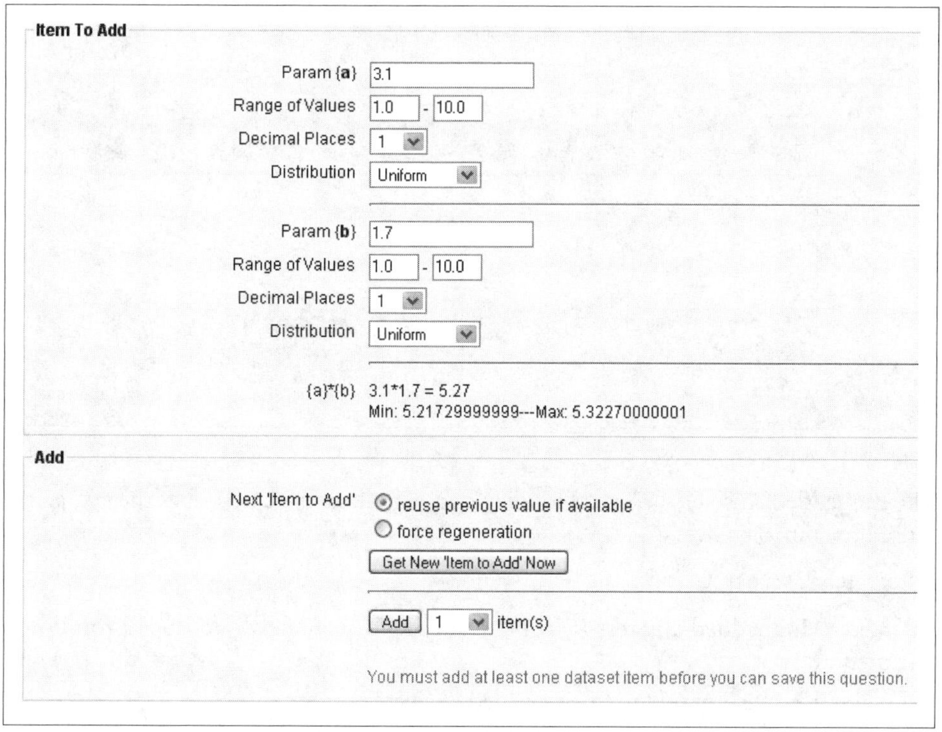

Figure 6-10. Editing calculated question datasets

To create an essay question:

1. Select Essay from the "Create new question" drop-down menu.
2. Give the question a descriptive name.
3. Enter the question text.
4. Select an image to display if you want to add a picture to the question (see step 3 in the section "Multiple-choice questions" for more details).
5. If you wish, add general feedback and/or specific feedback.
6. Click the "Save changes" button to add the question to the category.

Embedded answers (Cloze)

Embedded answer (Cloze) questions consist of a passage of text (in Moodle format) that has various answers embedded within it, including multiple choice, short answers, and numerical answers.

There is currently no graphical interface to create these questions—you need to specify the question format using the text box or by importing it from external files.

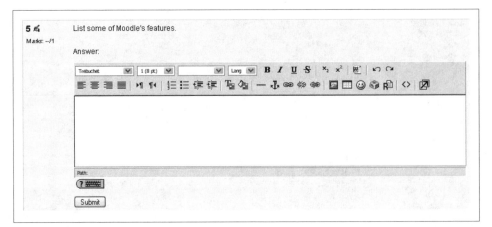

Figure 6-11. An essay question

The Embedded Answers (Cloze) Moodle documentation page describes the syntax required to embed answers.

To create a Cloze question:

1. Select "Embedded answers (Cloze)" from the "Create new question" drop-down menu.
2. Type the question text with embedded answers.
3. Continue to add text and embed questions until complete.
4. Click the "Save changes" button to add the question to the category.
5. Add the question to the quiz, then preview it, using the edit icon next to the question number to make additional edits if required.

Importing Questions

If you have questions from a textbook question bank, or if you don't want to use the web interface to create your questions, you can import them from a text file. Moodle supports a range of formats and provides an easy way to create new importers if you know a little PHP.

Once you get to know a format, it may be easier to type the questions into a text file than to use the web interface. You can just keep typing instead of waiting for new web pages to load for each question.

The default formats include:

GIFT
With GIFT format, you can write multiple-choice, true/false, short-answer, matching, and numerical questions.

Missing word

If you're going to write a lot of missing-word multiple-choice questions, the missing-word format is an easy way to create them.

Blackboard

If you're converting from Blackboard to Moodle, you can export your course and import the question pools into Moodle using the Blackboard format.

WebCT

Currently, the WebCT format supports only the importing of multiple-choice and short-answer questions.

Course Test Manager

This format enables you to import questions from the Course Test Manager from Course Technology.

Embedded answers (Cloze)

The Cloze format is a multiple-answer question with embedded answers. These questions can be a bit tricky to develop, but they provide a unique approach.

Moodle XML

This Moodle-specific format imports quiz questions that have previously been exported in the same format. It allows you to import image files used in the questions.

To import questions:

1. From the Question-editing page, click the Import link just below the tabs in the middle of the page.

2. In the "Importing questions" page, as shown in Figure 6-12, select a category into which the imported questions will go.

3. Select a file format. The help pop up next to the file format drop-down menu contains further details of each format.

4. Choose "Nearest grade if not listed" from the "Match grades" drop-down menu. Otherwise, a question will not be imported if its grade is not included in the list of accepted grades found in the help pop up.

5. Either browse for an import file on your computer and click the "Upload this file" button, or use the "Choose a file" button to browse for a file in your course files area and then click the "Import from this file" button.

Exporting Questions

You can share questions you have created by exporting them to a text file. Possible export formats are to GIFT, IMS QTI 2.0, Moodle XML, and XHTML.

To export questions:

1. From the "Editing question" page, click the Export link just below the tabs in the middle of the page.

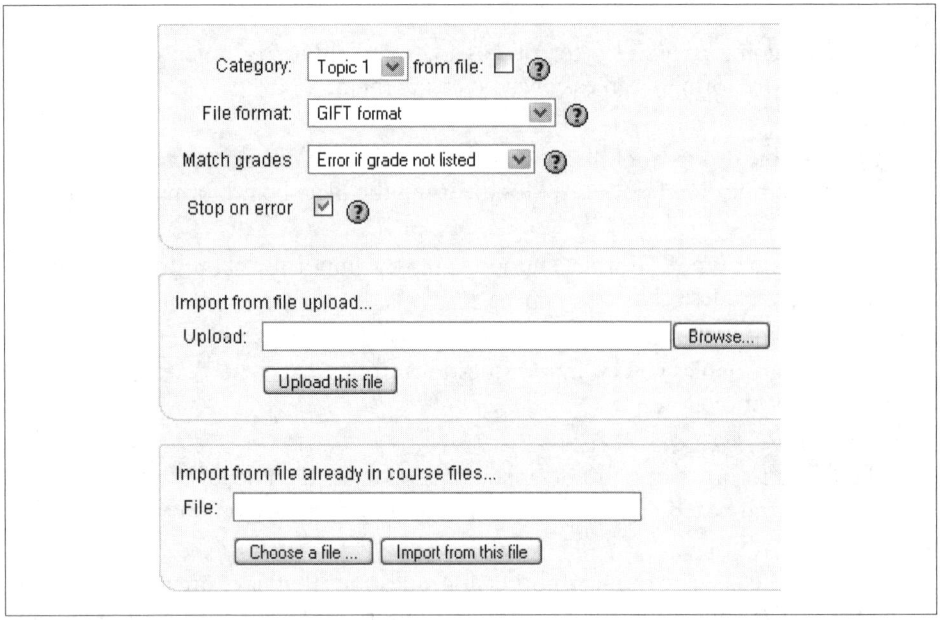

Figure 6-12. Importing questions

2. Select a category from which the exported questions will be taken.

3. Select a file format. The export questions page in the Moodle documentation contains links to further information on each export format.

4. Click the "Export questions to file" button.

The export file will be saved in your course files area in the backupdata folder.

Adding Questions to a Quiz

Once you've created your questions, you need to add them to the quiz.

On the "Editing quiz" page, as shown in Figure 6-13, click on the "Add to quiz" icons (<<) to add individual questions, or select a number of questions using the checkboxes and then click the "Add to quiz" button below the question list.

If you want to add all of the questions you created to the quiz, click the "Select all" link and then click the "Add to quiz" button.

Once you've added a question to the quiz, it appears on the left side of the page in the quiz question list. The question is still selectable on the right, but you can add it to the quiz only once. If you select the question in the category list again and add it to the quiz, nothing will happen.

If you have created a lot of questions, you may want to sort the question list by type and name or by age. You can also choose to display the question text below each

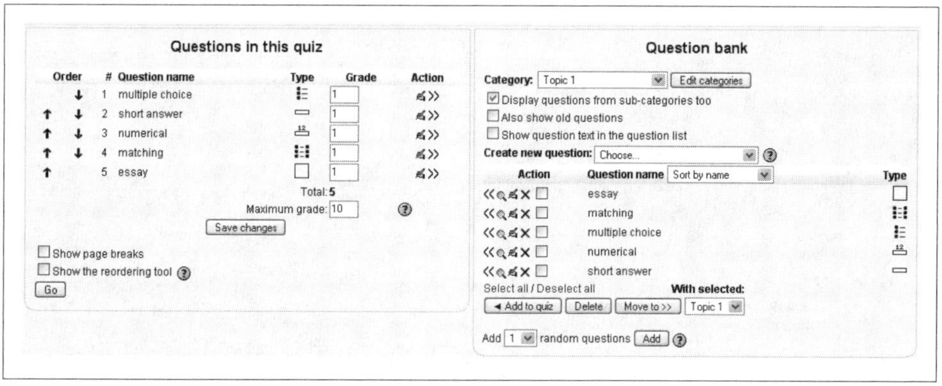

Figure 6-13. Editing a quiz

question name by checking the box "Show question text in the question list" above the question list.

Once you've added the questions to the quiz, you can change the order of the questions by clicking the arrow buttons in the Order column on the left side of the list of quiz questions.

If you have more than just a few questions, it's a good idea to limit the number of questions displayed per page. Check the box "Show page breaks," then set how many questions should be displayed per page and click the Go button.

You will also need to set the grade for each question. You can set the number of points for each question in the Grade column. You may want to make certain questions or question types worth more than others. Remember, the questions will be weighted to match the total points possible for the quiz you set in the quiz body. You should also set the "Maximum grade" for the whole quiz. This does not have to be equal to the sum of the grades for the individual questions. The grades achieved by the students will be rescaled to be out of this maximum grade. When you're done, click the "Save changes" button.

You can preview the quiz by clicking on the Preview tab at the top of the page. If you answer the questions, you can submit the quiz by clicking the "Submit all and finish" button and see the feedback and responses your students will see, as shown in Figure 6-14. Your students will see two scores at the top of the page. The first is the raw score representing the total points they scored out of the maximum possible points from each question. The second score is the weighted score representing the number of points out of the maximum possible points for the quiz.

If you've enabled feedback after answering, each question will be displayed below the scores with the answers marked correct or incorrect. If you've enabled the display of correct answers, they will appear highlighted.

In the next section, we'll discuss how to manage your quizzes.

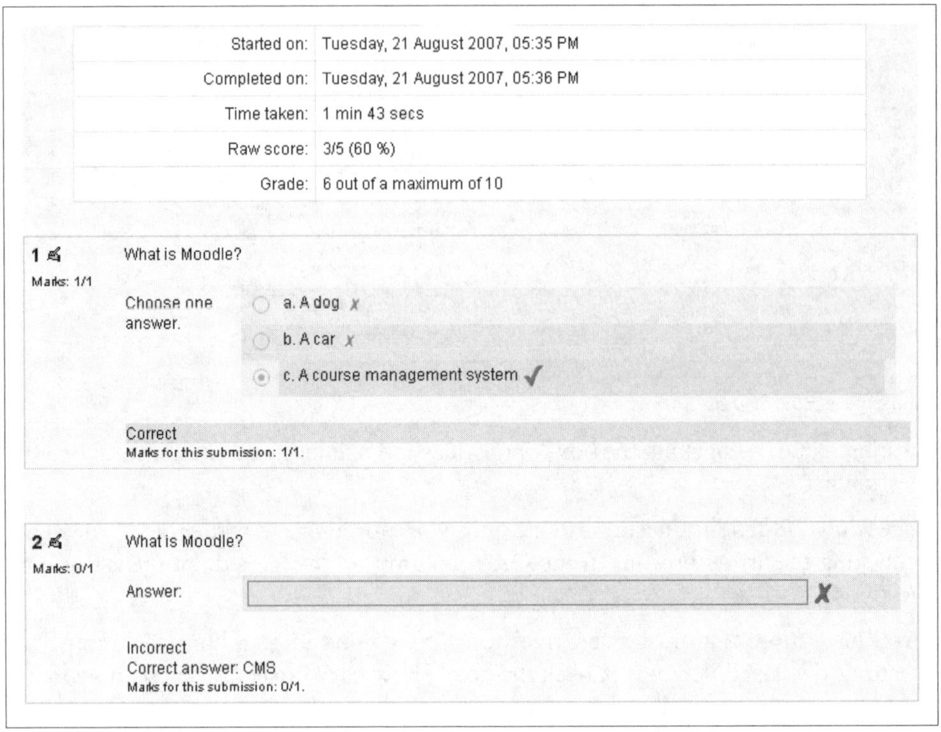

Started on:	Tuesday, 21 August 2007, 05:35 PM
Completed on:	Tuesday, 21 August 2007, 05:36 PM
Time taken:	1 min 43 secs
Raw score:	3/5 (60 %)
Grade:	6 out of a maximum of 10

1 ✍ What is Moodle?
Marks: 1/1

Choose one
answer.

    ○ a. A dog *x*

    ○ b. A car *x*

    ◉ c. A course management system ✓

Correct
Marks for this submission: 1/1.

2 ✍ What is Moodle?
Marks: 0/1

Answer: [   ] ✗

Incorrect
Correct answer: CMS
Marks for this submission: 0/1.

Figure 6-14. Quiz preview

Random questions

A random question is a placeholder for a randomly selected question. One of the advantages of a computer-generated quiz is the ability to generate a quiz from questions randomly selected from a category. Each random question will pull a question randomly from the question category and insert it into the quiz. This means that different students are likely to get a different selection of questions. When a quiz allows multiple attempts for each student then each attempt is likely to contain a new selection of questions. The same question will never appear twice in an attempt. If you include several random questions then different questions will always appear for each of them. If you mix random questions with nonrandom questions then the random questions will be chosen so that they do not duplicate one of the nonrandom questions. This means that you need to provide enough questions in the category from which the random questions are chosen, otherwise the student will receive a friendly error message. The more questions you provide the more likely it will be that students get different questions on each attempt.

To add random questions to the quiz:

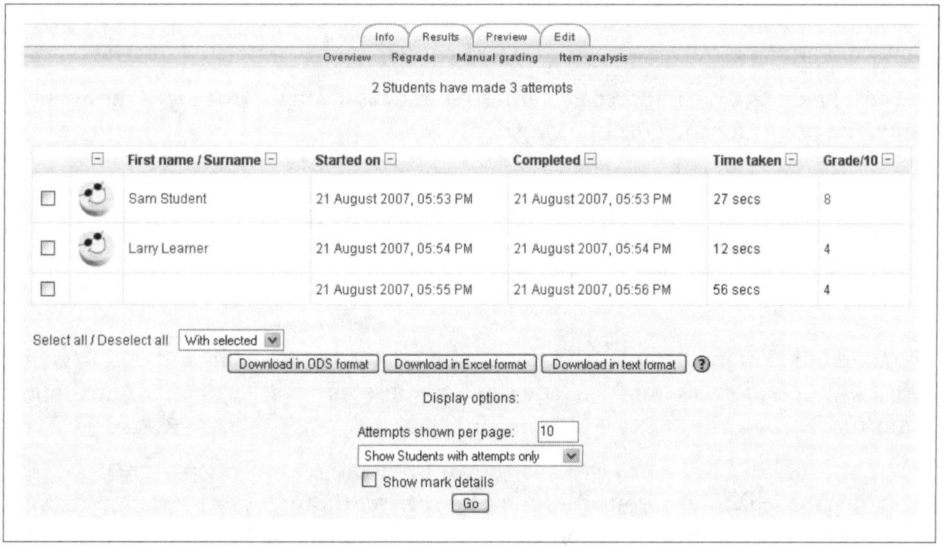

Info
Results
Preview
Edit
Overview
Regrade
Manual grading
Item analysis
2 Students have made 3 attempts
First name / Surname
Started on
Completed
Time taken
Grade/10
Sam Student
21 August 2007, 05:53 PM
21 August 2007, 05:53 PM
27 secs
8
Larry Learner
21 August 2007, 05:54 PM
21 August 2007, 05:54 PM
12 secs
4
21 August 2007, 05:55 PM
21 August 2007, 05:56 PM
56 secs
4
Select all / Deselect all
With selected
Download in ODS format
Download in Excel format
Download in text format
Display options:
Attempts shown per page:
10
Show Students with attempts only
Show mark details
Go

Figure 6-15. Quiz results

1. Select the number of random questions you wish to add from the drop-down menu below the question list.
2. Click the Add button.

Managing Quizzes

Once students start to take the quizzes, you'll have a lot of data available. If you click on the quiz link in the middle column of your course page, you'll immediately see the number of quizzes that your students have completed. If you click on the Results tab, you'll see the quiz results overview page, as shown in Figure 6-15. From here, you can see every quiz attempt and drill down into the individual responses. Clicking on the date and time of the attempt provides each question and answer.

If you want to delete an attempt, click on the checkbox next to the student's name and then select Delete from the drop-down menu below the attempts list.

> If you decide to add additional questions to the quiz, you will need to delete all attempts before being allowed to do so.

There is a choice of three formats for downloading the table of results: Open Document Spreadsheet, Excel, or text.

If you want to see the marks for each question, check the "Show mark details" box, then click the Go button.

Above the attempts list, there are four links. The first link, Overview, shows the list of completed attempts you saw when you first clicked on the completed quiz link.

The next link, Regrade, is for recalculating quiz grades if you have changed the possible number of points for the quiz or a question.

 If your students come up with a correct answer to a short-answer question that you had not previously thought of, you can edit the short-answer question, then regrade the quiz.

The third link, "Manual grading," is for grading essay questions. In addition to giving each essay question attempt a grade, you can also provide feedback by writing a comment.

The fourth link is "Item analysis," as shown in Figure 6-16. This is a great tool for evaluating the reliability of your questions. You can see the three most common answers to each question, the percentage of students who got each question correct, the standard deviation, the discrimination index, and the discrimination coefficient. The discrimination index correlates students' overall performance on the quiz to their performance on each item; stronger students should have a better chance of getting each individual question correct, and weaker students should have a lower chance of getting each item correct. If the distribution of correct and incorrect responses is flat (everyone has an equal chance of being correct), then everyone is guessing. If everyone is getting it right (or wrong), then the question is too easy (or too hard). The higher the discrimination index, the better the question is at providing useful data about student performance.

Below the item analysis table are various analysis options, such as restricting the analysis to students' first attempts. Low scores, perhaps for trial attempts, may be rejected by setting a low limit for the score of the attempts to analyze.

Again, there is a choice of formats for downloading the item analysis table for further analysis.

Quiz Capabilities

The quiz module has a range of capabilities that allow you to create a number of student roles:

View quiz information
    This allows a user to view the quiz introduction but not attempt the quiz itself.

Attempt quizzes
    This allows a user to attempt the quiz as well as view the quiz introduction.

Q#	Question text	Answer's text	partial credit	R. Counts	R.%	% Correct Facility	SD	Disc. Index	Disc. Coeff.
(16) multiple choice : What is Moodle?		A course management system	(1.00)	4/4	(100%)	100 %	0.000	-0.50	-999.00
		A dog	(0.00)	0/4	(0%)				
		A car	(0.00)	0/4	(0%)				
(17) short answer : What is Moodle?		CMS	(1.00)	2/4	(50%)	50 %	0.577	0.50	0.61
		course management system	(0.00)	0/4	(0%)				
(18) numerical : What is 2 + 2?		4 (4..4)	(1.00)	2/4	(50%)	50 %	0.577	0.00	0.43
(19) matching : Match the term to its definition.		Moodle: A CMS	(1.00)	1/4	(25%)	25 %	0.500	0.50	0.65
		Quiz: An activity in Moodle	(1.00)	1/4	(25%)				
		Firefox: A web browser	(1.00)	1/4	(25%)				
(22) essay : List some of Moodle's features.			(0.00)	0/4	(0%)	13 %	0.250	0.00	0.05
		Moodle has quizzes!	(0.00)	1/4	(25%)				

Analysis options:

Attempts to analyze per user: all attempts

Don't analyse if score is less than: 0 %

Questions per page: 10

Go

Download in ODS format   Download in Excel format   Download in text format

Figure 6-16. Item analysis

Manage quizzes

This allows a user to edit and delete quizzes. Editing quizzes allows the user to add and subtract questions and change the quiz settings.

Preview quizzes

This allows a user to preview the quiz as part of the editing process.

Grade quizzes manually

This allows a user to change the scores on a quiz, and manually grade quiz essay questions.

View quiz reports

This allows a user to see the reports detailing user responses and question statistics.

Delete quiz attempts

This allows a user to delete both their own and other users' quiz attempts.

Ignores time limit on quizzes

A user with this capability can take as long as he wants to complete a quiz.

You may wish to allow the capability "Ignores time limit on quizzes" for students with learning disabilities that require they be given additional time to take assessments.

Effective Quiz Practices

As we've seen, the Moodle quiz engine is a powerful, flexible tool for monitoring and diagnosing a student's understanding of certain types of knowledge. Using this tool effectively can boost your course's effectiveness and promote student performance. While a computer-scored quiz is a different evaluation than more open-ended assessments, it does give valuable insight into student thinking, especially when you use good strategies and a little creativity.

Quiz Strategies

Of course, using the quiz engine effectively takes some work and practice. The first thing to do is use effective question-design strategies. If you ask good questions, you'll get useful data about your students' performance and understanding of the material. Of course, the converse is also true. There is a ton of literature about effective assessment design available. We'll just highlight a few of the most important ideas:

- Tie each question to a course goal. After all, you want to know whether your students are achieving the goals of the course, so why not ask them directly?
- Try to ask multiple questions about each important idea in the class. This gives you more data points about a student's understanding.
- When writing a multiple-choice question, be sure each wrong answer represents a common misconception. This will help you diagnose student thinking and eliminate easy guessing.
- Write questions requiring your students to think at different levels. Include recall questions, comprehension questions, and application and analysis questions. You can determine where students are having problems in their thinking. Can they recall the material but not apply it?
- Test your questions. After you've established an initial question bank, use item analysis to determine which questions are useful and which aren't. As you write new questions, give them a lower point value and throw in a few to establish their reliability.

Once you have a few well-written test banks, be sure to use the quiz reports and statistics to monitor your classes' performance. The detailed reports and statistics are valuable tools for measuring your students' understanding of the material.

Creative Quiz Uses

With the Moodle quiz engine, it's easier to utilize educationally sound assessment strategies that would be too difficult to implement with paper and pencil. Most people think of tests as an infrequent, high-stakes activity, such as midterms and finals. Better strategies involve frequent, low-stakes assessments you and your students can use to guide student performance during the course of the semester.

Creating a series of mini-tests gives you a very flexible system for gauging performance and keeping students engaged in the class. Here are a few ideas for quick quizzes you can use as part of a larger assessment strategy.

Chapter checks

Getting students to complete reading assignments has to be one of the hardest motivational tasks in education. Reading is critical to understanding most material and fundamental to success in many classes. The problem for most students is that there is no immediate punishment for procrastinating on a reading assignment. If they haven't done the reading for a class discussion, they can either keep quiet or skim-read it in class. There's almost no need to do the reading for a lecture course, since the lecturer usually covers most of the material in class anyway.

Creating a mini-test for each reading assignment solves a number of problems. First, it encourages students to do the reading so they can do well on the quiz. Second, it gives the students feedback on how well they understood the reading assignment. Third, it gives you data about which aspects of the reading students found confusing, and which they have already mastered, so you can refocus your class activities.

For a reading mini-test, setting a limited-time quiz that students can take only once is recommended. Because it's a low-stakes activity that students should use for self-assessment, you could also display feedback and correct answers. If you're concerned about students sharing answers after they've taken the quiz, randomize the question and answer order. If you have a test bank, make some of the questions random as well. As an additional assignment, you could ask students to write down one question about a question they got wrong and bring it to class.

Test practice

They key to effective practice is to have a realistic practice environment. Many students worry about tests, especially high-stakes tests, because they have no idea what to expect. What question format will you use? How detailed will the questions be? What should students study?

You can help alleviate test anxiety by creating a practice test students can take to help answer these questions. These tests are usually based on old questions similar to the upcoming test questions. Using last year's final as an example test will force you to write new questions every year. This is a good idea anyway, since you can be sure someone has a copy of last year's test and is sharing it with others.

To set up a practice test, you could create a zero-point test with questions from the year before in random order with random answers. You could also allow students to take the test as many times as they like so they can test themselves as much as they need. Display feedback, but not correct answers, so the test presents more of a challenge.

Data gathering

As an expert, you know a lot about your field. Your challenge as a teacher is to translate your knowledge for a novice who doesn't share your conceptual understanding or experience. An example or lecture you think is brilliant may leave your students completely confused. It can be hard to tell what students really understand and what's leaving them baffled.

A data-gathering quiz is similar to a chapter check, but it takes place after a class meeting or lecture. Your goal is to quickly get some feedback on your students' understanding of a lecture. What did they really understand? What do you need to spend more time on? It can be difficult to gauge what students find difficult and what they find so easy that it bores them.

Setting up a post-class data-gathering quiz is similar to creating a chapter check. Set the quiz for a limited time, such as a day or two before the next meeting. Allow your students to take it once and display feedback and correct answers.

Progressive testing

A very nice example of using the new feedback system with other options is the idea of progressive testing. To implement this, you need to create a series of increasingly difficult quizzes. The first quiz should be open to anyone, with the later quizzes protected by a password. In the feedback for each quiz, decide a cutoff percentage which you feel represents mastery of the skills tested. If the students' score is greater than the cutoff score, the feedback message includes a link to the next quiz with the appropriate password.

In this way, students gradually have access to increasingly difficult tests, and it allows them to concretely demonstrate their progress. But they don't become frustrated with questions that are too difficult.

Quiz Security and Cheating

Of course, online testing also presents another chance for the cheaters in your classes to try to game the system. Most online quizzes are meant to be taken at home, or at least outside of class. Students can download the questions and print them out. They can take the tests with other students or while reading their textbooks.

Fortunately, you can counter many of these strategies, making them more trouble than they are worth. Let's look at a few strategies for countering most cheating schemes:

Printing and sharing questions

If you display feedback and correct answers, students can print the results page and share it with their friends. Or they can simply print the questions themselves directly from the quiz. The key to discouraging this behavior is to randomize the question order and answer order. It makes the printouts a lot less useful. Creating larger question banks and giving tests with random subsets is also an effective strategy. If students can print only a small number of questions at a time, they will need to view the test again and again, and then sort the questions to eliminate duplicates.

Using the textbook

Students will frequently look up the answer to questions in the textbook or a reading. If you are giving a chapter-check quiz, then this is what you want them to do. Otherwise, you need to come up with creative ways to make the textbook less directly useful. Timed quizzes are the single most effective tool for eliminating this strategy. If you include enough questions and make the time to take the quiz short enough, students won't have time to look up all the answers.

Jason: I usually allot about 30 seconds per multiple-choice question. If they answer them faster and have time to look up some answers afterward, I figure they knew enough to deserve the option of looking up an answer or two.

Assume there will be printed copies of your questions available to students who want them. Most instructors don't realize students frequently have copies of old paper-based tests, and delivering a test electronically is another way for students to get copies of the questions.

Jason: I know one professor who had over 1,100 questions in his online test bank. At the end of the semester, he confiscated a printout from a student. It had every question with the correct answer, neatly formatted and divided by textbook chapter. We decided if students wanted to memorize 1,100 questions to the level where they could answer a small number of them displayed at random, then they would have learned more than if they had just studied. Of course, we used timed quizzes and other strategies to minimize using the printout as a reference manual.

Asking students to apply their knowledge to novel situations can also make a difference. Synthesis and application questions can't be looked up. Students have to understand the material and apply it creatively to answer the questions. So while they may take the time to review the text, they will still need to understand what they've read to successfully answer the question.

Working with friends

If your students are on the same campus, they may meet in a lab and try to take the quiz together. This strategy is easily thwarted with random question order, random answer order, and random questions pulled from a test bank. If my screen doesn't look like yours, then it's harder for us to quickly answer all of the questions. A timed quiz also makes it harder for the two of us to cheat if we have different questions and only a short amount of time to answer.

Have someone else take the test

The old adage goes, "On the Internet, no one knows you're a dog." And no one knows who is actually taking the test. Students will sometimes pay classmates, or others who have taken the course in the past, to take online quizzes for them. There are two ways to counter this strategy. One, have an occasional proctored exam where students need to show ID. If they haven't taken the quizzes or done the work until then, they will do poorly on the proctored exam. Second, to eliminate current classmates from taking each other's quizzes, make them available only for a short time. You could require everyone to take the test within a two- to four-hour block. If the test is properly randomized, it will be very difficult to take it more than once during the testing period. The test-taker will worry about her own grade first, then about her employer's grade.

Obviously, there are many strategies students can use to cheat. While it would be naïve to assume there isn't cheating, the vast majority of your students want to succeed on their own merits. The anonymity of the online environment may open up new avenues for the cheaters, but it's not really much different from your face-to-face classes. A few people will go to great lengths to cheat, but most will be honest as long as it's not too easy to get away with it. A few precautions will eliminate most of the cheaters, and the classic strategies will work for the others.

CHAPTER 7

Assignments

This chapter covers the following MTC skills: 5.1 Assignments

After the complex and powerful quiz module, assignments are a refreshingly simple method for collecting student work. They are a simple and flexible catch-all for things you want to grade that don't fall into any of the other tool types.

The assignment module gives you an easy way to allow students to upload digital content for grading. You can ask them to submit essays, spreadsheets, presentations, web pages, photographs, or small audio or video clips. Anything they can store on their hard drives can be submitted in response to an assignment.

Assignments don't necessarily have to consist of file uploads. You can create offline assignments to remind students of real-world assignments they need to complete. Alternatively, you can ask students to input their answer directly into the assignment itself.

Assignments are a useful tool you can use in creative ways to collect more authentic responses from your students than is possible with the quiz engine.

Assignment Types

There are four assignment types:

Upload a Single File
    This allows each student to upload a single file in any format, including a ZIP file.

Offline Activity
    This is useful when the assignment is performed outside of Moodle. It could be something face-to-face or on paper. Students can see a description of the assignment, but they can't upload any files.

Online Text
    This allows students to input text online. You can grade the assignment online and, if necessary, add inline comments or changes.

Advanced Uploading of Files

This allows each student to upload one or more files in any format. As the teacher, you can also upload one or more files for each student, either at the start or in response to their submission. A student may enter notes describing their submitted files, progress status, or any other relevant information.

Creating Assignments

Compared to some of the other tools we've looked at, assignments are easy to create. Once you've decided on the basic type of assignment, you can very quickly create a place for students to upload or enter their responses to the materials.

To create an assignment:

1. Click "Turn editing mode on."
2. Select an assignment type from the "Add an activity" drop-down menu.
3. On the "Adding a new assignment" page, as shown in Figure 7-1, give your assignment a descriptive name.
4. In the Description area, carefully describe your assignment. It's a good idea to be very detailed here, even if you've already detailed the requirements in your syllabus. In fact, you might want to copy and paste from your syllabus to avoid confusion.
5. Choose the grade scale you want to use for the assignment.
6. Set the "Available from" date and "Due date" for your assignment or check the Disable boxes.
7. Decide whether to prevent late submissions.
8. Choose the options for the type of assignment you have chosen:

   Advanced uploading of files
   - Set the maximum size for a file upload. (The top of the scale is set by your system administrator. There is also a maximum upload size in your course settings.)
   - Choose whether students may delete uploaded files at any time before grading.
   - Set the maximum number of files each participant may upload. Note that students can't see this number, so it's a good idea to write the actual number of requested files in the assignment description.
   - Choose whether to enable students to enter notes into the text area. This can be used for communication with the grading person, for assignment progress description, or for any other written activity.
   - Decide whether to hide the assignment description prior to the date when the assignment is available.

- Choose whether teachers should be alerted via email whenever students add or update their submission.

Online text

- Decide whether to allow students to resubmit assignments after they have been graded (for you to regrade).
- Choose whether teachers should be alerted via email whenever students add or update an assignment submission.
- Choose whether the student's submission will be copied into the feedback comment field during grading, making it easier to comment inline or to edit the original text.

Upload a single file

- Choose whether to allow students to resubmit assignments after they have been graded (for you to regrade).
- Choose whether teachers should be alerted via email whenever students add or update their submission.
- Set the maximum size for a file upload. (As mentioned previously, the top of the scale is set by your system administrator and there is also a maximum upload size in your course settings.)

9. Select the common module options:

Group mode

Another location to set the group mode for the activity. If group mode is forced in the course settings, then this setting will be ignored.

Visible

This determines whether students may view the activity or not.

10. Click the "Save changes" button to make your assignment available.

Your assignment will appear in your course page. It will also be added to your course calendar and will appear in the Upcoming Events block to remind students when it's due.

To see how your assignment appears for your students, select Student from the "Switch role to" drop-down menu in the top-right corner of the course page, next to the "Turn editing on" button. The "Return to my normal role" link at the bottom of each page restores your teacher status.

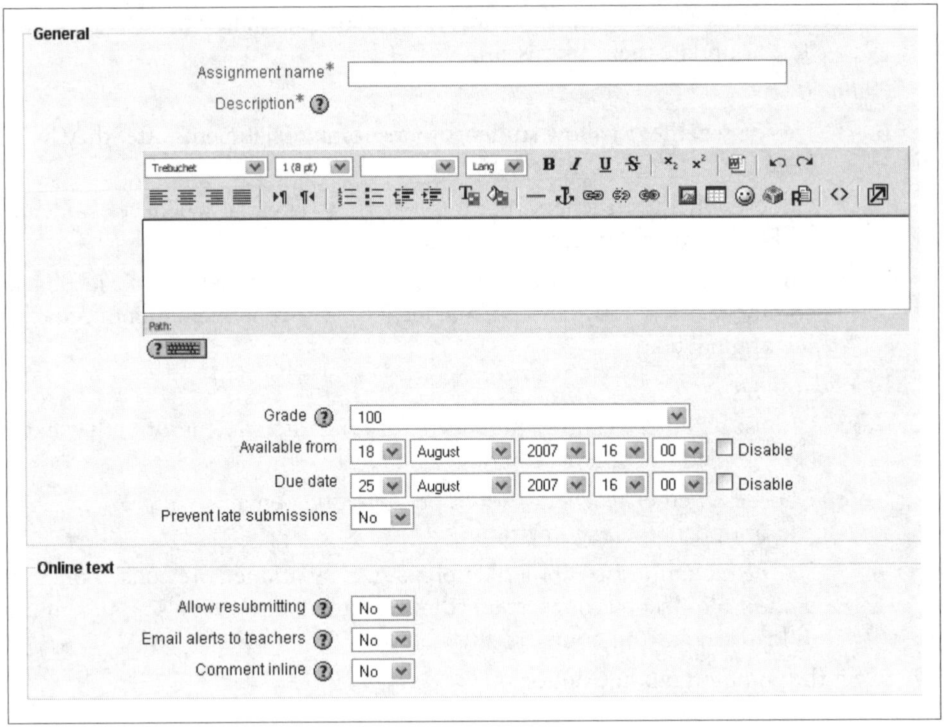

Figure 7-1. Adding a new assignment

Assignment Capabilities

The assignment module has only three capabilities:

View assignment
> This allows a user to view the assignment but not submit anything.

Submit assignment
> This allows a user to make an assignment submission.

Grade assignment
> This allows a user to view all assignment submissions and grade them.

Managing Assignment Submissions

To view your students' submissions, click on the assignment name in your course page. You'll see the assignment name and details and a link in the upper-right corner of the page telling you how many assignments have been submitted. Click on this link.

The assignment submissions page, as shown in Figure 7-2, contains a table with these headings: First name/Surname; Grade; Comment; Last modified (Student); Last modified (Teacher); and Status. The list may be sorted by clicking on a particular heading.

	First name / Surname ↓ □	Grade □	Comment □	Last modified (Student) □	Last modified (Teacher) □	Status □
First name : **All** A B C D E F G H I J K L M N O P Q R S T U V W X Y Z
Surname : **All** A B C D E F G H I J K L M N O P Q R S T U V W X Y Z
😊	Larry Learner	-		📄 First_topic.doc Saturday, 18 August 2007, 06:07 PM		Grade
😊	Sam Student	**95 / 100**	Excellent work!	📄 Topic_1.doc Saturday, 18 August 2007, 05:38 PM	Saturday, 18 August 2007, 05:56 PM	Update

Submissions shown per page: 10 (?)

Allow quick grading: ☐ (?)

Save preferences

Figure 7-2. Assignment submissions

Clicking twice on the same heading sorts the list in the opposite order. If the table is too large, then columns may be collapsed by clicking on the Hide icon next to a particular column heading.

By default, 10 submissions are shown per page, though this may be changed at the bottom of the page.

To grade a submission, click on the Grade link opposite a particular student's name. A new window will open containing a feedback area (see Figure 7-3).

For *Upload a Single File* and *Advanced Uploading of Files* assignments, there is a link to download the file together with the date it was last submitted. You will need to open it in another application, unless it's a web page. So if your student submits a Word document, you'll need to save it to your desktop and open it in Word.

For an *Advanced Uploading of Files* assignment, you have the option to upload a response file. Students may upload draft files for you to review at any time. When their assignment is finished, they can mark it as final by clicking the "Send for marking" button. Prior to grading, you may choose to revert an assignment back to draft status.

For an *Online Text* assignment, the text is displayed in a box with the word count above. If comment inline has been enabled, then the text is copied into the feedback comment field.

Once you've reviewed the student's assignment, pick the grade for the assignment from the drop-down list. (You set the scale when you created the assignment.) Below the grade scale, you can type comments regarding the student's work. When you're done, click "Save changes" or "Save and show next."

To quickly grade multiple assignments all on one page, rather than one by one in a new window, check the "Allow quick grading" box at the bottom of the assignment submissions page. Simply add the grades and comments, then when you're done click "Save all my feedback" at the bottom of the page.

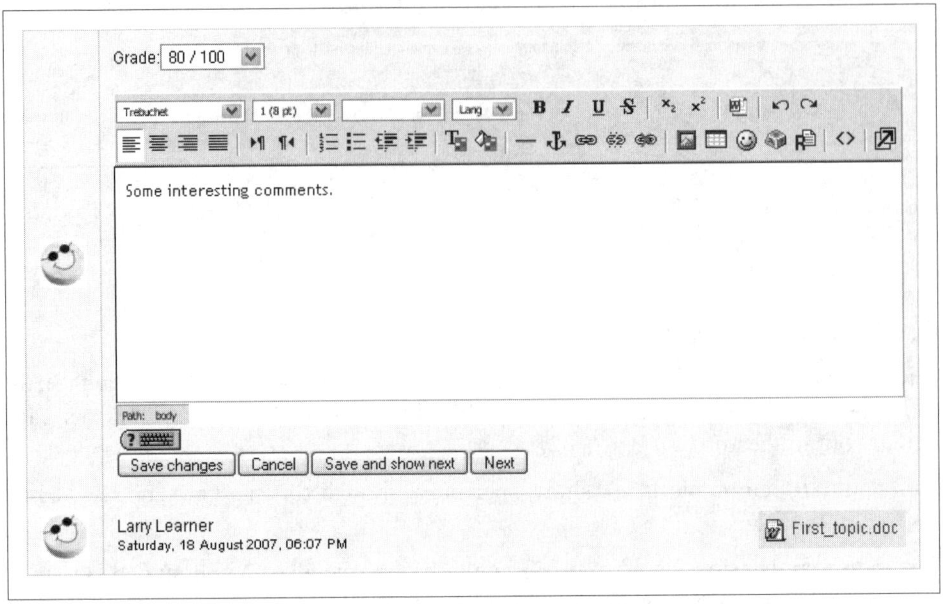

Figure 7-3. Assignment feedback

If you've set an *Offline Activity* assignment, you can enter grades and comments in the same way as for the other types of assignments.

Students can see their grades and comment in two ways. First, they can click on the assignment link again. They will see their grades and comments below the submission block. Alternatively, they can click on the Grades link in the course Administration block. They will see the grade for the assignment and can then click on the assignment name to get the written feedback.

Effective Assignment Practices

The two most basic assignment types, offline and upload, are so generic you may find it difficult to use them effectively at first. You may find it useful to think about them as two separate modules sharing a common interface.

Offline assignments are useful for recording grades for real-world activities. Currently, they are a sort of hack that allows the creation of manual columns in the grades module. If you look at the grades area (which we'll cover in Chapter 13), you'll notice there is no way to add a column in order to add grades not automatically generated by a quiz or other tool. The offline assignment gives you a way around this limitation by adding a column in which you can record any grade at all. This limitation will be addressed in Moodle 1.9, which includes a completely rewritten gradebook.

The offline assignment is more than just a hack, however. You can use this tool to record scores or feedback for student presentations, class participation, performances, sculptures, or any other nondigital performance. You can create a scale to give nonnumeric feedback if you don't want to give a numeric score to a creative performance. Again, we'll cover creating scales in detail in Chapter 13.

Uploaded assignments are probably what most people expect when they think about assignments. Remember, you can use these assignment types for any sort of digital content. Most instructors use assignments to collect essays and other word-processing assignments. You can also use them to collect other types of student work. Students could upload PowerPoint slides prior to a presentation. You could assign a what-if scenario using a spreadsheet and ask students to submit it. Students could take a digital photograph of a sculpture or mechanical project and submit it for evaluation.

As long as the file is smaller than the upload maximum, you can create assignments for any sort of digital content. Consider the types of work products you want your students to produce during your course. How many of them could be digital files submitted using an assignment?

Creative Assignment Practices

Simple, flexible tools can lend themselves to creative problem solving. The uses for the assignment module are limited only by your imagination. Let's take a look at case studies, an advanced use of assignments, to get the creative process started.

Case studies are important learning tools in a number of professional fields. Medical schools, business schools, and others use case studies to convey information in a narrative context and give students a chance to immediately apply their new knowledge.

Designing a good case study does take some time, but an iterative approach works well. Start small and build up over time. Eventually, you could follow one case study across an entire semester, or build a set of cases, forming the basis for your students' practice.

Jason: My wife's engineering capstone course used one case study in several parts, over the course of a semester, to test the students' abilities to apply the engineering concepts they had learned over the previous four years. Each phase of the course introduced new challenges they had to solve using different techniques and concepts.

Case studies have a few basic parts. There's a narrative setup, background data, and a problem statement. The problem statement should be an interesting challenge linked to course goals and solvable by applying concepts and procedures learned in class. The narrative setup is important because it contextualizes the assignment, giving students a feel for the people involved in the problem. You can make the case easier or harder depending on how ambiguous your narrative and data are. For more advanced challenges, you may want to create a case where there is no clear-cut answer, to encourage student discussion.

Most case studies require combining assignments with resources to present the case and give students a way to submit their answers. Add your narrative and data as resources using the files and resources tools discussed in Chapter 3. Then add your problem statement as the description of an assignment.

Students should use the narrative and data to solve the problem posed by the assignment. The response should show how the resolution of the problem is supported by the data.

Summary

Assignments are an easy way to gather and track student submissions. Students can submit any type of electronic file to fulfill the requirements. Instead of collecting unwieldy stacks of paper, you can let Moodle track who has turned in a paper and when. The feedback options provide you with an easy way to send grades and/or comments back to the students about their work.

CHAPTER 8

Glossaries

This chapter covers the following MTC skills: 5.5 Glossary

Part of becoming an expert in any field is learning the vocabulary used by practitioners. Experts in an area of study develop new language and word usage to communicate new ideas or subtle variations of old ones. As communities develop within a field and experts communicate with each other over time, new languages emerge. Many experts find it increasingly difficult to communicate with novices as they become more immersed in the language of their field. For example, computer experts have developed an entirely new vocabulary of acronyms, names, and shorthand to help them rapidly communicate complex ideas to each other.

Jason: As someone with a degree of expertise in computer technology, I know I need to be careful not to confuse others when I explain technical concepts. If you've ever been privy to a discussion among geeks, you know it can be nearly impossible for an outsider to follow the three- and four-letter alphabet soup that passes for geek speak.

Fortunately, Moodle has a tool to help you and your students develop glossaries of terms and embed them in your course. On the surface, the glossary module doesn't seem to be more than a fancy word list. In practice, however, it's a powerful tool for learning. The glossary module has a number of features that make it easy for you and your class to develop shared vocabulary lists, add comments to definitions, and even link every appearance of a word in a course to its glossary entry.

Creating Glossaries

Each Moodle course has its own set of glossaries. Only teachers can edit the main glossary. Secondary glossaries may be configured to allow student entries and comments.

Your Moodle course may contain one main glossary and as many secondary glossaries as you want. You can export entries from any secondary glossary into the main glossary.

You can create the link to your glossaries anywhere in your course sections. We suggest that you add a main glossary to the general section at the top of your course page, then add secondary glossaries to the topic or weekly section where they are relevant.

To create a glossary:

1. Click the "Turn editing on" button.

2. Select Glossary from the "Add an activity" drop-down menu.

3. On the "Adding a new glossary" page, as shown in Figure 8-1, give your new glossary a descriptive name.

4. Write a description of the glossary and give directions to your students in the Description area.

5. Select the general options:

   Entries shown per page
   > This sets the number of words and definitions your students will see when they view the glossary list.

   Is this glossary global?
   > Administrators can make a global glossary, with entries linking throughout the whole site. Any course may contain a global glossary, though usually they are only included on the site front page.

   Glossary type
   > The glossary can be either main or secondary. As mentioned, you can export entries from any secondary glossary into the main glossary.

   Duplicated entries allowed
   > This allows the entry of more than one definition for a given word.

   Allow comments on entries
   > Students and teachers can leave comments on glossary definitions. The comments are available via a link at the bottom of the definition.

   Allow print view
   > This provides a printer-friendly-version link for students.

   Automatically link glossary entries
   > Moodle has a text-filter feature that automatically creates a link from a word in the course to its glossary definition. Linked words are highlighted.

   Approved by default
   > If students are allowed to add entries, you can allow entries to be automatically approved and added to the glossary, or they can require your approval before other students are able to see them.

   Display format
   > You can select how the glossary appears when students list the entries. There are a number of different options:

Simple, dictionary style

This looks like a conventional dictionary with separate entries. No authors are displayed and attachments are shown as links.

Continuous without author

This shows the entries one after other without any kind of separation apart from the editing icons.

Encyclopedia

This is similar to the "Full with author" format apart from attached images being displayed inline.

Entry list

This lists the concepts as links.

FAQ

This is useful for displaying a list of Frequently Asked Questions. It automatically appends the words QUESTION and ANSWER in the concept and definition respectively.

Full with author

This is a forum-like display format with attachments shown as links.

Full without author

This is a forum-like display format that does not show author's data with attachments shown as links.

Show "Special" link

When users browse the glossary, they can select the first character of a word from a list. The Special link displays special characters such as @, #, $, etc.

Show alphabet

You can use this option to display the alphabet for easier glossary browsing.

Show "ALL" link

If you want students to see all of the glossary entries at once, set this to Yes.

Edit always

If you want entries to be always editable, set this to Yes.

6. Select the grade options:

Allow entries to be rated

You can grade entries yourself or allow students to grade entries as well. Select "Only teachers" or "Everyone" from the Users menu. Then select a grading scale. You can also restrict when entries can be graded to a specific date range.

7. Select the common module options:

Group mode

Another location to set the group mode for the activity. If group mode is forced in the course settings then this setting will be ignored.

Visible

This determines whether students may view the activity or not.

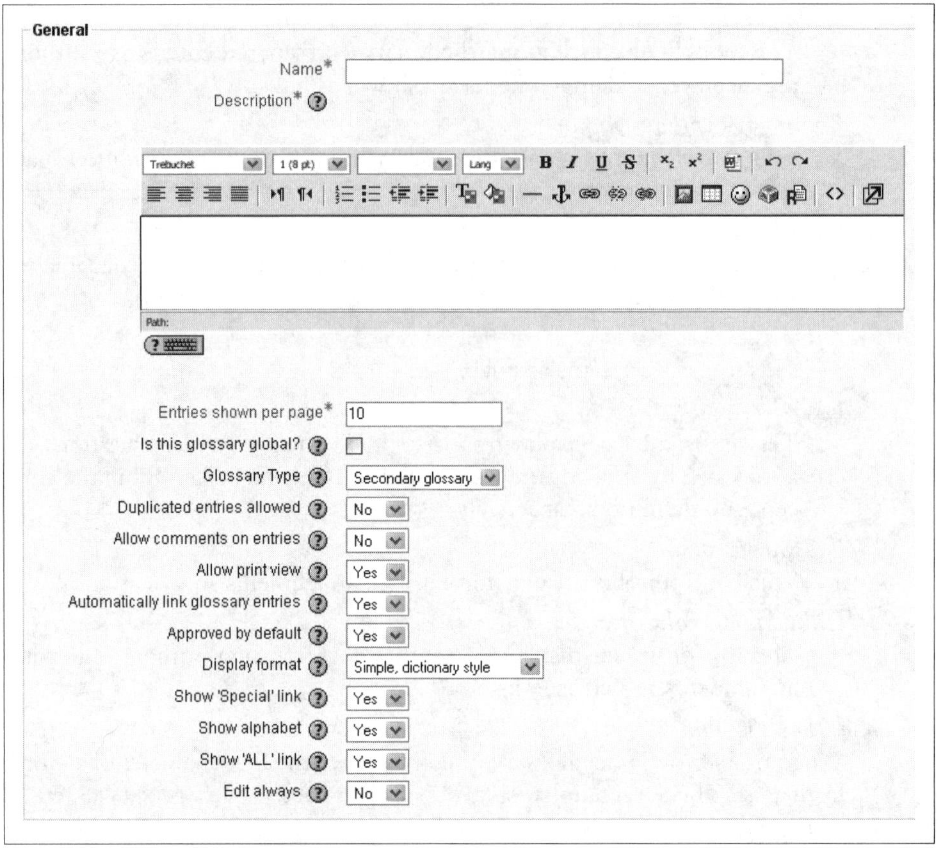

General

Name* [_____]

Description* (?)

| Trebuchet ▾ | 1 (8 pt) ▾ | ▾ | Lang ▾ | **B** *I* <u>U</u> S̶ | ×₂ x² | 🖹 | ↻ ↺ |

≡ ≡ ≡ ≡ | ¶▸ ◂¶ | ☰ ☰ ⇥ ⇤ | Tₐ ᵃⁿₐ | — ⚓ ∞ ⇔ ∞ | 🖼 🔲 ☺ 🌐 🗐 | ‹› | ⬚

Path:

(?) ⌨

Entries shown per page* [10]

Is this glossary global? (?) ☐

Glossary Type (?) [Secondary glossary ▾]

Duplicated entries allowed (?) [No ▾]

Allow comments on entries (?) [No ▾]

Allow print view (?) [Yes ▾]

Automatically link glossary entries (?) [Yes ▾]

Approved by default (?) [Yes ▾]

Display format (?) [Simple, dictionary style ▾]

Show 'Special' link (?) [Yes ▾]

Show alphabet (?) [Yes ▾]

Show 'ALL' link (?) [Yes ▾]

Edit always (?) [No ▾]

Figure 8-1. Adding a new glossary

8. Click the "Save changes" button at the bottom of the page.

There are a lot of options to choose from in the glossary setup. They open up some interesting possibilities that we'll explore later in the chapter. For now, let's take a look at how to add glossary entries and use some of the more advanced features.

The autolinking feature will work only if your system administrator has enabled it in the Modules > Filters section of the Site Administration block. Autolinking can be very processor-intensive, so if it doesn't seem to be working for you, your system administrator may have turned it off to speed up the system.

Using Glossaries

Once you've created your glossary, it's a good idea to seed it with a couple of entries so students have a model to work from.

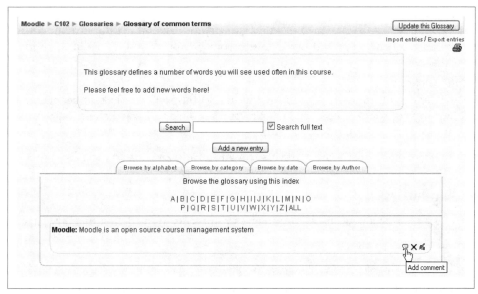

Figure 8-2. A glossary

The main view of the glossary can be a bit confusing at first, as you can see from Figure 8-2. Under the main Moodle navigation bar, you'll find the glossary description. Directly below the glossary description, you'll see the search bar. Checking the "Search full text" box allows searching for a given word in any position in the text.

Below the search bar is the "Add a new entry" button, then four browse tabs:

Browse by alphabet
Students can look for glossary entries by the first letter of a word when they select this tab.

Browse by category
You can create word categories and make them available for students to use when they are searching the glossary.

Browse by date
You can view entries based on the date they were last edited.

Browse by Author
If you want students to add entries, this is a useful way to keep track of who has entered what.

At the top right of the page, below the "Update this Glossary" button, are a few links:

Import entries
You can import glossaries from within this course or from other courses.

Export entries

> You can use this to export your course glossary to an export file stored in the course files area. You can then download it to your computer and upload it to another course.

Waiting approval

> If your default approval is set to No, this link will appear with the number of entries waiting approval in brackets. Clicking on the link will list the entries, with an approve tick icon opposite each one.

Once you've oriented yourself to the page, you can add an entry to the glossary.

Adding Entries

Clicking the "Add a new entry" button gives you access to the definition entry page.

To add a glossary entry:

1. From the Glossary page, click the "Add a new entry" button.
2. Enter the word you want to define in the Concept text field, as shown in Figure 8-3.
3. Add the definition of the word or concept.
4. If you've defined categories in the "Browse by category" tab, you can categorize your entry here. We'll cover how to add a category in the next section.
5. If there are synonyms you want to include with the entry, add them to the Keyword(s) text area. Enter one word per line.
6. If you want to add an attachment, such as a picture or an article, you can attach it below the Keyword(s) text area.
7. If you want this particular entry to be linked automatically within the course, check the "This entry should be automatically linked" checkbox. If you select automatic linking, the checkboxes below determine whether the links are case sensitive and whether only whole words are linked.
8. Click the "Save changes" button to add your word to the glossary.

Glossary Categories

Categories can help organize your glossary entries. If you've enabled autolinking, the category names can be linked along with individual entries.

To create a glossary category:

1. Click the "Browse by category" tab in the main page of the glossary.
2. Click the "Edit categories" button on the left side of the page.
3. Click the "Add category" button on the resulting Categories page.
4. Give the category a name.

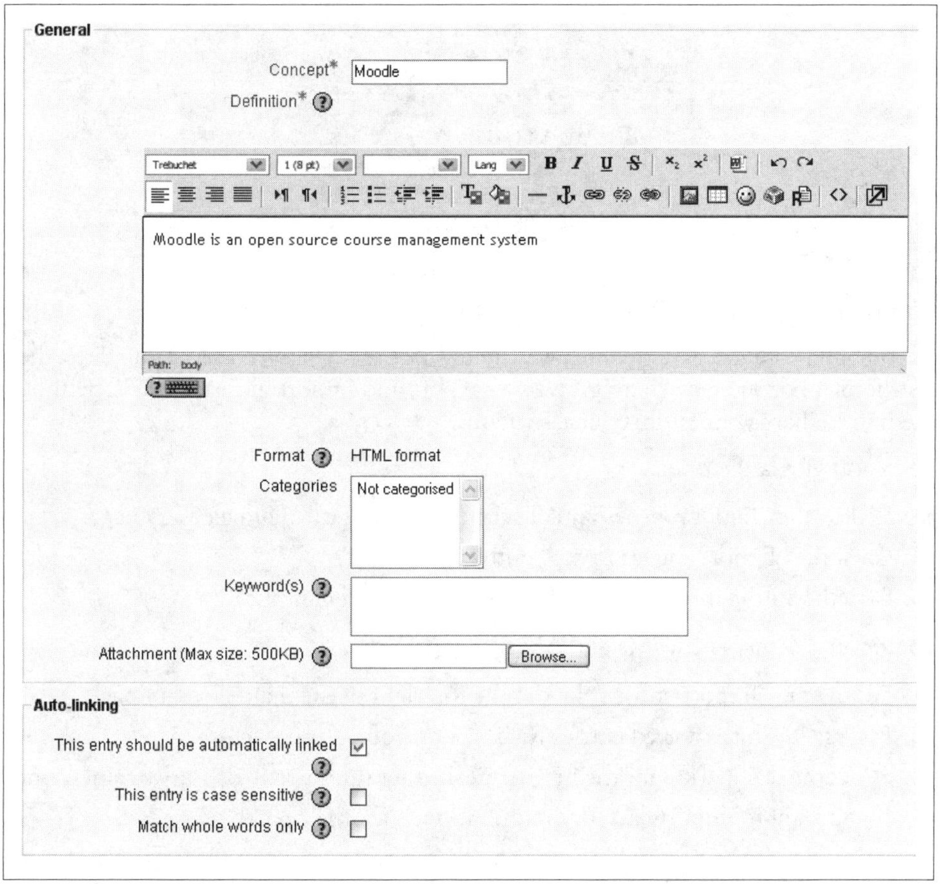

Figure 8-3. Adding a new glossary entry

5. Choose whether you want the category name autolinked as well.

6. Click the "Save changes" button.

If you autolink the category name, any occurrence of those words will be linked. When a student clicks on the link, he will be taken to the "Browse by category" page of the glossary.

Autolinking

Once you've added an entry to the glossary and enabled autolinking, any instance of a glossary term anywhere in Moodle will have a link to its definition. For example, if you create an entry for the word "Moodle" in the glossary, whenever someone uses the word in a forum, assignment, HTML or text page, or even in a description field, it will be clickable, as shown in Figure 8-4.

Once you click on the word, a new window with the glossary entry will pop up.

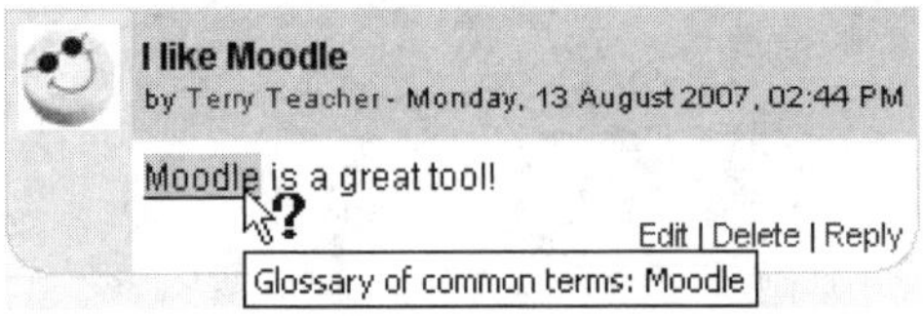

Figure 8-4. An autolinked word in a forum

Importing and Exporting Glossary Entries

As you build your glossaries, you may want to share them between classes or with other instructors. Fortunately, there's a way to export and import glossary entries without needing to share your entire course structure.

To export glossary entries:

1. Follow the "Export entries" link at the top right of the main glossary page.
2. Click the "Export entries to file" button.
3. Save the automatically generated XML file on your computer.

To import glossary entries via an XML file:

1. Follow the "Import entries" link at the top right of the main glossary page.
2. Browse for the exported entries XML file on your computer.
3. Select the destination for the new entries, either the current glossary or a new one.
4. If you want to import category information, click the checkbox.
5. Click the "Save changes" button. You'll then see a report of the entries and categories added to the glossary. If you enabled duplicate entries when you created the glossary, the import process will add all of the new definitions. Otherwise, it will not allow you to import any duplicate entries.

Commenting on Entries

If you enabled comments on the glossary entries, users can annotate the definitions in the word list. When you look at a word in the glossary list, you'll see a little cartoon speech balloon icon in the lower-right corner of the definition block, as shown previously in Figure 8-2.

When you click on the balloon, you're taken to the comment entry page. Add your comment then click the "Save changes" button.

Once you've saved your comment, Moodle will display all of the comments for the entry. When you return to the main glossary page, you'll see a new message next to the speech balloon telling you how many comments there are for the entry.

Printing a Glossary

If you've set "Allow print view" to Yes, then you'll see a little printer icon at the top right of the main glossary page. If you click the icon, Moodle will open a new browser window and present all the words and definitions in a printer-friendly format.

To print the glossary:

1. Click the printer icon at the top of the main glossary page.
2. From the newly opened window, choose Print from the File menu of your browser.
3. Once the word list has printed, close the printer-friendly format window.

Glossary Capabilities

The glossary module has a number of capabilities available to create roles. With capability overrides, you can enable your students to have a high degree of control over their glossaries.

Glossary capabilities are:

Create new entries
>   This allows a user to add new entries. If you want a glossary in which only teachers can add entries, you can use a role override to prevent students from adding entries.

Manage entries
>   A user with this capability can edit and delete other users' entries.

Manage categories
>   This allows a user to edit and delete glossary categories for organizing the terms.

Create comments
>   This allows a user to add comments, if commenting is enabled in the glossary. By default, both teachers and students are allowed to add comments. If you want only teachers to be able to add comments, you can use a role override to prevent students from doing so.

Manage comments
>   This allows a user to edit and delete other users' comments.

Import entries
>   This allows a user to import glossary entries.

Export entries
>   This allows a user to export glossary entries.

Approve unapproved entries
>   If the glossary is set to hide entries until they are approved, a user with this capability can approve new entries. This is a capability to consider giving trusted student moderators.

Rate entries
> This allows a user to rate entries, if rating is enabled in the glossary.

View ratings
> This allows a user to view all glossary ratings.

Effective Glossary Practices

A glossary can be an important part of your course. As we discussed earlier, acquiring vocabulary in a new field can be one of the biggest challenges to new learners. As an expert in your field, you are comfortable using the important terms and concepts in your area of expertise. Your students, however, are not experts. They may be just starting to learn new words representing new ideas and concepts. More advanced students will need to refine their learned definitions with subtle improvements to make the definitions more useful.

 As an experiment, go to the library and randomly choose a journal article in an area outside your field. As you read the article, does it make sense to you? Notice the number of unfamiliar terms, or familiar terms that seem to be used in a different way than you are used to.

Glossary Basics

At its most basic, Moodle's glossary can be used like a regular word list for a class. You can develop a list of terms you know students find difficult or confusing and make the list and definitions available for your class.

If you want to get more in-depth, we recommend creating either a weekly or chapter-based word list. Students can use it as they do weekly readings and assignments. A weekly glossary can make it easier for students to organize their learning process.

Creative Glossary Strategies

While a basic glossary is important, creatively applying the glossary can really make an impact on your class. Autolinking is very useful for integrating glossaries with other course activities. In addition, you may want to make use of the Random Glossary Entry block to display glossary entries on your course page. With the introduction of the database module, many activities can now be either glossary or database activities. Glossary has two advantages over the database at this point. First, many instructors find using the Random Glossary Entry block motivates students to submit high-quality entries, because they know the entries will be shared with the class on the front page of the course. The automatic term-linking is also useful to integrate the glossaries with other activities in the course.

Collaborative glossaries

Instead of creating a glossary on your own, why not have the students create it as they encounter unfamiliar terms? A collaborative glossary can serve as a focal point for collaboration in a course. Each member of the class could be assigned to contribute a term, a definition, or comments on submitted definitions. Multiple definitions can be rated by you and by the students, with the highest-rated definitions accepted for the final class glossary.

When students are responsible for creating the definitions, they are much more likely to remember the word and the correct definition. Engaging in the process of learning, debating, and refining a glossary can go a long way toward helping students begin using new terms. Moodle community member Leslie Smith has created a glossary for students to submit entries that contain the definition, part of speech, an original sentence using the word correctly, and some type of mnemonic or visual device to help classmates remember the word's meaning. The visual devices the students use are quite creative and definitely help with memorization.

You can also structure multiple glossaries over the course of a semester. Break them up by unit, chapter, week, or any other organizational structure. Another Moodle community member, Andy Diament, has his students create as many entries as they can in 20 minutes after a topic review, which creates both a framework for further discussion and a nice study aid when printed out.

If you have a large class, assign student teams to come up with definitions and answers. One strategy for managing large courses is to make each team responsible for one week's worth of definitions, while all the other teams must rate and comment. Alternatively, each team could be responsible for one definition per chapter and then rate and comment on the other teams' work.

To set up a collaborative glossary, create a new glossary for each unit with the following options:

* Glossary type: Secondary glossary
* Duplicate entries allowed: If you want teams to be able to submit multiple definitions for rating, select Yes
* Allow comments on entries: Yes
* Approved by default: Yes
* Allow entries to be rated: Yes—by everyone

The other options are up to you. Once you've selected the above options, students can add their own definitions, rate each other's, and add comments.

Mini-projects

Mini-projects are small research projects where students create small resources for each other. One high school teacher has the students do research on organs in the body, then create an encyclopedia-style entry in the glossary, including pictures and other resources. Moodle community member A. T. Watt uses the glossary for students to share biographies of people in the field they are studying. In both of these uses, the automatic linking makes this a very valuable resource, as anytime someone mentions the organ or person in a lesson, forum, or wiki, the word is linked back to the definition in the glossary.

Collaborative quiz questions

One of the most creative uses we've heard about is using the glossary to create collaborative quiz questions. Students are given the Moodle question formats and they create questions in the glossary matching one of the import types. The teacher has the glossary set to require approval, which hides the submitted questions from other students. When the students have all submitted their questions, the teacher exports the glossary and then imports it into a question bank. The quiz can then be built from student-submitted questions.

Credit for word use

This is a combination strategy using the forum and the autolink feature of the glossary. After you and your students have defined the glossary terms, it's important for students to begin practicing using the words in realistic contexts. Students, however, are usually reluctant to experiment with new terms. With the autolinking feature, it's easy to spot when a glossary word has been used in a forum or in a posting on the web site.

To encourage word use, assign a portion of the credit students receive for their forum postings for correct use of glossary terms. As you or other students rate posts, you can quickly scan for highlighted glossary words and award points for usage. You may even want to break the score down further. Perhaps award one point for using the word and two points for using it correctly.

Summary

At first glance, the glossary doesn't seem to be a very interesting tool. You could simply create a word list in a word processor and upload it. The power of the glossary tool in Moodle comes from its ability to automatically create links in your course for every word in the list, and to easily build collaborative glossaries.

Use the glossary tool to help your students learn the vocabulary of your field and encourage them to experiment with new terms. Collaborative glossaries give your students even more practice using the new words and negotiating their meaning.

In the next chapter, we'll take a look at a tool for developing linear lessons that combines multiple resources and little quizzes to help students progress through the course materials.

CHAPTER 9

Lessons

This chapter covers the following MTC skills: 5.11 Lesson

Jason: When I was growing up, I enjoyed reading a series of books called *Choose Your Own Adventure*. Written in second person, they placed the reader into the story as the main character. Each chapter was a page or two long, and ended with a choice of actions. I could choose the action I wanted to take and turn to the appropriate page to see what happened. I could then make another choice and turn to that page, and so on until the story ended or my character died, which happened with disturbing regularity.

The Moodle lesson tool is a lot like the *Choose Your Own Adventure* books. Each page in the lesson can have a question at the bottom of the page. The resulting page depends on the answer the student gives. You can create branching paths through the material based on the selections students make at each page.

With branching lessons, you can create programmed learning opportunities in which each correct answer brings up a new piece of information and a new question. You can also easily create flash-card lessons and, with a little creativity, use the lesson module to create simulations and case studies to respond to student input, which results in a degree of interactivity.

There are two basic page types in the lesson module. The question page presents the student with a question, and the student has to enter a correct answer. After a student submits his answer, he will see the response you've created and will be taken to another page or looped back. Question pages are scored and added to the student's cumulative grade.

A branch tables page presents the user only with the option to select a branch. There is no correct or incorrect answer for each response, and the student's selections do not impact his grade.

The authors of the lesson tool envision branches as tables of contents giving students access to chains of questions. At the end of a chain, the user will return to the branch table, access another one, or end the lesson. Of course, you don't have to create a lesson this way. You can use the branch table to create a simulation in which the student's choices present him with consequences and new decisions. At the end of the chapter, we'll explore some other creative ways to apply the lesson module.

Creating a lesson isn't complex, but the math of branching lessons means you have to plan carefully. Unless you prune your branching lesson, you will end up with a huge number of options for students and a large number of pages to write.

Creating a Lesson

Before you begin creating a lesson, it's a good idea to draw a flowchart. Lessons require more advanced planning than many of the other tools. They have the potential for branching on each page, so advanced planning is critical before you begin to develop your lesson. Even with two choices per page, if every choice results in a new page, you will quickly need a very large number of pages. The first page will require two additional results pages, and each of these will require two more—for a total of seven pages from an initial two choices. The key to minimizing the number of pages is to reuse as many as possible.

Take a few minutes to draw a flowchart for your lesson. What will the first page display? What are the options? Where will the options take the student? It's important to answer these questions for each page of the lesson to avoid getting lost while you are actually creating the content.

Once you have your flowchart, it's time to start creating a lesson.

To create a lesson:

1. Click the "Turn editing on" button.

2. Select Lesson from the "Add an activity" drop-down menu in the appropriate course section.

3. On the "Adding a new lesson" page, as shown in Figure 9-1, give the lesson a descriptive name.

 Don't be put off by the long list of settings—they can generally be left as default or you can change them at a later time.

4. Choose whether a lesson attempt should be timed, and if so, what the time limit should be. If a time limit is used, then a student may finish the lesson activity after the time is up, though any questions answered after the time limit is up are not counted.

5. Choose the maximum number of answers/branches per page. This is the maximum number of selection options you want per page.

6. Select the grade options:

Practice lesson

> If set to Yes, then students' grades are not recorded.

Custom scoring

> This allows you to add a score (positive or negative) for each answer.

Maximum grade

> Choose a value between 0 and 100 percent. If the maximum grade is set to 0, then the lesson does not appear in the gradebook.

Student can re-take

> You can set this only to Yes (to allow students to re-take the lesson) or No. You can't set the number of times a student can re-take a lesson.

Handling of re-takes

> If you allow students to re-take the lesson, you need to set a grading policy. You can use the mean of the student's grades for each lesson attempt or select the maximum grade.

Display ongoing score

> Set to Yes to show the student's ongoing score on each page.

7. Select the flow control options:

Allow student review

> If set, the last page of the lesson contains a "Review Lesson" button for the student to navigate through the lesson again from the start. Maximum number of attempts should be set to more than 1.

Display review button

> If set, a Review button appears after an incorrectly answered question, enabling the student to reattempt it. The Review button cannot be used for essay questions.

Maximum number of attempts

> This represents the maximum number of attempts a student can make on any question. If a student has difficulty with a short-answer or numerical question, she can make this number of attempts before being moved to the next page.

Action after correct answer

> This determines how the system responds after a correct answer. Most of the time, you'll want the system to show the page you've selected as a response. You can also elect to have the system randomly display a question the student hasn't seen yet or one he hasn't answered.

Display default feedback

> If set, for questions without specific feedback, the responses "That's the correct answer" and "That's the wrong answer" are used.

Minimum number of questions

With this option, you can set the number of questions used as a base for calculating the student's grade. If you set a minimum number of questions, the student must answer at least this many questions to receive full credit.

Number of pages (cards) to show

Set this parameter only if you are creating a flash-card lesson (see the following section, "Effective Lesson Practices"). If this is set to a number greater than 0, students will be shown that number of cards, then the lesson will end. If this is set to a number greater than the number of cards you've created, Moodle will display every card.

8. Select the lesson formatting options:

Slide show

If set, the lesson is displayed as a slide show, with a fixed width, height, and custom background color, which you can also set.

Display left menu

If set, the list of the pages is displayed.

Progress bar

If set, a progress bar is displayed at the bottom of each page.

9. Set the "available from" and deadline for your lesson.

10. Set dependency options, if required:

Dependent on

Access to this lesson can be made dependent on student performance in another lesson. Unless you have more than one lesson in a course, this menu will only allow you to select none.

Time spent (minutes)

You can make access to this lesson dependent on the amount of time students have spent in a previous lesson.

Completed

To access this lesson, the student must have completed a previous lesson.

Grade better than (%)

You can make access to this lesson dependent on the student scoring higher than a certain percentage in another lesson.

11. Choose or upload a file for a pop-up window at the beginning of the lesson, if required.

12. Select the other options:

Link to an activity

To add a link to another activity on the last page of the lesson, select the activity from the drop-down menu.

Use this lesson's settings as defaults

If set, the settings you have chosen for this lesson will be the default settings the next time you create a lesson in the same course.

Visible

This determines whether students may view the activity or not.

13. Click the "Save changes" button.

You are then asked what you would like to do first:

Import questions

You can import questions from a variety of formats. The lesson module will create a page for each question you import.

Import PowerPoint

PowerPoint slides get imported as branch tables with previous and next answers.

Add a branch table

A branch table is a lesson page without responses to student selections. Instead, each selection option branches to another page. Branch tables do not impact a student's grade. A lesson may start with a branch table that acts as a table of contents.

Add a question page

A question page consists of a title, some content, and a question at the bottom of the page. When a student answers a question, she sees the response for her answer and a Continue button. The Continue button takes the student to the appropriate branch page.

To add a question page, fill in the form as shown in Figure 9-2:

1. Select a question type for the page by clicking a tab. Your options are multiple choice, true/false, short answer, numerical, matching, and essay. If you want to use multiple-answer multiple-choice questions or case-sensitivity in the short-answer responses, click the checkbox below the tabs.

2. Give the page a title. The title will also be visible to the student as he completes the lesson. You can also use it to organize your pages as you build the lesson.

3. Enter the page contents. The contents will need to include the question you want the students to answer as well. If you are creating flash cards, you'll want to enter only the question here.

4. Enter the correct answer to the question in the Answer 1 box.

5. Enter the response generated by the answer.

By default, the first response takes the student to the next page while all other responses return the student to the same page. After you've created a page, you can come back and edit this behavior. The lesson automatically presents the

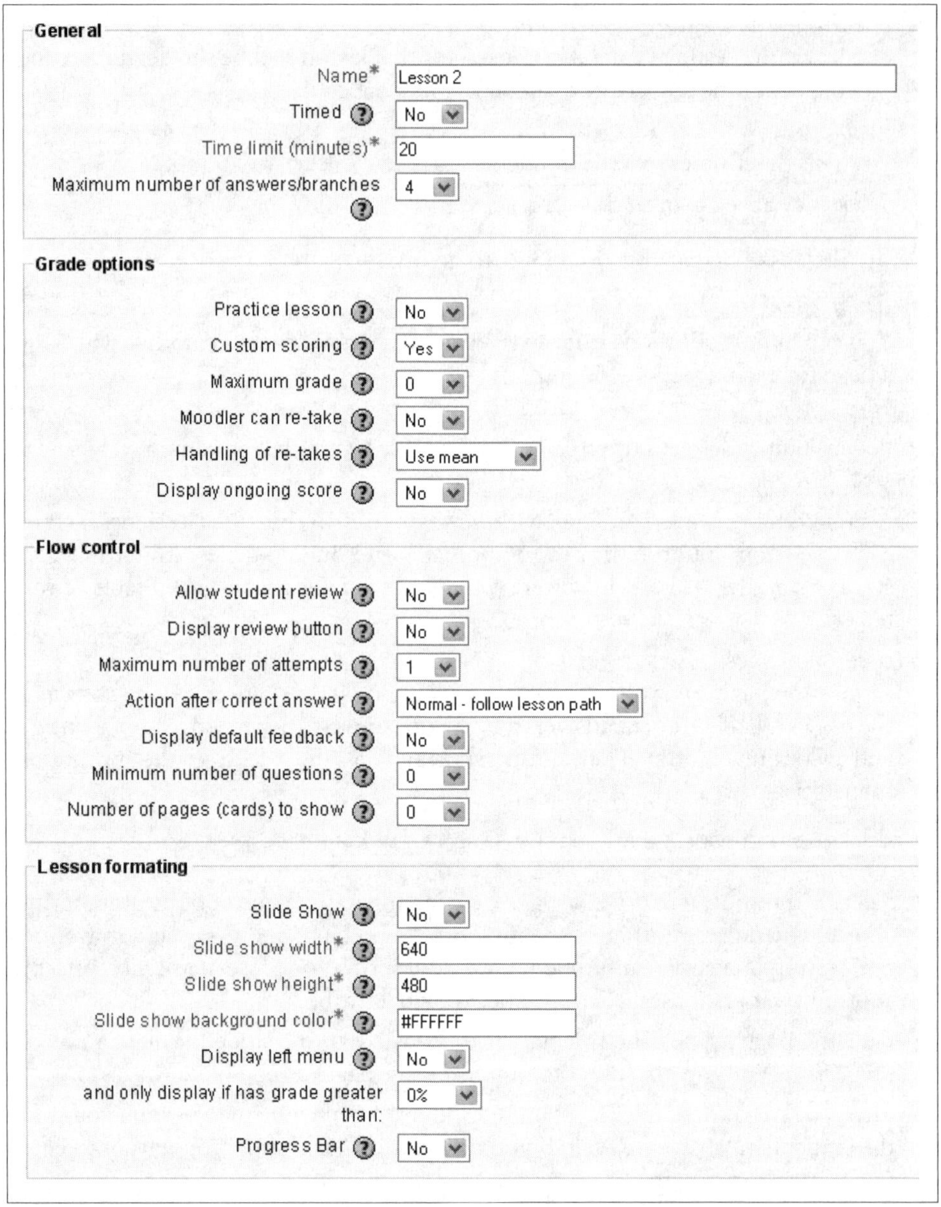

General

Name* `Lesson 2`

Timed (?) `No`

Time limit (minutes)* `20`

Maximum number of answers/branches (?) `4`

Grade options

Practice lesson (?) `No`

Custom scoring (?) `Yes`

Maximum grade (?) `0`

Moodler can re-take (?) `No`

Handling of re-takes (?) `Use mean`

Display ongoing score (?) `No`

Flow control

Allow student review (?) `No`

Display review button (?) `No`

Maximum number of attempts (?) `1`

Action after correct answer (?) `Normal - follow lesson path`

Display default feedback (?) `No`

Minimum number of questions (?) `0`

Number of pages (cards) to show (?) `0`

Lesson formating

Slide Show (?) `No`

Slide show width* (?) `640`

Slide show height* (?) `480`

Slide show background color* (?) `#FFFFFF`

Display left menu (?) `No`

and only display if has grade greater than: `0%`

Progress Bar (?) `No`

Figure 9-1. Adding a new lesson

question choices in random order so you don't have to worry about the first response always being the correct one.

6. Enter any other answer choices you want to student to consider, with responses for each.

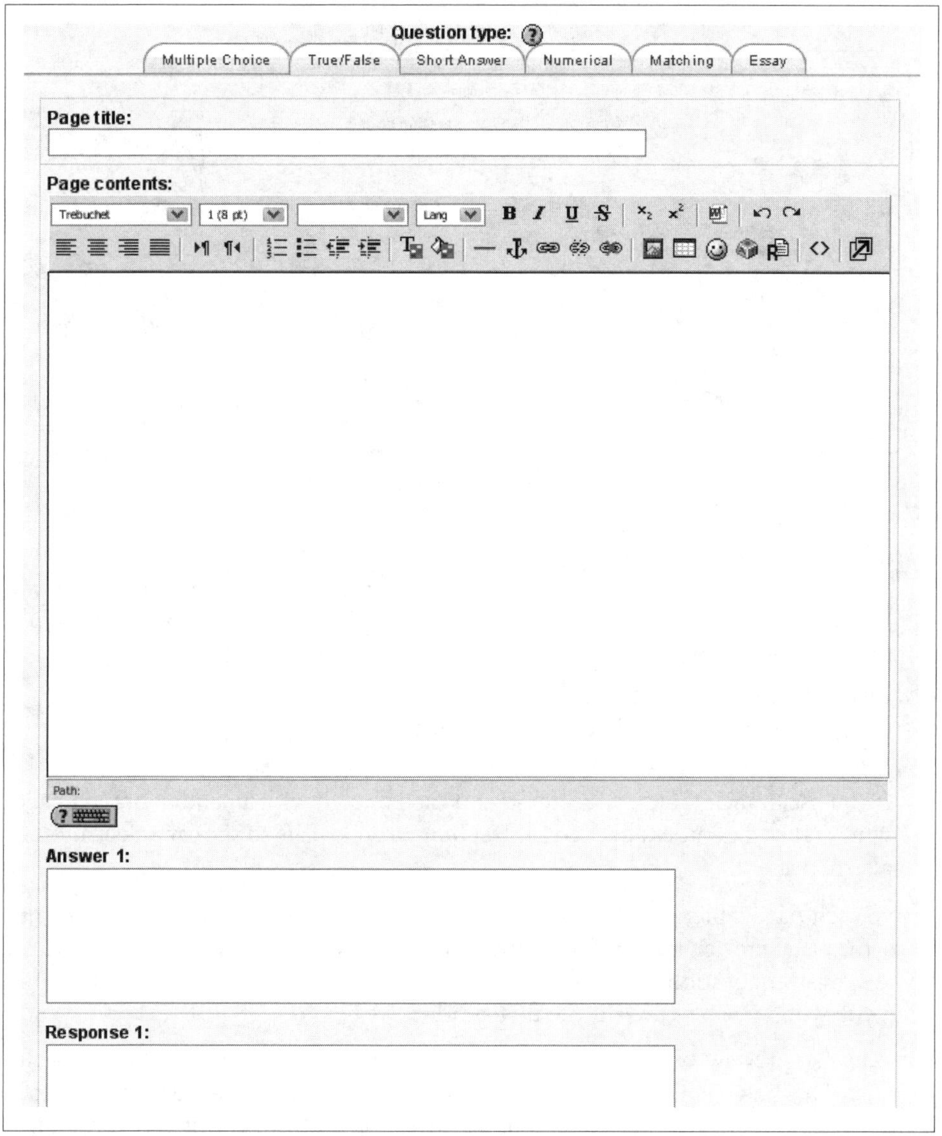

Figure 9-2. Adding a question

7. Click the "Add a question page" button at the bottom of the page.

You'll then see the lesson construction page, such as the one shown in Figure 9-3. Each page you create will be listed here with a number of options above and below it.

In addition to the options covered previously, you also have the option to:

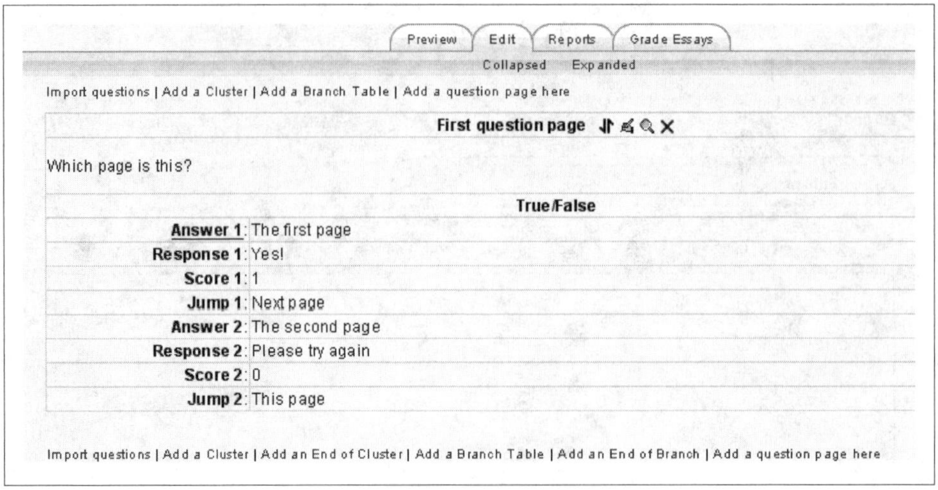

Figure 9-3. Lesson construction

Add a cluster

A cluster is a set of question pages from which one or more may be randomly chosen. Questions within a cluster are randomly selected by choosing "Random Question within a Cluster" as a jump.

Add an end of cluster

Clusters should be completed with an end of cluster page.

Add an end of branch

If you use branch tables, you should end each branch with an end of branch page, which takes the student back to the last branch table page so she can select another alternative.

Above each page table, you'll see the icons for moving, updating, previewing, or deleting the page. Previewing the page shows the lesson from the student's point of view. You can answer questions, check out branches, and interact with the lesson. The only thing you won't be able to see is the final grade.

You can also preview your whole lesson by clicking the Preview tab at the top of the page list. This link will take you to the first page in your lesson as a student would see it. You can then start from the beginning of the lesson and work your way through.

Once you've created your first page, you can add a new page, add a branch table, or edit an existing question. You'll need to add each page you want students to be able to view.

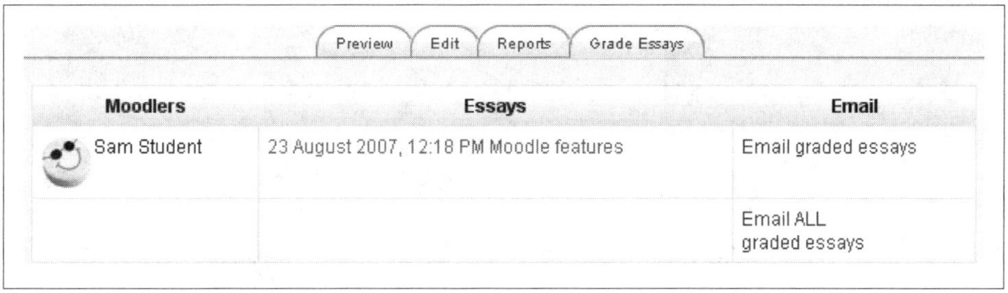

Moodlers	Essays	Email
Sam Student	23 August 2007, 12:18 PM Moodle features	Email graded essays
		Email ALL graded essays

Figure 9-4. Grading an essay

Managing Lessons

Once you've created your lesson, there isn't much management involved, unless you have included essay questions. Essay questions require manual grading with an optional comment.

To grade an essay question:

1. Click the "Grade essays" tab at the top of the lesson page.
2. Click the essay link in the middle column of the page, as shown in Figure 9-4.
3. Give the essay a score and add some comments.
4. Click the "Save changes" button.
5. When you have finished grading essays, click the "Email ALL graded essays" link to notify your students.

As students complete the lesson, their scores will be recorded in the gradebook (see Chapter 13). If you've allowed students to attempt each lesson multiple times, their scores may change as they repeat the lesson.

Lesson Capabilities

The lesson module has only two capabilities:

Edit a lesson activity
 This allows a user to edit a lesson. If you create a blank lesson and allow students to edit it, they can create a new lesson for the rest of the class.

Manage a lesson activity
 This allows a user to manage a lesson and grade essay questions.

Effective Lesson Practices

Lessons can be an interesting change of pace for your students. They may require more upfront development time than many other types of tools, but they do provide some

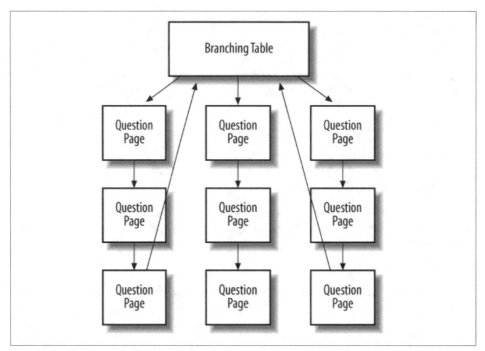

Figure 9-5. Branching quiz schematic

benefits. The two basic lesson types, branching quizzes and flash cards, are relatively easy to set up.

Branching Quizzes

The most basic lesson structure is a branching quiz. You use branches to organize sets of questions around different topics or concepts in your course. Each branch of the quiz leads to a linear series of pages and test questions, then returns to the main branch. The main-branch page acts as a table of contents for the lesson, as shown in Figure 9-5.

If you decide to build this type of lesson, be sure to include a link to the end on the main page. If not, the students will have no way of ending the lesson and recording their scores.

If you create a lesson with a branch table and strings of questions, be sure to set a reasonable minimum number of questions. Otherwise, students will be able to visit one branch and receive a maximum score for the lesson, even though they didn't look at any other branches.

To create a branching quiz:

1. Create the lesson and the first question page by following the instructions.
2. Create a question page for the first question in each branch.

3. Create a branch table with a branch for each of the questions you just created.

4. Be sure to make the last branch a link to the end of the lesson.

5. After you've saved the branching table, move it to the top of the pages list.

6. Under the first question for the first branch, create the second question page for the next step in the branch.

7. Fill in the question page for the second question. Put the correct answer in the first answer slot if you are creating a true/false or multiple-choice question.

8. Continue adding questions to the branch until you are finished.

9. Add an end of branch after the last question in the branch.

10. Below the first question for the each of the remaining branches, repeat steps 6 through 9.

11. When you have added all your pages, review your lesson by clicking the Check Navigation link.

Flash Cards

Flash cards can be a useful way to practice recalling basic facts and definitions. As we discussed in Chapter 8, learning vocabulary can be one of the most difficult tasks for novices in any field of study. Flash cards allow students to practice rapidly recalling definitions as an initial step toward learning how to communicate in a new field.

The lesson module can act like a deck of flash cards, presenting either the whole deck or a subset of cards to students when they want to study the new terms. Each question page is a separate card, and students can rapidly react to each one in turn. This is a very different structure than the branching quizzes.

Setting up a flash-card lesson requires specifying options when you first create the lesson. To create a flash-card lesson:

1. Follow steps 1 through 4 for creating a lesson in the "Creating a Lesson" section.

2. Consider setting a low value for the maximum grade. You want to reward students for using the flash cards but also make them a valuable learning tool.

3. Use the following options:

   Maximum grade
   > Consider setting a low value for the maximum grade. You want to reward students for using the flash cards but also make the cards a valuable learning tool.

   Student can re-take
   > Unless you have a very specific reason for limiting re-takes, it's best to set this to yes. Flash cards are used to practice recalling information rapidly. Save the assessment of students' recall skills for a quiz.

Handling of re-takes
> If you set this to use maximum, it will encourage students to reuse the flash cards to attempt to get the maximum score.

Action after correct answer
> Set this to unseen or unanswered. This tells the lesson module you don't want it to present the next page in order.

Minimum number of questions
> Keep this at zero. The students shouldn't have a choice about the number of cards they see.

Number of pages (cards) to show
> If you want to limit the number of questions students see each time they practice with the cards, set this to a nonzero number. Make it large enough to give students enough practice, but not so large that they become fatigued by the sheer volume of questions.

4. Once you save the lesson options, simply create question pages. The order doesn't matter. You're basically creating a deck of questions to draw from.

Once you've created the deck of flash cards, you can release it to your students so they can practice answering the questions you've created.

Creative Lesson Uses

While branching quizzes and flash cards are interesting applications, there is a hidden potential in the lesson module that makes it much more interesting than it at first appears. If you take advantage of the ability of each answer in a question page to link to any other page, you can create branching *Choose Your Own Adventure*-style simulations or case studies.

Simulations and case studies

A branching simulation can be a great learning tool. On each page, the student reads some information or looks at a picture (or both), then decides what to do next. For example, a medical simulation may start out by presenting a patient's complaint. Possible choices could then be to order a test or to do nothing. If the student orders a test, each branch would present the results and ask the student what to do next. Each page could include an option to switch from diagnosis to treatment, which would branch the student to a different set of options.

To successfully create a branching simulation, you will definitely have to map out each page in advance. The first page should introduce the situation. You'll need to include enough details in the first page to get the students started. If you have other materials you want them to use in the simulation, you may want to create a resource link for the students to access before they start the lesson.

If you just want students to engage in the decision-making process and not receive a grade, simply create a series of branch tables. Otherwise, you can create a combination of branching tables and questions.

To create a simulation:

1. Create a lesson as you would a branching-quiz lesson. If you're just using branch tables, assign a point value of zero to the lesson.

2. Create the first question page. If the first question page will be the first page in the simulation, be sure to provide enough details about the case so the students can start making decisions.

3. Create the first set of decision-result pages from the first page.

4. Go back and edit the first page and assign each answer a link to a resulting page.

5. Create the decision-result pages for each of the other decision pages.

6. You'll need to create all of the pages in advance or, after you create each iteration of decision-result pages, go back and add the links to those pages in the decision page.

7. After you've added all of the pages and links, test your simulation by clicking the Preview tab at the top of the page list.

CHAPTER 10

Wikis

This chapter covers the following MTC skills: 5.8 Wiki

A wiki is a collection of collaboratively authored web pages. A wiki starts with one front page. Students can edit the page or add more pages to the wiki by creating links to new pages that don't yet exist. Old versions of each page can be viewed by checking the page history.

Moodle's wiki is built on top of an older wiki system, called ErfurtWiki (*http://erfurt wiki.sourceforge.net/*).

In Moodle, wikis can be a powerful tool for collaborative work. The entire class can edit a document together, or you can create group wikis which are only editable by group members.

Creating Wikis

Creating a wiki is relatively simple and involves far fewer steps than the lesson module. Most of the work involved with creating wikis becomes easier once you start using them.

To create a wiki:

1. Click the "Turn editing on" button.
2. Select Wiki from the "Add an activity" drop-down menu in the course section where you would like to add the wiki.
3. On the "Adding a new wiki" page, as shown in Figure 10-1, give the wiki a descriptive name.
4. In the summary field, describe the purpose of the wiki and what you expect students to contribute.
5. Select the wiki type: groups, student, or teacher. The wiki type interacts with the groups setting for your course, resulting in nine options, as shown in Table 10-1.

Table 10-1. Wiki group permissions

	No groups	Separate groups	Visible groups
Teacher	Creates a single wiki that only the teacher can edit. Students can view the wiki but not make changes.	Each group has a wiki that only the teacher can edit. Other groups can't view the page.	Each group has a wiki that only the teacher can edit. Other groups can view the page.
Groups	There is one wiki for the class. All students can edit the wiki.	There is one wiki per group. Students in that group can edit the wiki. Other students can't view the page.	There is one wiki per group that group members can edit. Other groups can view the page.
Student	Each student has their own wiki that only the teacher and student can edit.	Each student has their own wiki that they can edit. Students in the same group can view the page as well.	Each student has their own wiki that they can edit. All the other students in the course can view the page as well.

6. Click the Show Advanced button to display the following additional options:

Print wiki name on every page

If you select this option, the top of each page will have the name of the wiki.

HTML Mode

There are three options: No HTML, safe HTML, or HTML only. No HTML will display all HTML tags as tags (for example, a bold tag will look like a <b> instead of making the word bold). Safe HTML will allow certain tags to be displayed. HTML only enables the HTML editor.

Allow binary files

Binary files are graphics, audio, video, and other nontext resources. If you want students to be able to add files as attachments, be sure to set this to Yes.

Wiki autolinking options

A new page can be created in the wiki by typing a word using CamelCase, i.e., with a capital letter at the beginning and a capital letter somewhere else in the word. It's called CamelCase because the two capital letters resemble a two-humped camel. CamelCase combines all the words for the link into one word. Each word in the link is capitalized. When a word is added in CamelCase, the wiki automatically creates a new page and makes the word a link. You can disable this feature if you wish, so that typing a word enclosed in square brackets is the only way of creating a new web page.

Student admin options

When students can edit a page, you can allow them certain administrative privileges in the wiki. We'll cover each of these options in more detail in the "Managing Wikis" section later in this chapter.

Page name

If you want the first page of the wiki to be different from the name of the wiki, then add a page name. Otherwise, leave the field empty.

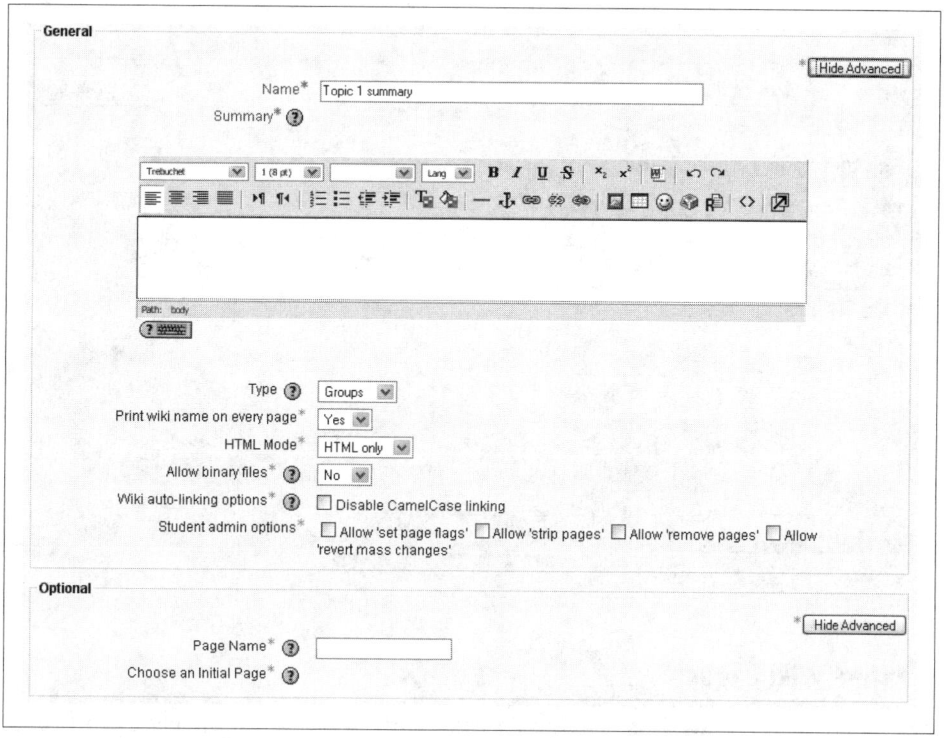

Figure 10-1. Adding a new wiki

7. Select the common module options:

Group mode
> This is another location in which to set the group mode for the activity. If group mode is forced in the course settings, then this setting will be ignored.

Visible
> This determines whether students may view the activity or not.

8. Click the "Save changes" button. You will then be taken to the editing view of the wiki page you just created.

Once your wiki is up and running, you and your students can begin collaborating on creating content.

Managing Wikis

After you've created your wiki, it's available for editing. You and your students can create wiki pages, link them together, and collaboratively create a collection of web pages.

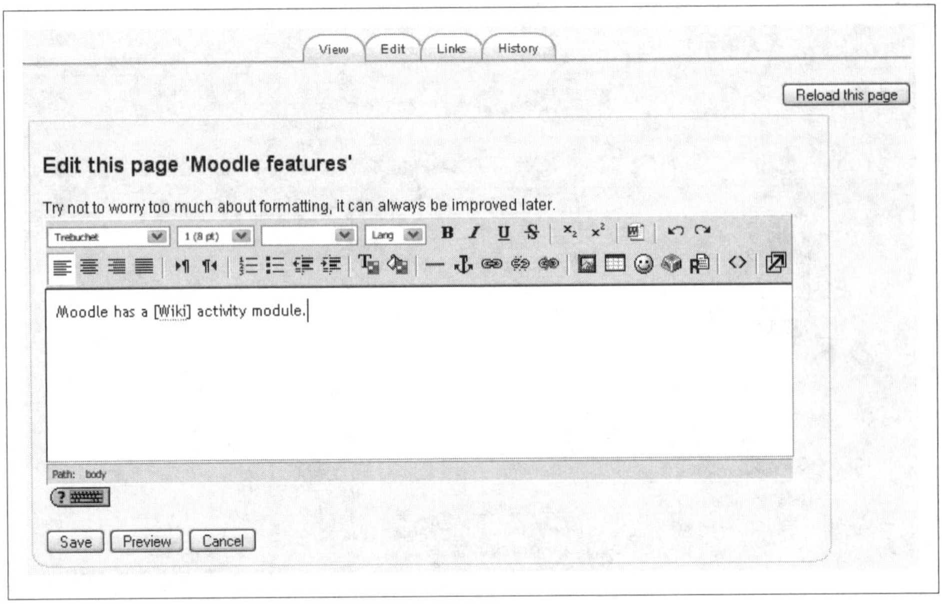

Figure 10-2. Editing a wiki page

Creating Wiki Pages

After you create the wiki itself, Moodle will take you to the first page, as shown in Figure 10-2.

In the center of the page, you'll see the editing area for your wiki page. If you've chosen the HTML only mode, you'll be able to use the HTML editor as you would for any other document. You can add images, tables, and any formatting you need.

To add other pages to your wiki, simply type a word enclosed in square brackets. If you haven't created a page with that name already, Moodle will put a question mark next to the word.

For example, if you type the word "[Wiki]" in the page, Moodle will look to see if a page with the name "Wiki" has already been created. If it hasn't, when you view the page you'll see the word in bold with a question mark after it, as shown in Figure 10-3.

If you click on the question mark, you'll be taken to the editing view of the new wiki page. Once you add some content and save the page, it becomes active. Whenever you type the same word in square brackets, Moodle will automatically create a link to the page.

There are four tabs above the editing area: View, Edit, Links, and History, as shown in Figure 10-2. When you browse a wiki, every page is displayed in view mode. If you want to edit a page, click the Edit tab and you'll see the editing area for that page. The Links tab will display the pages that have links pointing to the page you are viewing.

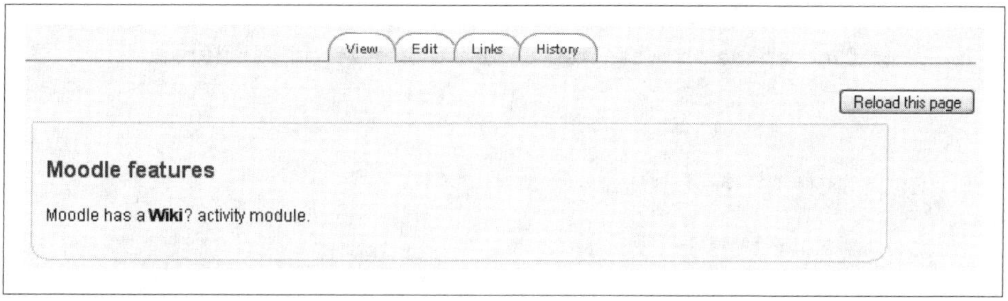

Figure 10-3. Viewing a wiki page

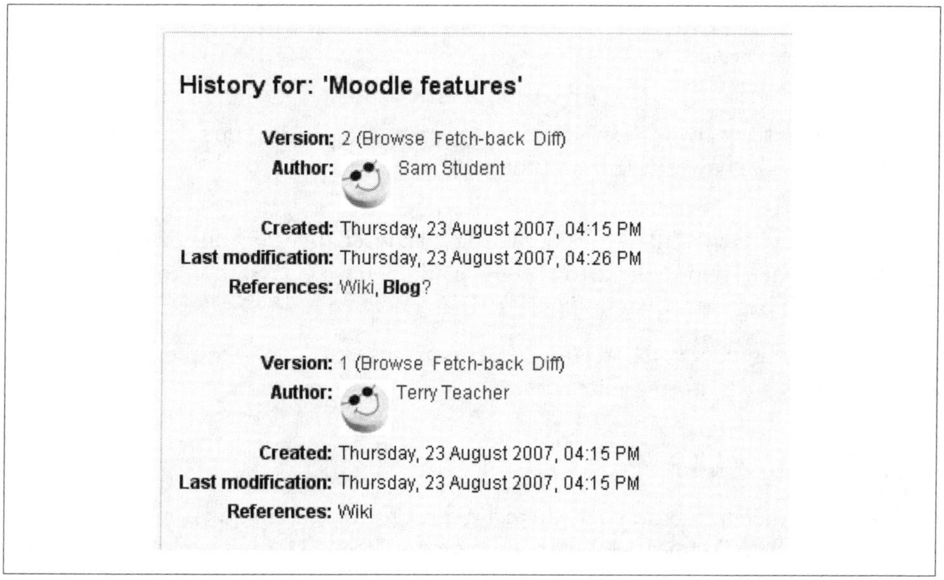

Figure 10-4. A wiki history page

You can use this to backtrack and see where this page is referenced elsewhere in the wiki.

The History tab gives you access to the version history of the page. Whenever someone clicks the Save button, they create a new version of the wiki page. Moodle tracks all these versions until you strip them out (see the strip tool in the administration menu in the next section). Figure 10-4 shows the history page for our wiki's first page.

Each version has three tools you can use:

Browse
> You can view every version of a page.

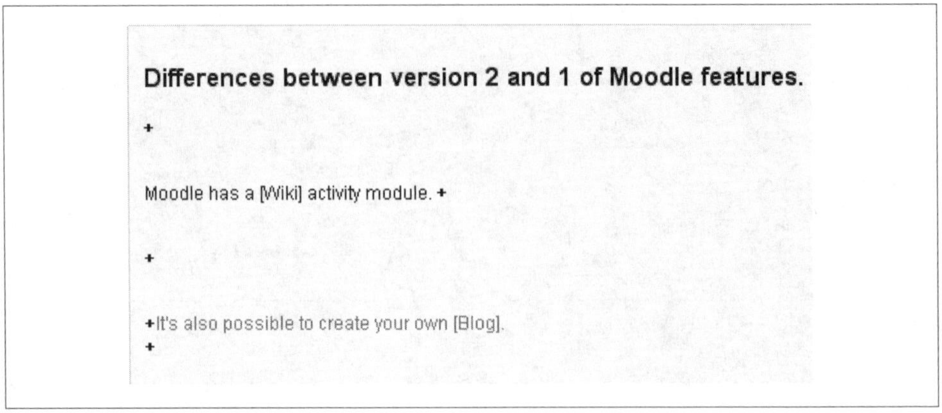

Differences between version 2 and 1 of Moodle features.

+

Moodle has a [Wiki] activity module. +

+

+It's also possible to create your own [Blog].
+

Figure 10-5. A version diff

Fetch-back
> This brings back an old version of the page for editing. Once you save your changes, it becomes the newest version of the page.

Diff
> This highlights the differences between two consecutive versions of a page. Additions have a + symbol next to them. Deletions have a – symbol next to them. A simple diff page is shown in Figure 10-5.

As you build your wiki, you and your students can use these very simple tools to create a very sophisticated information space.

Administering a Wiki

Under the Moodle navigation bar, there are three tools: search, links, and administration. The Search Wiki button allows you to search the wiki for key terms. Moodle will return all the pages containing your search term.

The Choose Wiki Links drop-down menu provides you with tools to view your wiki in different ways. The tools include:

Site map
> A hierarchical view of the pages and links in the wiki, starting with the first page.

Page index
> An alphabetical list of all the pages in the wiki.

Newest pages
> A list of the most recently created pages.

Most visited pages
> A list of pages with the most views.

Most often changed pages
> A list of most frequently edited pages.

Updated pages

Lists all the pages in the wiki by date and time of last edit.

Orphaned pages

A list of pages that were created and had all the links to them deleted.

Wanted pages

A wiki page where people can list pages they want to see in the collection.

Export pages

You can wrap up all your wiki pages and export them as regular HTML to a ZIP file for download or to a Moodle directory.

File download

Download binary files attached to wiki pages.

The Administration drop-down menu gives you tools that keep your wiki running smoothly. As you and your class generate the wiki, pages may become orphaned or you may need to manage a student's contributions.

Set page flags

Page flags are properties you can set on a per-page basis. Every page can be set with different permissions:

TXT

Indicates whether the page can contain text.

BIN

Flag for allowing binary (graphics) content.

OFF

Stands for "offline." The page is still there; it just can't be read by someone who doesn't have editing permissions.

HTM

Allows HTML content instead of wiki text.

RO

Stands for "read-only." You and your students can only read the file, not make changes.

WR

The writable flag allows anyone in the course to make changes to the document.

Remove pages

The wiki engine automatically tracks pages that aren't linked from anywhere else (they were created and then the link was deleted) and empty pages. This tool allows you to remove these orphaned wiki pages, which can't be reached through the ordinary wiki interface.

Strip pages
> While the wiki engine tracks changes, it stores old versions in the database. To declutter the data, you may occasionally want to delete all the old versions and just keep the new one.

Revert mass changes
> Use this tool to roll back changes to all pages if a particular author makes a mess of many pages in the wiki.

Wiki Capabilities

Wiki capabilities enable you to allow your users to engage with the wiki in very different ways. There are three wiki-specific capabilities:

Edit wiki pages
> This allows a user to add or delete content from pages within the wiki. Students have this capability allowed by default, but you could use it to restrict editing after a certain date.

Manage wiki settings
> This allows a user to edit the settings for the wiki (all the options we've described above).

Override locked pages
> When a page is edited by someone, the wiki locks the page so multiple people can't edit the same page at the same time (which would mean the last person to save their changes would overwrite the first person's work). Sometimes, however, a student will open a page for editing, but forget to save his changes. This will keep the page locked for other students for an unreasonable amount of time. A user with this capability can override the lock, freeing the page for editing by someone else.

 If you have group wiki projects, consider assigning the "Override locked pages" capability to the students so they can manage their own wikis.

Effective Wiki Practices

Wikis are gaining popularity as a collaborative tool in many environments. There are now several commercial vendors offering wikis for group collaboration in corporate settings. Many social web sites also have wikis to allow their members to collaborate on documents. Effective management practices are the key to a wiki's success. You'll need to think about your wiki's editorial policy, as well as its educational objectives.

Wiki Basics

Wikis are a simple, flexible tool for collaboration. They can be used for everything from simple lists of web links to building entire encyclopedias. Wikipedia is the largest wiki in the world (*http://www.wikipedia.org*). As of August 2007, Wikipedia contained over 2,000,000 articles in English alone, on everything from general topology to split infinitives. The entire Wikipedia site is written by volunteers from around the world. An article is started by someone with an interest in the subject, and then anyone in the community can add content, edit other people's work, or add another page elaborating on a sub-topic. It has become so large and so frequently used that there is a lively debate about how authoritative a collaborative work without a central editor can be.

Of course, wikis in your own class won't be that extensive. But it's important to have a plan for your wiki before you release it to the class. Students need to know the purpose of the wiki and how it fits in with the class. If it's a personal wiki, will they be graded? Is it simply a staging area for group work that will be submitted later? Students need to know so they can submit appropriate work. A brainstorming wiki is very different from one that will be submitted for a grade.

You'll also need to decide on an editing policy. Will you be a central editor? Or will you let the students be completely responsible for the work? How will you deal with offensive content?

In most circumstances, you'll find that you can trust students. But on the rare occasion a student does do something offensive, you will need to have a policy to deal with it. Will you roll back the changes by that author? Or will you create a new version by deleting her content? Creating a new version leaves a trail you can use for evidence later, but it also makes it easier for the perpetrator to restore her comments.

Creative Wiki Practices

The free-form, collaborative nature of wikis makes them easy to apply in creative ways. Any sort of group process can be facilitated using a wiki.

Group lecture notes

Usually, lecture notes are a solitary activity. But one person can easily miss an important point during a lecture, whether by daydreaming or by trying to understand a prior point.

Students also have difficulty deciding what information is important and what is elaboration or example. Creating a wiki for group lecture notes after a lecture gives students a chance to combine all their notes. Those who missed information can get it from their peers. The group can also decide what information is critical and give it proper emphasis.

Group lecture notes could be done with the entire class, if it is small enough, or with small working groups. Groups can also compare notes for further discussion and refinement.

Group project management

The most straightforward use of a wiki is as a tool for group collaboration for creating group projects. If you assign a group project, give your students a place to work by creating a wiki with the group mode enabled. This will give each group their own space to record their research, create outlines, and even create the final product. You may even want to create a submission date where you turn off editing capabilities for students and then grade the final projects. Afterward, consider enabling visible groups so everyone can see each other's work.

Brainstorming

Brainstorming is a creative process in which ideas are elicited from a group of people. In a face-to-face meeting, a brainstorming facilitator will usually stand in front of a big piece of paper and elicit ideas from the participants in the room. You can use a wiki to create an online version of this process. Set up a wiki for the entire class, or for student groups, and ask people to submit ideas around a brainstorming topic. People can add ideas as they occur and link to other pages for elaboration.

Contribute to other wikis

Consider assigning your class the task of contributing to Wikipedia, or to another wiki on the Web, on a topic in your class. Assign your students to groups (or make it a class project if the class is small enough and the topic broad enough) and challenge them to collaboratively create an article they would feel confident posting to a public-information space. Your students will use the course wiki to create drafts of the article they will publish to the community at the end of the semester.

This type of assignment has a number of benefits:

- It gives students additional motivation to do their best, since they know their work will be viewed and critiqued by the public instead of just their instructor.
- It can act as a summarizing activity for an entire semester's worth of material.
- Students will know their work will be used by other people, not just graded and filed away.

CHAPTER 11

Blogs

The word "blog" is a contraction of "web log." Blogs are a form of online journal that millions of people around the world use for self-expression and communicating with family and friends. The author of a blog usually organizes it as a chronological series of postings. Although some groups of people contribute to blogs, there is usually only one central author for each.

Blogs are growing in importance around the world. They are used by everyone from teenagers posting who they like or dislike at school to CEOs communicating directly with their customers to dissidents in oppressed populations expressing their political views.

In version 1.6, Moodle released a blog tool for users. The Moodle blog has some advantages and disadvantages when compared to other blogging platforms.

Using Blogs

This chapter covers the following MTC skills: 3.16 Blogs

Blogs in Moodle are user-based—each user has his own blog, which is non-course-specific. Your profile page contains a Blog tab for accessing your blog page, as shown in Figure 11-1.

 If your profile page doesn't contain a Blog tab, contact your system administrator and ask if blogs are enabled.

Adding Blog Entries

To add a blog entry:

1. Click on the Blog tab in your profile page.

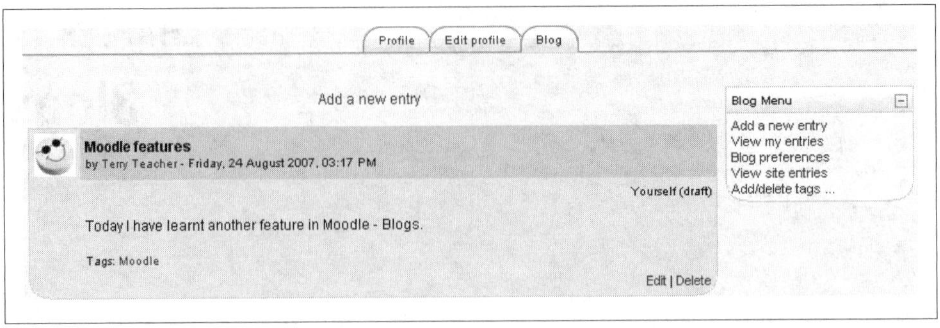

Figure 11-1. A blog page

2. Click on the "Add a new entry" link in the Blog Menu block.

3. In the "Add a new entry" page, as shown in Figure 11-2, write your entry and give it a title.

4. If you want to attach a file, such as an RTF document or a picture, click the Browse button, find the file on your computer, and click Open. Be sure your document is smaller than the maximum attachment size (set by the system administrator).

5. Choose who you wish to publish the entry to (i.e., who may see the entry). There are three options:
   - Yourself—so your blog entry is a draft
   - Anyone on your site
   - Anyone in the world

6. Select appropriate official tags for your entry and/or add one or more user-defined tags (which we'll cover in the next section).

7. Click the "Save changes" button.

You can edit your blog entry at any time using the Edit link at the bottom of the entry. You may want to change the publish option from yourself to anyone on the site. You can also delete the blog entry completely if you wish.

Viewing Blog Entries

You can view your own blog entries via the Blog tab in your profile page or the "View my entries" link in the Blog Menu block. You may view blog entries for all students in your course, or for all students in a particular group, via the Blogs tab in the course participants page.

Alternatively, you can choose to view all blog entries with a particular tag via links in the Blog Tags block (which we'll cover in the next section).

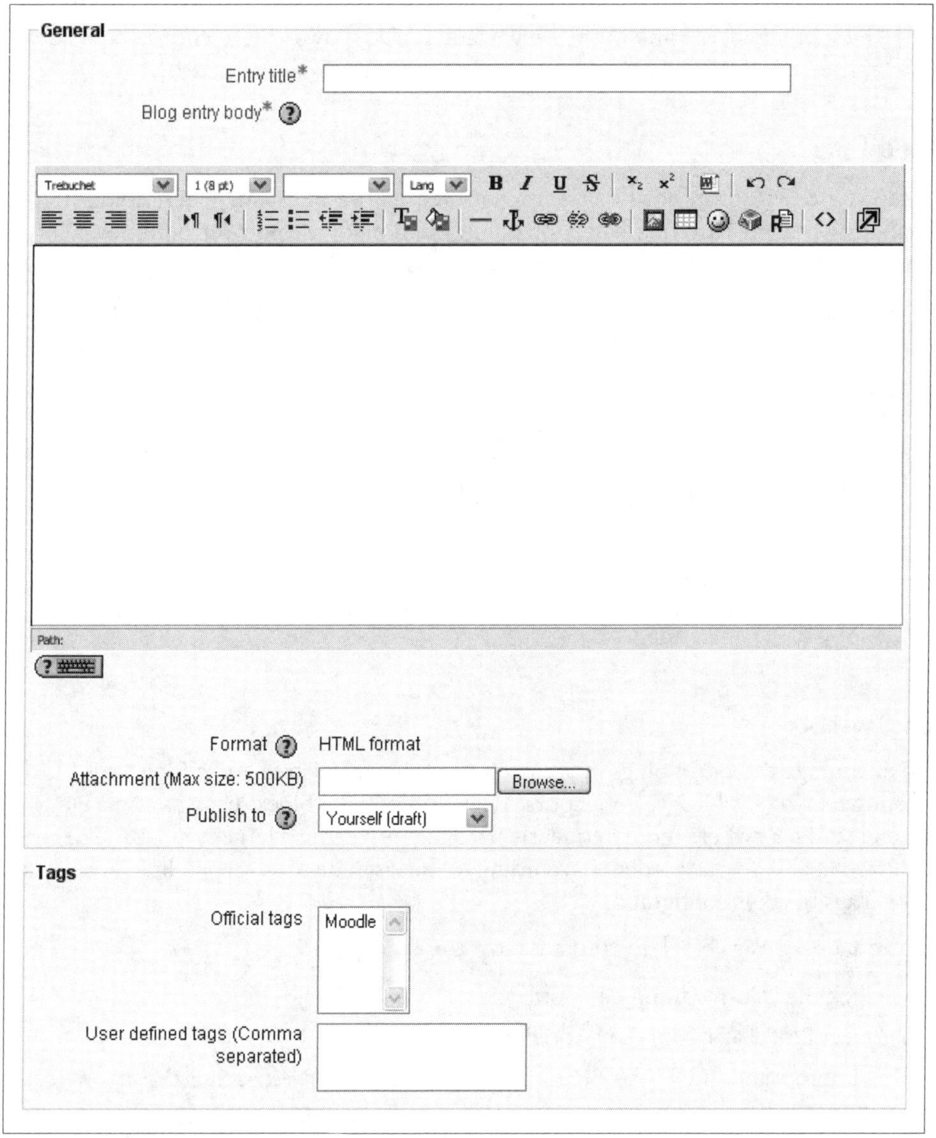

Figure 11-2. Adding a new blog entry

Blog visibility

By default, all site users can view all blog entries via the "View site entries" link in the Blog Menu block. However, your system administrator may have restricted blog visibility site-wide so that users can only see blog entries for people with whom they share a course or a group.

Blog preferences

The "Blog preferences" link in the Blog Menu block allows you to choose how many blog entries are displayed on a page. The default number of entries is 10.

Blog Tags

A tag is a relevant keyword or term associated with a blog entry, describing it and enabling keyword-based classification of information for the purpose of retrieval. Typically, a blog entry will have one or more tags associated with it.

You can add new blog tags when adding or editing a blog entry. There are two types of tag:

User-defined tags
> Personal tags that any user can add

Official tags
> Added by an administrator and available for any site user

 If you need to add official tags as a teacher, contact your system administrator and ask for the capability to be allowed.

Blog Tags block

To encourage the use of blogs in your course, you may wish to add a Blog Tags block, as shown in Figure 11-3, to your course page. A Blog Tags block displays a "tag cloud," i.e., a list of tags where more frequently used tags appear in a larger font size. Tags can be listed in alphabetical order or according to the last date used, depending on how the Blog Tags block is configured.

To add a Blog Tags block to your course page:

1. Click the "Turn editing on" button.
2. Select Blog Tags from the "Add blocks" menu.
3. If appropriate, move the Blog Tags block up and/or left, using the arrow icons under the block title.

To configure a Blog Tags block:

1. Click on the edit configuration icon in the block header.
2. On the Blog Tags configuration page, as shown in Figure 11-4, adjust the settings as required or leave them as default.
3. Click the "Save changes" button.

Blog Tags

About Me Blogs
moodle
Conference
Development
EDUCACION Education
Moodle Moodle
1.6 **Moodle Günlüğü**
Moodlemoot NZ
Newsletter
Teaching Türkçe
blog coding
e-Learning groups
personal training wiki

Figure 11-3. The Blog Tags block from Moodle.org

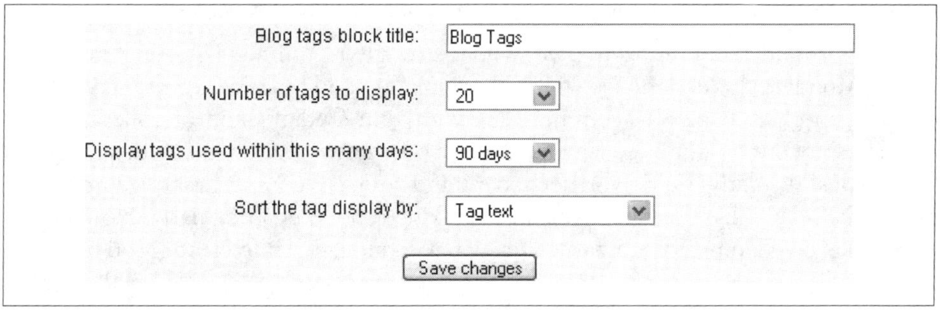

Blog tags block title:	Blog Tags
Number of tags to display:	20
Display tags used within this many days:	90 days
Sort the tag display by:	Tag text

Save changes

Figure 11-4. Configuring a Blog Tags block

Blog Capabilities

Blog capabilities focus on entries and tags, as you might expect.

These capabilities are set at the global level, so as a teacher you may not have the ability to change them.

View blog entries
> This allows a user to view entries in other users' blogs. If you prohibit this capability, the user will not be able to read any blogs on the system.

Create new blog entries
> This allows a user to create entries in her own blog.

Edit and manage entries
>   This allows a user to manage entries, giving her the ability to change and delete other users' entries.

Manage personal tags
>   This allows a user to create and delete user-defined tags that others may use. (Users are always allowed to add their own user-defined tags.)

Manage official tags
>   This allows a user to create and delete the official tags that all users see.

Effective Blog Practices

Blogs in Moodle are a relatively new feature, which many people are still learning how to use. There are currently very few examples of good usage of blogs. Most blogs are either blogging for the sake of blogging, or an ill-defined "learning journal" where students engage in unstructured reflection on what they are learning. It's difficult to maintain students' motivation for either of these activities. Students who are engaging in purposeful blogging for the first time will have a difficult time successfully posting without scaffolding and some clear goals. Perhaps a weakness in blogging assignments comes from a lack of first-hand experience on the part of teachers.

To begin to understand blogging, we would strongly recommend starting your own blog in Moodle. This experience will help you understand blogs better, and it will also give you another channel to communicate with your students and/or colleagues. As you develop your blog, notice which posts are easy to write and which are a struggle. Do you post regularly? Or do you need to remind yourself to post? Creating interesting posts on a regular basis is not easy, nor is making time to post regularly. However, if you set a good example for your students, you will find it easier to create good blogging activities.

The most important element of running an effective blog as part of your course is to have a clearly defined goal for student blogging.

At the beginning of a course, do a quick poll of your students. How many of them are blogging now? Why are they blogging? Many of your students will have either MySpace or Facebook accounts where they can post updates of their activities to their friends. But social blogging is different from blogging in a learning environment, and you will need to work closely with your students to create effective blogs.

It's recommended that you allow each student to create his own blogging goals. As David Hawkins writes in his book *The Roots of Literacy*, "Children can learn to read and write with commitment and quality just in proportion as they are engaged with matters of importance to them, and about which at some point they wish to read and write."

Blogging is essentially a writing exercise. It can be a personal, reflective exercise, or it can be a forum for posting about the ideas and concepts important to the author.

Once your students have started blogging, they may respond better if they have an audience. Knowing someone is reading your posts is a great motivator to continue writing. Be sure to comment, either via messages or in class, on posts students have made public. If students want to keep their posts as private reflections, allow them to do so. Blogging is always personal, and your blogging authors need to feel a sense of control over their personal posts.

Creative Blog Practices

As blogs are so new, there is a lot of room for new and creative applications. As the blogs continue to develop in future versions of Moodle, there will be more capabilities to apply to interesting activities. But even now, there are a few creative activities you can develop using the blog tool.

Group work with tags

Blog tags are used to categorize and locate blog entries. Usually general categories are used, like "teaching" or "trips." However, creating assignment-specific tags can turn the blog tool into a brainstorming tool. If you have an assignment on understanding evolution, create a set of tags for your students to tag research findings, claims, counter-claims, evidence, etc. Once students have begun to create entries, they can collate the work of the entire class by selecting the appropriate tags, and every post with that tag will be displayed.

One-minute responses

Effective feedback is important for learning. This is true for both the teacher and the student. One-minute-response blog posts are an easy way to get informal feedback from students about a lesson or activity and keep them posting in their blogs. Usually, the instructor gives the students a few prompts to get quick feedback on the effectiveness of the lesson.

You can use three questions when asking for a one-minute response to a lesson:

- What was the muddiest (i.e., least clear) point in the lesson?
- What was the most important point?
- How useful/interesting was the lesson?

Obviously, there are many more prompts you can use to get the feedback you want from your students. You may want students to reflect on how they feel about the class itself, or about a test, or ask other questions about how they perceive various aspects of your course. Alternatively, you could ask them for quick answers to more specific, content-related questions that you know students frequently have problems with.

Jason: One of the most effective Geography classes I've seen uses one-minute responses on a daily basis. In each lesson, the instructor hands out a page asking students what they didn't understand, what the strongest point was, and what they wanted to know more about. The instructor then takes a few minutes at the beginning of the following lesson to address the issues raised in the reflections from the day before.

Assign students a one-minute response as a blog assignment. Post the questions in a prominent place in your course, and ask them to tag the post with the name or date of the activity. Clicking on the tag will make it easy to collate all of the student responses.

CHAPTER 12

Databases

This chapter covers the following MTC skills: 5.12 Database

The database module provides a tool for collaborative development of a database within the course. For those of us old and geeky enough to remember, it's Moodle's answer to Apple's FileMaker program: a simple, easy-to-use, general purpose database. It's not meant to be very complex or powerful, it's simply a way for multiple people to add structured data to a shared resource.

Only your imagination limits the potential uses of the database module. You could use the database to create glossaries, catalogs, taxonomies, registrations, paper submissions, maps, or anything where the students in your class can fill in a form to add data.

Creating database activities is a little more involved than most of the Moodle activities, but it's not as complex as lessons. You also have the option of using a preset of an empty database activity, rather than creating your own from scratch. An image gallery preset is currently included in the database module, though more database presets will be available in the future. For now, however, let's create a database activity from scratch, based on the goals you have for the students in your course.

 The database module should not be confused with the database that powers your Moodle site. The database module is an activity type, which uses the Moodle database to store data. The Moodle database stores data for all modules and for your Moodle site.

Creating Databases

A database is made up of fields and templates. Fields define the type of data the database will store: text, dates, files, URLs, etc. Templates allow you to control the visual layout of information when listing, viewing, or editing database entries.

A database activity has three basic template types:

List template
> The list template allows you to control the fields used and their layout when viewing multiple entries. Usually an overview of each entry is provided, with more detailed information available by clicking on an entry to access the single view.

Single template
> The single template is for displaying the detailed view of a single entry. All the data the user entered should be visible here.

Add template
> The add template creates the interface form used when adding or editing database entries.

As with many of the activity modules, a little preplanning can go a long way when you are thinking about developing a database activity. The field definitions determine the fields in the add template, which determine the data you can display on the list and single templates. Before you being digging into the database, try to sketch out the fields you think you need the students to enter, and how you might want to lay them out in each template.

Once you have a rough sketch, creating the database itself will be easier and you will less likely need to go back and add fields later (although you can if you need to).

> *Moodle.org* has three good examples of database activities:
>
> - Moodle Buzz (*http://moodle.org/mod/data/view.php?id=6140*), a database of the titles, authors, and web links to news articles mentioning Moodle
> - Themes (*http://moodle.org/mod/data/view.php?id=6552*), a database containing screenshots, download links, and user comments about Moodle themes
> - Modules and plug-ins (*http://moodle.org/mod/data/view.php?id=6009*), a database containing a number of web links and information about the modular components of Moodle
>
> Browsing these activities can give you ideas for each of the template types.

Adding a Database

The first step to creating a database is adding it to the appropriate section of your course. As with most Moodle activities, you first set the options for the database, then create the fields and templates.

To create a database activity:

1. Select Database from the "Add an activity" drop-down menu in the course section where you would like to add the activity.

2. On the "Adding a new database" page, as shown in Figure 12-1, give the database a name and a description.

3. Select the general options:

    Available from/to
    The dates the database is both visible to students and open for data entry.

    Viewable from/to
    The dates the database is available for viewing, but not open for data entry.

    Required entries
    The number of entries each student is required to enter before the database activity can be considered complete. The student will see a reminder message if she has not submitted the required number of entries.

    Entries required before viewing
    The number of entries the student needs to submit before he can see entries by other students. If the student has not submitted the required number of entries, he will only see the entry page and not the list or single view pages.

    Maximum entries
    The maximum number of entries the student can submit before she is blocked. This prevents people from spamming the system, either in the hope that one entry is good enough or, on a public site, as a way of advertising.

    Comments
    Enables commenting on entries. The comments field appears on the single view template when this is enabled.

    Require approval?
    Allows you to require each entry to be approved by someone with the appropriate role before other users can view it.

    RSS articles
    Enables you to publish an RSS feed of entries in the database. The option here sets the number of entries available in the feed.

     RSS feeds need to be enabled by your system administrator.

    Allow posts to be rated?
    Lets you allow posts to be rated, which will enter a score in the gradebook for the student's submissions in the database. The grade is set using the drop-down menu below this option.

4. Select the common module options:

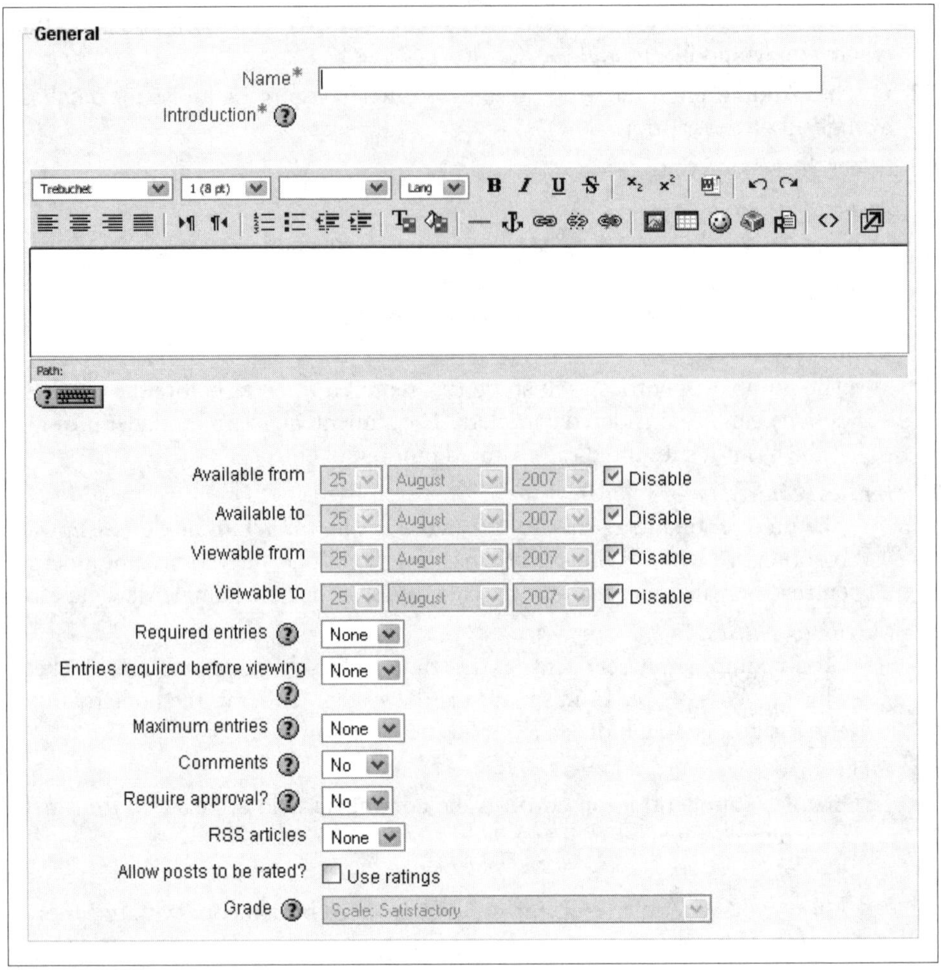

Figure 12-1. Adding a new database

> *Group mode*
>> This is another location in which to set the group mode for the activity. If group mode is forced in the course settings then this setting will be ignored.

> *Visible*
>> This determines whether students may view the activity or not.

5. Click the "Save changes" button and you will be taken to the database setup page.

Creating Fields

The field definitions create the basic structure of the database and determine what kind of information students can enter into your database. You are provided with a choice of 12 data field types:

Checkbox

>　For students to select one or more checkboxes. To add multiple checkboxes, enter each option on a different line in the options text field.

 If you want to ensure that a student actively selects only one of the options, it's better to use the radio buttons field.

>　Multiple checkboxes can be useful, for example, for different film genres in a movie database. You can check more than one in the case of Horror-Comedies or Comedy-Westerns. The menu (multiselect) field also achieves this, but clicking multiple checkboxes is usually a more obvious interface.

Date

>　For students to enter a date by picking the day, month, and year from a drop-down list.

File

>　For students to upload a file of any type from their computer.

 If you want students to upload image files, it's better to use the picture field.

Latitude/longitude

>　For students to enter a geographic location by specifying the location's latitude and longitude. When students view the entry, links are automatically generated to geographic data services such as Google Maps, Google Earth, or Multimap.

Menu

>　For students to select an option from a drop-down menu. Enter each option on a different line in the options text field.

Menu (multiselect)

>　For students to select multiple options from a drop-down menu (by holding down the Control or Shift key as they click).

The checkbox field offers the same options as menu (multiselect) but with a more obvious user interface.

Number

For students to enter a number (positive, negative, or zero).

Picture

For students to upload an image file from their computer.

Radio buttons

For students to select just one option from a list. If used, "radio buttons" is a required field; a student may only submit his database entry after selecting an option.

Text

For students to enter text up to 60 characters in length. For longer text, or for text that requires formatting—such as headers and bullet points—the textarea field should be used.

Textarea

For students to enter text longer than 60 characters in length and/or include formatting such as headers and bullet points.

URL

For students to enter a URL. Selecting "Autolink the URL" will make the URL a clickable link, and entering a forced name for the link means that the name will be used for the hyperlink.

To create the fields for your database:

1. On the database setup page, select the field type you want to add from the "Create a new field" drop-down menu.
2. Enter a field name and a field description. The field name is used to create the templates, so make it unique and long enough to be descriptive, but not too long to retype.
3. If necessary, add/select the options for each field type. For example, you can set the height and width of the text area generated by the textarea field.

Once you've defined the fields you want to use in your database, as shown in Figure 12-2, you are ready to begin editing your templates.

Editing Templates

Once you have created the fields for your database, you will probably want to edit the templates that define the user interface. Creating the fields produces a default template,

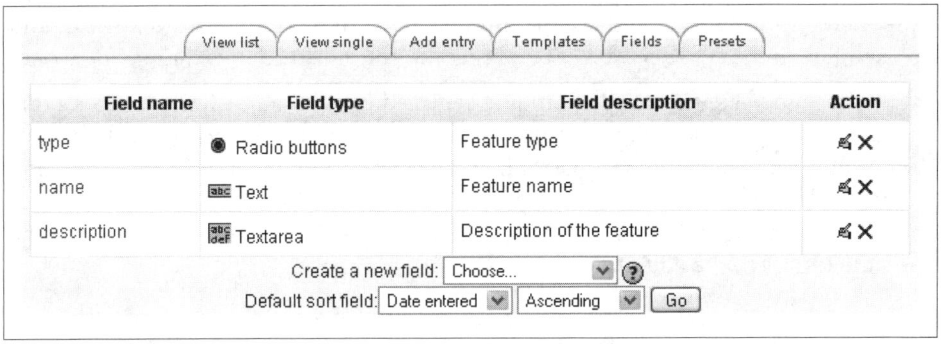

Figure 12-2. Database fields

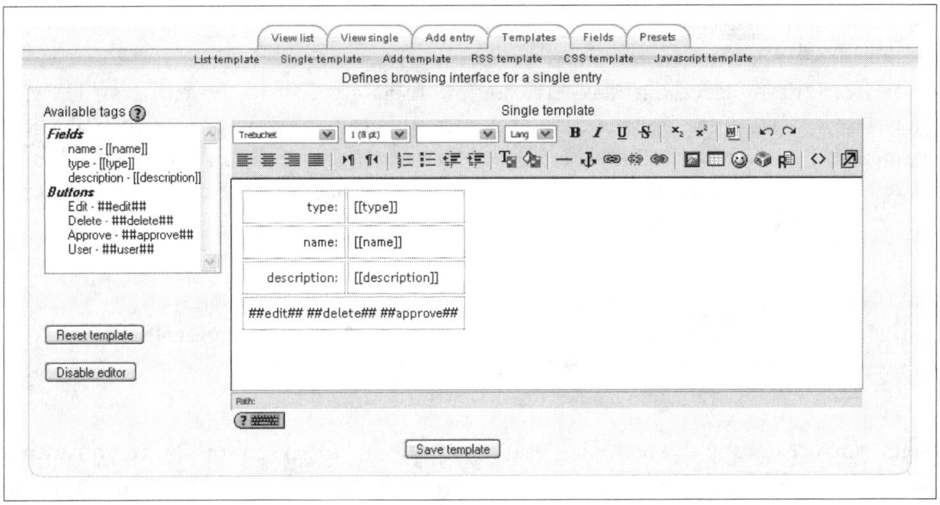

Figure 12-3. A single template

as shown in Figure 12-3. However, with a little work, you can improve the defaults considerably.

Database templates all work on the same principle. They are basically HTML pages with a new set of tags for the database module to interpret. When editing a template, Moodle displays a list of available tags on the left side of the editing screen. Double-clicking on any of the tags adds it to the template. The database activity interprets these new tags before sending the template's HTML to the browser for display. It looks for words enclosed in either two square brackets ([[) or two hash signs (##), representing two different types of interface elements it can add to the template.

The square brackets define data tags, which tell the module to replace the word in the brackets with the value or form element of the field with the same name. So if you have a database with a name field, you would represent it in the template with [[name]]. In the single or list template, the module would replace it with the data in the name field for that entry. In the list template, the module would replace it with a text field, and put the value in the text field if you're editing the entry instead of creating a new one.

The ## tags indicate the word should be replaced by an icon or link for interacting with the module. These tags are used to place the edit and delete icons, and links for More, Approve, Comments, and User. If you want to add the edit icon to a template, you just add a tag that looks like ##edit##. When the user looks at the page with the tag, the database module replaces it with the edit icon. If the user then clicks on the icon, it takes her to the edit template.

The edit and delete icons only appear for users with appropriate capabilities allowed. The Approve and Comments links only appear if these options are enabled AND only for users with appropriate capabilities allowed.

Aside from the replacement tags, creating a template is just like creating an HTML page. Use a table to lay out the data elements (this is an acceptable use of tables for layout), add descriptive text around the replacement tags, and publish. The database makes it easy to rapidly view your changes by flipping between the Templates tab and the tab for the template you are working on.

Don't forget to save the template before you switch views! It's easy to forget, and very frustrating to switch views and have the template look exactly the same because you forgot to save!

When you are editing the template, you may find the HTML editor gets in your way, especially when editing the list template (more on the list template below). Fortunately, Moodle has a toggle button for enabling and disabling the HTML editor in the template editing screen. Just below the "Reset template" button on the left side of the template page, you'll see the "Enable/Disable editor" button. Disabling the editor allows you to get your hands dirty with the raw HTML code rather than trying to use the editor's GUI. Most of the templates are quite simple, and switching the editor off is a great way to learn how the templates are structured.

As mentioned previously, there are three basic templates necessary to use the database: list, single, and add. The three other templates—RSS, CSS, and JavaScript—are more advanced templates and aren't necessary for basic database use.

To edit a template:

1. On the database page, click the Templates tab.

2. Click one of the template links below the row of tabs.

3. When you are done, click the "Save template" button.

Add template

Add template is used to create and edit new entries. In this template, data tags are replaced with the form element for the field. If the user is editing an entry, the field will have the data from the field in the form element for editing as well.

 It's important to list every field you want the user to fill in on this template. If you leave off a field, the user won't be able to add or edit its data.

If you have a lot of form elements, consider grouping them together logically. For example, if you have a database asking students to build a catalog of insects found during a field trip, you may want to separate the description and taxonomy from the location data. It will make it easier for students to fill in and organize their data.

Single template

The single template, as shown earlier in Figure 12-3, is the detailed view of an entry. This template should list all of the available data. Again, consider organizing the data if you have a lot of fields in your database.

List template

The list template is the first page students will see when they come to your database. The list template should give an overview of the entries and enable users to click through to the single or edit template.

Organizing a good list template is a bit of a challenge. First, you should identify the fields that will be most helpful to users for selecting the entries they want to view. The default layout almost always has too much information and is not laid out well.

The form has three areas: the Header, Body, and Footer. If you lay out the list template as a table, you'll want to use the Header area as the table header, the Body for the data, and the Footer to close the table, as has been done for the *Moodle.org* modules and plug-ins and Moodle Buzz databases. But the HTML editor puts a full table in each area, which makes it difficult to get proper alignment of the elements and not repeat the headers for every entry.

 A knowledge of tables in HTML is required in order to lay out the entire list template as one table.

To make the entire list template as one table:

1. On the list template page, turn off the HTML editor. Figure 12-4 shows the list template from the *Moodle.org* modules and plug-ins with the HTML editor turned off.

Figure 12-4. The list template from the Moodle.org Modules and plug-ins database

2. In the Header area of the template, open the table and add a row for your header text. Each column should contain one element of the header.

3. In the Body, create another row with the data and command replacement tags.

4. In the Footer, close the table.

5. Save the template. DO NOT switch the HTML editor on while editing this template. If you turn the editor back on, it will create tables in each of the areas.

RSS template

The RSS template allows you to structure the RSS feed from the database. If you have enabled RSS feeds for the database in the database options, the database will publish the entries in a feed. This template allows you to structure how the entries in the feed appear to the readers.

CSS template

The CSS template defines the CSS styles for all of the templates in the database. If you know CSS, you can adjust the template's fonts, spacing, colors, and other display information.

JavaScript template

Like the CSS template, the JavaScript template is used by the other templates. The JavaScript template allows you to add new behaviors to the templates by defining JavaScript routines that can be loaded when the template page loads. At the time of this writing, the JavaScript API isn't yet documented, but the image gallery preset uses JavaScript to define the size of images in the list and single templates.

Managing Databases

Once you have set up your database, you and your students can begin to enter data. Managing your database as students begin to populate it with data is an important factor in the success of a database activity. Someone will need to maintain the quality of the entries and give students credit for participating.

Quality Data

Once students have started to add entries to your database, you will need to track their data to help ensure they are making useful contributions. Managing the quality of database entries can be a tedious exercise, but it can also be a learning opportunity for your students. Students will enter their data according to their interpretation of the activity and their abilities. An inaccurate or disorganized entry from a student is a potential opportunity for feedback to help the student learn.

The database module has a few tools that will be useful to you in ensuring data quality:

Comments
> Comments are a great tool for feedback to motivate your students and help them improve their entries.

Require approval
> The ultimate quality assurance tool is the "Require approval" option in your database options. As mentioned earlier, this option hides an entry from the rest of the class until you or someone with approval capability approves it. You might want to use this capability to help students produce good material by giving them feedback before approving an entry.

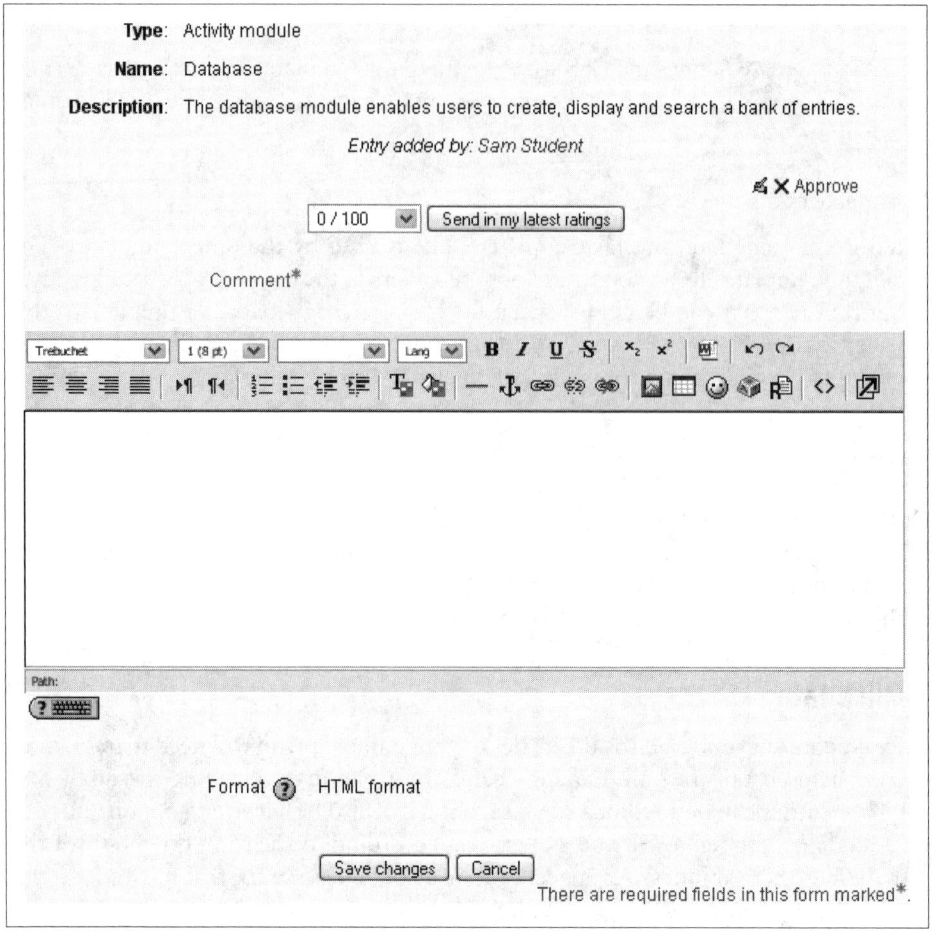

Figure 12-5. Rating and adding a comment to a database entry

Rating

Giving grades for entries is the single most powerful motivator for students. It also rewards students for their time and effort. As always, if you don't want to assign a numerical grade to an entry, you can create a custom scale and assign a qualitative grade. (We'll cover grades and scales in Chapter 13.) When you rate an entry, the grade is added to the gradebook, like a rated forum post.

We would strongly recommend combining rating and comments, as shown in Figure 12-5. Rating allows you to assign a numerical value to an entry, but it doesn't give you a method to tell the student why she received her particular grade. The comments box enables you to communicate the reason.

Rating and comments can be turned into a collaborative venture with your students. By default, students are allowed to add comments, but only teachers are allowed to rate entries. However, you can enable collaborative rating by setting a student role override.

 If you don't see the "Override roles" link in the Roles tab, ask your system administrator. By default, teachers are unable to override roles, so this ability must be granted by your system administrator, as well as setting which roles can be overridden by the teacher role.

To enable student rating of entries:

1. On the Updating database page, select the Roles tab.
2. Click the "Override roles" link just below the tabs.
3. Select the student role from the list of roles in your course.
4. Select Allow for the "Rate entries" capability, as shown in Figure 12-6.
5. Click the "Save changes" button.

Database Presets

To avoid the necessity of always having to create a new database from scratch, the database module has a presets feature. As mentioned already, an image gallery preset is currently included in the database module to help get you started. You can create your own presets as well and share them with others.

To use a preset:

1. On the database page, click the Presets tab.
2. Either click the "Choose file" button, browse for the preset ZIP on your computer and click Import, or choose a previously loaded preset.

 If you have already created fields in your database, you need to map them to the new fields in the preset or they will be deleted. For example, if you load the image gallery preset, you can map three fields to the image, title, and caption fields in the preset. Any other fields will be deleted and any data in them will be lost.

3. If you desire, customize the fields and templates.

That's all there is to using a preset. All the hard work of setting up the templates has been done for you.

If you wish to share your database presets with others, you have two options:

1. Export as a ZIP file, which can then be imported to another course or Moodle site.
2. Save as a preset, which publishes the database for other teachers on your site to use. It will then appear in the preset list. (You can delete it from the list at any time.)

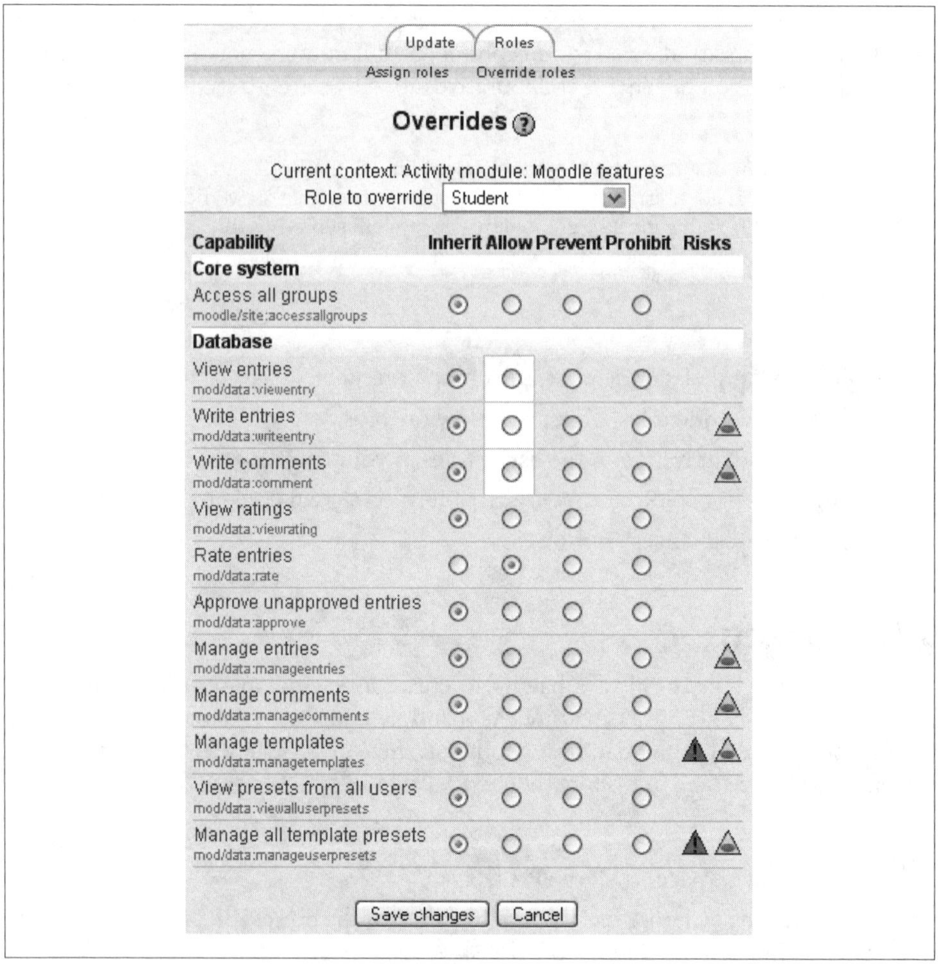

Figure 12-6. Setting a student role override

 Only the fields and templates of the database are copied when exporting or saving it as a preset, not the entries.

Database Capabilities

The database module has a number of capabilities you can use to fine-tune your users' interaction with the activity.

View entries

This allows a user to view database entries submitted by other users. This capability is moderated by any submission requirements in the database options, such as the number of entries required before viewing.

Write entries

This allows a user to create new database entries.

Write comments

This allows a user to add comments to database entries. This capability is only active if the comments option is enabled.

By default, students are allowed to add comments. If you only want teachers to be able to add comments, you can prevent this capability with a student role override.

View ratings

This allows a user to view all ratings.

Rate entries

This allows a user to rate entries by other users. This capability is only active if the "Allow posts to be rated" option is enabled.

The capabilities to write comments and rate entries together allow students to provide feedback on entries.

 You may want to select a small group of students as moderators and create a role for them to provide feedback to others.

Approve unapproved entries

This allows a user to approve entries before they are viewable by everyone. This capability is only active if the "Require approval" option is enabled.

Manage entries

This allows a user to edit and delete other users' database entries.

Manage comments

This allows a user to edit and delete other users' comments.

Manage templates

This allows a user to edit and delete the interface templates of the database. If you want students to create database activities for each other, you can enable this capability for them.

View presets from all users

This allows a user to view the list of site presets and select them for use.

Manage all template presets

This allows a user to delete site presets.

Effective Database Practices

The database activity is both powerful and complex. It is probably the most technical module to set up, though a complex lesson may take longer, but it has tremendous power. The database is a veritable Swiss Army knife, useful in many situations with a little ingenuity and work.

To reduce your workload creating databases, make use of one of the presets available on *Moodle.org*. If a preset doesn't meet all of your requirements, it's easier to customize an existing database than create one from scratch.

You can also share the work of creating a database. If you want your students to create and submit a database for a project, you can override the student role and grant them authoring capabilities. If you then use the separate groups mode, each group can create its own database of research and submit it at the end for grading.

Remember to use roles and groups functionality to create additional flexibility to your database.

Creative Database Practices

With a little creativity, the database activity can become a useful tool for collaboration. The structure provided by the field definitions and the templates makes it easier for students to understand what you expect of them and to provide each other with good data. Combined with less structured activities, like wikis and forums, you have a powerful combination of thinking tools to enable your students to produce good work.

Student files area

Long-time Moodle community member and high school German teacher Art Lader uses the database module to create a student storage tool. Creating a database to allow students to upload files and then download them in a different location produces a very simple-to-use content repository.

If you want to make a private student storage tool, so that only the student and teacher can access the student's files, you can set the database so that entries require approval, but never approve the students' entries. This will keep them invisible to everyone except the student and the teacher.

 You could use a file storage area in a small business as a repository of proposals or other work products for sharing amongst your team.

Collaborative research

In addition to allowing students to store files, you can also use the database to collect information and references for collaborative research projects in a course. If you use the groups mode, each workgroup can have their own collection and work together to find books, articles, URLs, and other resources to share.

Voting and comments

The database module can also be used to gather feedback on a list of ideas for a project or a guest lecturer. The rating and commenting fields can be used to capture group feedback, as well as give you a tool for providing feedback to students. To set up voting, select an appropriate scale when you set up the database options. To allow students to comment, enable commenting in the database options.

CHAPTER 13

Grades and Scales

Grades are a necessary evil in modern education. They take a complex task—learning a new subject—and reduce it to a single measure. Grades can function as both carrot and stick for motivating students, and they are the primary measure of success in a course. Tracking and calculating grades are serious and tedious tasks. Fortunately, Moodle has a great tool to help.

The Moodle grades area is a sophisticated tool for tracking student scores in your course. You can use it for scored activities both in the classroom and in Moodle. Moodle 1.8 introduces a number of useful improvements, including options to assign extra credit, grade on a curve, and exclude a particular score from a student's total grade.

With the new improvements, you should consider using the Moodle gradebook as your primary tool for recording scores and calculating grades. Students will appreciate being able to check their grades at any time and to compare themselves to the class average.

Grades aren't the only way to give feedback to students. With Moodle's scales, you can create lists of nonnumeric feedback options for assessing student work. Moodle comes with one scale by default, "Separate and Connected ways of knowing," which we'll discuss later in this chapter. You can easily create your own additional scales for feedback options that are meaningful to you and your students.

Using Grades

This section covers the following MTC skills: 7.4 Grades

You can access the grades area by clicking the Grades link in the Administration block on your course page.

The View Grades page, as shown in Figure 13-1, contains a table listing students in the course together with their grades for each activity.

You can sort the table by student last name or first name by clicking the respective links under the student column on either the left or right side. Initially, it's sorted by last name.

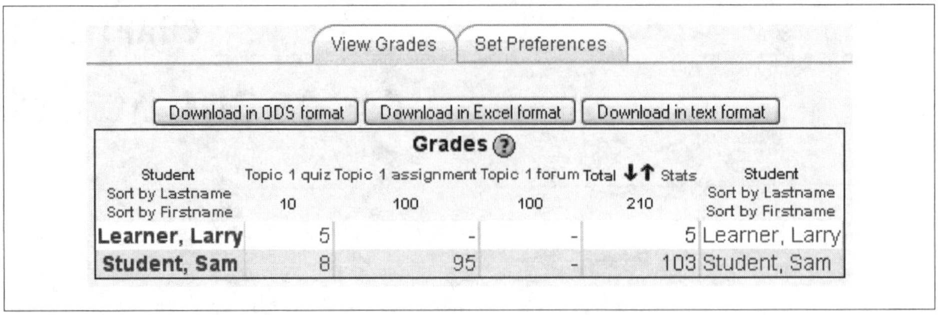

Figure 13-1. Viewing grades

To display the grades for one particular student only, click on his name. This is useful when you are looking at grades together with a student and you need to protect the privacy of other students.

On the right is the Total column. There are two arrows for sorting student totals in descending or ascending order. There is also a Stats link, which displays statistics for the class in a pop-up window.

Each graded activity name links to the grades for that particular activity.

Buttons above the grades table enable you to download course grades in a choice of three formats: Open Document Spreadsheet, Excel, or text. Also at the top of the page is the Set Preferences tab.

Set Preferences

The Set Preferences page contains the following settings:

Reprint Headers
> This preference sets the frequency with which Moodle will display a row with the column labels rather than scores. With a large class, this feature can make it easier to view a large number of graded activities without losing track of individual grades.

Show Hidden Items
> You can choose whether to show or hide hidden graded activities on the View Grades page.

Advanced Features

Clicking the "Use Advanced Features" button on the Set Preferences page reveals further settings, as shown in Figure 13-2. Tabs for setting categories, weights, grade letters, and grade exceptions appear at the top of the page. The advanced features enables you to manipulate the raw grade scores however you see fit.

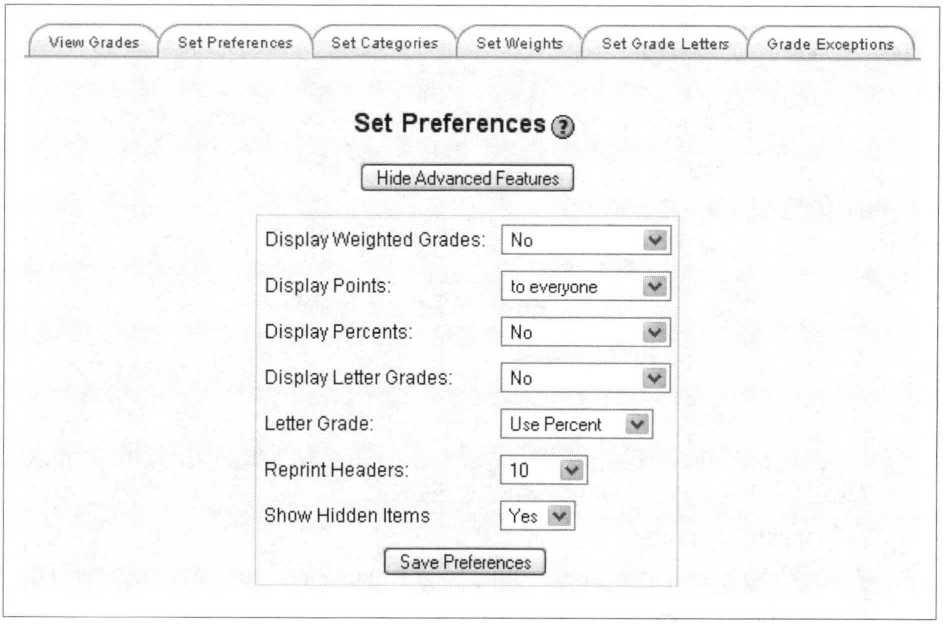

Figure 13-2. Setting preferences with advanced features

Display Weighted Grades

   This determines whether or not the weighted percent will be displayed for you and/or students.

Display Points

   This determines whether points are displayed for you and/or students.

Display Percents

   This determines whether percentages are displayed for you and/or students.

Display Letter Grades

   This determines whether a letter grade is displayed for the course total.

Letter Grade

   This determines whether the letter grade is calculated using a raw or weighted percent.

Set Categories

Categories are the key to using most of the advanced features. Categories are simply collections of graded activities that you can manipulate together. The Extra Credit, Curving, and Weighting features all use Categories to identify which grades to use.

Category

   If you have a lot of graded activities in your course, then arranging them into categories will make grade viewing easier, since the View Grades page can be set to

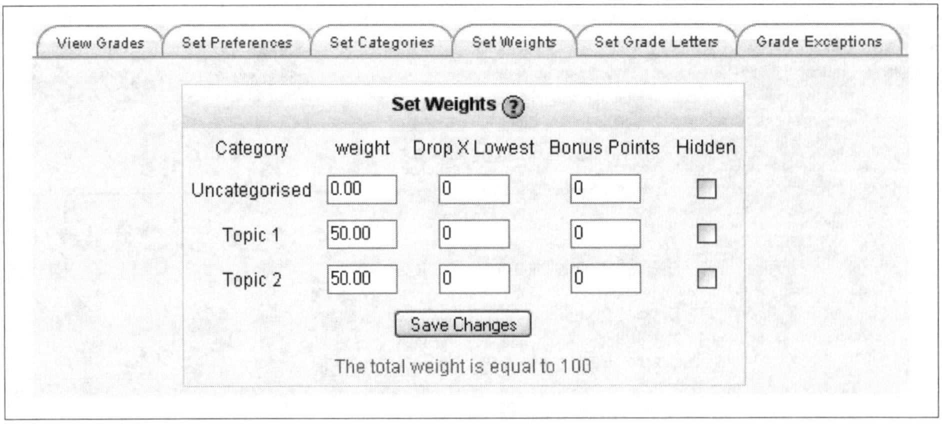

Figure 13-3. Setting weights

display grades for one particular category rather than for all activities. In addition, you will be able to set weights for the categories.

To add a new category:

1. On the Set Categories page, type a category name into the "Add category" box.

2. Click the "Add category" button.

You will then be able to categorize activities using the new category by selecting it from the Category drop-down menu next to the activity name.

Curve To

Curving sets a new maximum point total for the category. For example, if the maximum grade for an assignment is 30 and the curve to is set to 25, then students' grades and percentages will be calculated against a possible 25 points rather than 30.

Extra Credit

This checkbox is for giving particular activities extra credit. If an activity is marked as extra credit, the points earned by a student will be added to the point total for the category but won't increase the total possible points.

When you are done, click the "Save changes" button.

Set Weights

Once you have set up some categories, you can weight them appropriately on the Set Weights page, as shown in Figure 13-3. The options are:

Weight

This allows you to weight grades by category. The weight is the percent that a category will contribute to a grade's total. The individual weights must add up to 100.

Drop X Lowest

This allows you to choose to omit grades for activities in which a student has performed badly. However, if you use this feature, the point totals for all activities in the category must be the same.

Bonus Points

This is used to give extra points that do not change the point total for a category. For example, it can be used to adjust for unfair questions. Bonus points will be applied equally to all students.

Hidden

If this box is checked it will remove a category from display and grade calculation.

 The hidden category option provides a way of only adding items to the gradebook after they have been graded. Since graded items that have not been categorized will automatically be assigned to "Uncategorized," you can set the Uncategorized category to hidden and then, as you grade items, move them to an appropriate category.

When you are done, click the "Save changes" button.

Set Grade Letters

Here you can set an appropriate grade letter scale for the course total. You may choose letters (e.g., A, B, C, D, E) or words (e.g., Below Pass, Pass, Merit, Distinction).

To set your grade letter scale:

1. Edit the grade letters and/or low and high figures, or leave the default scale as it is. The figures must be written to two decimal places.
2. Click the "Save changes" button.

Grade Exceptions

Here you can exclude students from having particular activities graded. This is useful, for example, in cases of extended illness.

To exclude a student from having an activity graded:

1. Click on the name of the activity(s) in the middle column. Holding down the Ctrl key will allow you to select multiple items.
2. Click on the student's name in the left column.
3. Click on the "Exclude from Grading" button. The student's name will be moved from the left column to the right.

The figures in brackets after the activity names in the middle column denote the number of students excluded from having the activity graded.

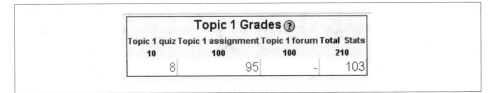

Topic 1 Grades ⓘ				
Topic 1 quiz	Topic 1 assignment	Topic 1 forum	Total	Stats
10	100	100	210	
8	95	-	103	

Figure 13-4. Viewing grades as a student

To include a previously excluded student:

1. Click on the name of the activity in the middle column.
2. Click on the student's name in the right column.
3. Click on the "Include in Grading" button. The student's name will be moved from the right column back to the left.

Student Grade View

Students can check their grades by clicking the Grades link in their Administration block. They can see only their own grades, not the other students', as shown in Figure 13-4.

As for the teacher view, on the right is a total column and a stats link, which displays statistics for the class in a pop-up window.

Creating Scales

This section covers the following MTC skills: 7.3 Scales

Scales are a nonnumeric way of evaluating students' performance. Instead of giving an assignment a number from 1 to 100 as a grade, you can give the student a word or a small phrase as standard feedback.

Moodle's default scale "Separate and Connected ways of knowing" gives you three options: Mostly Separate Knowing, Separate and Connected, and Mostly Connected Knowing. These phrases relate to a theory about how people approach the world. Separate knowers try to remain objective and avoid personalizing knowledge. They like to debate and critique new ideas. Connected knowers learn in a socially connected, empathetic way. They try to find consensus instead of confrontation.

This scale comes with Moodle as a default. Some people use it, but many people create their own. You can create a scale using any rating system you choose.

To create a new scale:

1. Click the Scales link in the Administration block.
2. On the Scales page, shown in Figure 13-5, click the "Add a new scale" button.

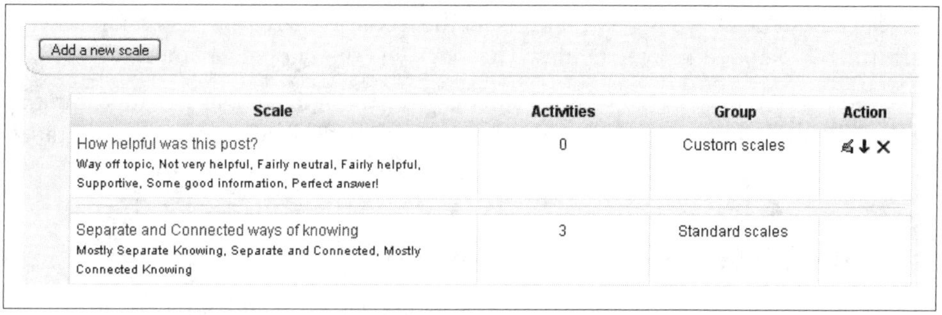

Figure 13-5. Viewing scales

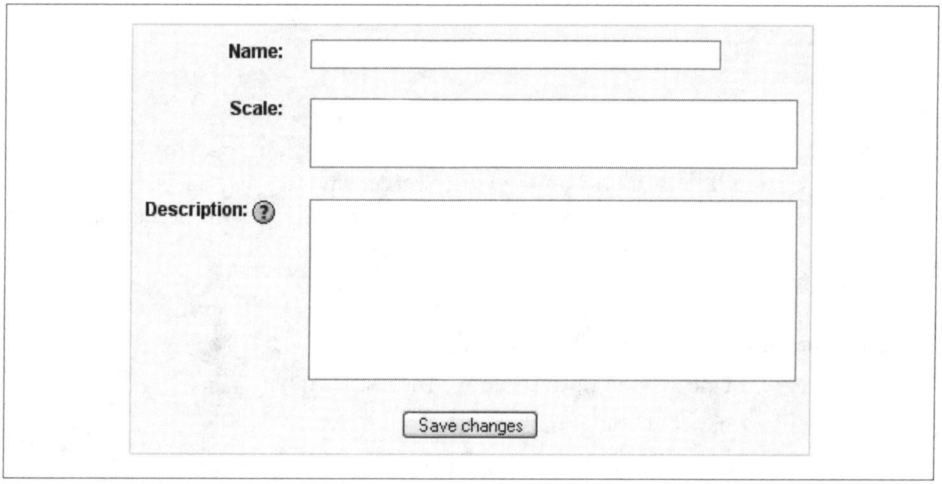

Figure 13-6. Adding a new scale

3. On the next page, shown in Figure 13-6, give your scale a name that will identify it clearly. This will appear in scale-selection lists.

4. In the Scale box, create your scale, ranging from negative to positive, separated by commas.

5. Write a meaningful description for your scale. Your students will have access to the description, and you can use this to give them additional feedback. The more details you put in the description, the more students will understand what each scale item means.

6. Click the "Save changes" button.

Once you've created your scale, you can use it in any activity where you would give a grade, except quizzes. Quizzes are the only tool where you have to use a numeric grade so Moodle can compute a score.

You can edit or delete your new scale, using the icons in the Action column, until you start using it in one or more activities. The icons will then no longer appear.

When you give feedback using a nonnumeric scale, the activity does not appear in the total grade column. Instead, the word you select for the feedback appears in the grades list.

Effective Grade and Scale Practices

Grades and scales are important tools for providing feedback to your students. Using these tools effectively can help you create a more powerful learning environment.

Grade Practices

Backups

We recommend that you regularly download your gradebook for backup. Your system administrator should be backing up the entire server on a regular basis, but you can never be too certain. After all, your students will complain to you if they lose their grades, not to the system administrator.

To download your gradebook:

1. Click the Grades link in the Administration block.
2. Click one of the download buttons above the grades table.
3. Save the file somewhere on your computer.
4. Rename the file to include the date of the download.

If you follow the backup procedure on a regular basis, you will have a record of student grades if there is a catastrophic loss of data on the server. You can always recover students' grades up to that point in the semester if you have a regular backup.

Extra credit

Teachers often want to be able to award extra credit. Fortunately, the gradebook's advanced features make awarding extra credit easy.

To give an activity extra credit:

1. Click the Grades link in the Administration block. From the Grades page, click the Set Preferences tab.
2. Click the Set Categories tab. (If you've not yet enabled the advanced features, click the Set Preferences tab, then click the "Use Advanced Features" button to reveal additional tabs.)
3. Click the extra credit checkbox opposite the activity you want to award extra credit for.

4. Click the "Save changes" button.

Curves and grade letters

Grading on a curve and translating numeric grades to letter grades are important tools for adjusting student grades to reflect the performance of students relative to each other rather than an objective standard. When the subject matter is very difficult, or if you are trying a new course design, this can be very useful for maintaining fairness.

The gradebook provides two tools for adjusting grades after you have awarded a raw score. On the Set Categories page you can set a maximum score for a scored activity below the original point amount. This is equivalent to grading on the curve. Usually, you will set the curve after the scores are completed. You may want to set the curve to equal the highest grade in the class. If you set the curve score below the highest score, students who score above that level will receive a score higher than 100 percent. Allowing scores above 100 percent may be a useful way of rewarding students who have done exceptionally well, and would have otherwise blown the curve.

You can also use the grade-letters scale to curve the total class score. There's no law that an "A" grade has to be 90 percent and above. You can use whatever scale you want, as long as you are clear about it up front.

Jason: One of my favorite teachers in high school challenged us by making an "A" 93 percent and above. The modified scale encouraged the students to put that much more effort into their work to try to meet his higher standard.

Categories and Weights

If you have a course design where it is useful to give a lot of low-stakes practice (like weekly or daily homework), it can be difficult to balance the number of points possible in the practice with the number of points in higher-stakes assessments, like finals. For example, if you have 10 homework assignments, each worth 10 points, you will have 100 possible homework points. But if you want homework to equal only 10 percent of the final grade, your midterm and final would each have to be worth 450 points (for 900 points of assessment) to balance out the homework.

Categories and weights make it much easier to manage activity types and give them the correct weight when you calculate the total grade. If you want homework to be worth 10 percent of the total grade, create a "homework" category and give it a weight of 10 percent. Then create a "tests" category and give it a weight of 90 percent. You can then create two 100-point tests and assign them to the tests category. Put all of the homework assignments in the homework category. It won't matter how many points the homework assignments are worth. All of them together will only count as 10 percent of the final grade.

Creative Grade Uses

The gradebook can be as useful in a business context as it is in traditional education. Most business training tends to be shorter and more focused than traditional education, but scores are still important. Usually, managers and trainers are only interested in exceptional/pass/fail or other simple scales for both activities and final scores. But trainees will still want to be able to track their progress and see how they are performing.

Gradebook scores can also be used to track progress against competency models. Try creating a category for each competency and track student scores on activities designed to measure the students' performance against the performance standard.

Scale Practices

Scales give you the ability to provide qualitative, rather than quantitative, feedback, but they require careful wording. When creating scales, ensure that your word choices are meaningful to the students and provide information they can use to improve their performance in the future.

CHAPTER 14

Surveys and Choices

Moodle has two tools specifically designed for collecting ungraded feedback from your students: surveys and choices.

A survey is a set of predetermined questions. It's not yet possible to create your own questions in a survey unless you install a nonstandard module such as Questionnaire or Feedback. The current survey focuses on getting feedback from students about the nature of the course.

Choices are small, one-question surveys. They act as small web polls that you may have seen on other web sites. You can use a choice to get rapid feedback from your students about any topic you wish, as long as it's only one question long.

Surveys

This section covers the following MTC skills: 5.6 Survey

There are three types of surveys you can give:

COLLES (Constructivist On-Line Learning Environment Survey)
> This is a set of 24 statements that asks students about the relevance of the course, provides opportunities for reflection and interactivity, provides peer and tutor support, and facilitates interpretation. These factors are based on social constructivist theory, as discussed in Chapter 1. Variations on the survey ask students to discuss their preferred learning environment or the actual learning environment. Moodle offers three types of COLLES surveys: preferred, actual, or a combination of the two. The preferred COLLES survey asks students to discuss how they think they want to interact with a course, while the actual COLLES survey asks them how they are interacting currently.

ATTLS (Attitudes to Thinking and Learning Survey)
> ATTLS seeks to measure the quality of interaction within a course. It builds on the "Separate and Connected ways of knowing" scale, which we discussed in Chapter 13.

Critical Incidents

The Critical Incidents survey asks students to consider recent events and answer questions about their relationship to those events.

Creating Surveys

The limited nature of the surveys tool makes surveys very easy to create. Basically, you select the set of prewritten questions you'd like to give, edit the introductory text, and you're done.

To create a survey:

1. Click the "Turn editing on" button.
2. Select Survey from the "Add an activity" drop-down menu in the course section where you would like to add the survey.
3. On the "Adding a new survey page," as shown in Figure 14-1, give the survey a name.
4. Select the type of survey you want to give from the drop-down menu.
5. If you wish, add an introduction to the survey.
6. Select the common module options:

   Group mode
   This is another location in which to set the group mode for the activity. If group mode is forced in the course settings then this setting will be ignored.

   Visible
   This determines whether students may view the activity or not.

7. Click the "Save changes" button.
8. The following page displays the question set you have chosen. Click the "Check and continue" button at the bottom of the page.

Administering Surveys

Once you've created the survey, students can begin to give their feedback. They simply click on the survey name in the course section and answer the questions. Once students have begun to answer the survey questions, you can track results via the "View xx survey responses" link at the top right of the survey page.

The survey report page contains links at the top right for viewing the data by course, by student, or by question. You can also download the data in a choice of three formats: Open Document Spreadsheet, Excel, or text.

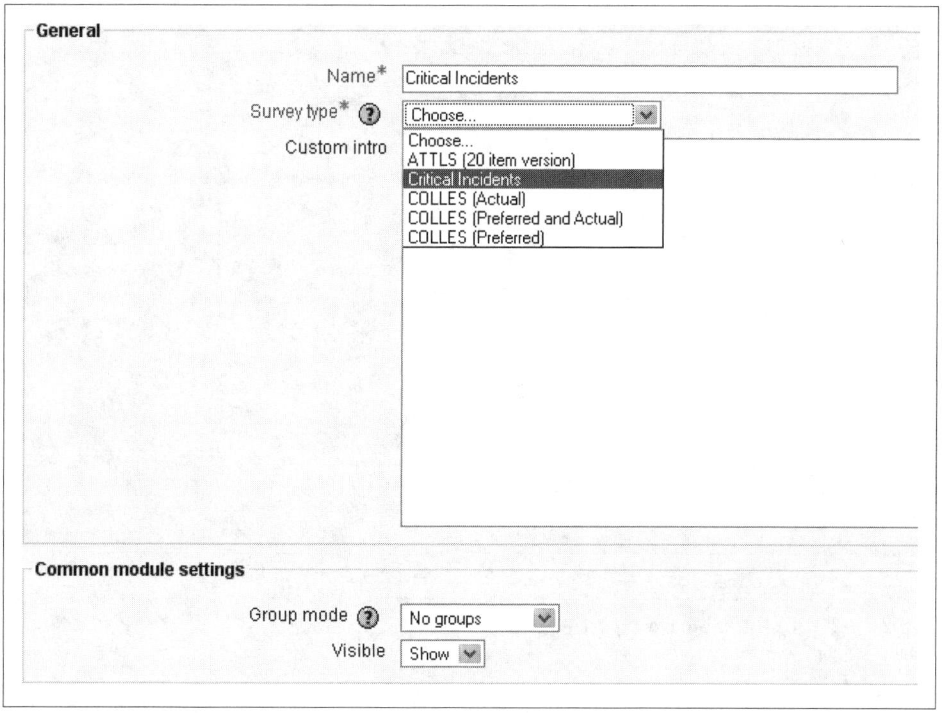

Figure 14-1. Adding a new survey

Moodle surveys are not anonymous. While students cannot see each other's results, you can view each student's survey. There is no way to ensure anonymity. If you are using these results for research, you must develop a scheme to download the data and assign participant numbers. You should also inform students of this limitation.

The COLLES and ATTLS questions are five-point scales that range in response from "Almost always" to "Almost never" for COLLES and from "Strongly agree" to "Strongly disagree" for ATTLS. These results are reported in graphical form when you view them, as illustrated in Figure 14-2.

The Critical Incidents survey is a free-response survey where students must type their answers. You can see what students have typed for each answer. Later in this chapter, we'll discuss how to apply the data you gather.

Survey Capabilities

The survey module has three capabilities:

Respond to survey
    This allows a user to participate in a survey.

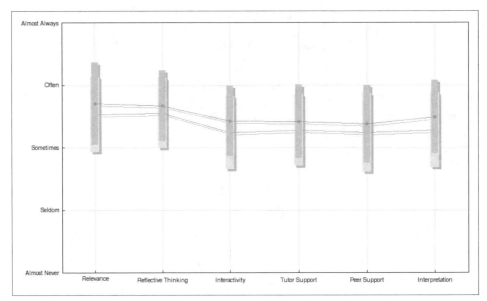

Figure 14-2. A COLLES survey report summary

View responses

This allows a user to read survey responses via the "View xx survey responses" link at the top right of the survey page.

Download responses

This allows a user to download survey responses.

Choices

This section covers the following MTC skills: 5.3 Choice

Unlike surveys, the choice tool allows you to ask any question you'd like, as long as it's multiple-choice. Once you've set up your choice, it acts as a poll in your course. Students click on the choice and select their answer. You can choose when and if students see the results of the choice and even let them change their minds.

Creating Choices

To create a choice:

1. Click the "Turn editing on" button.
2. Select Choice from the "Add an activity" drop-down menu.
3. On the "Adding a new choice" page, as shown in Figure 14-3, give the choice a descriptive name.

4. Enter the question text in the choice text area.

5. Choose whether to limit the number of responses allowed. If this is enabled, each response can be assigned a different limit. When the limit is reached, nobody else will be able to select the response. If limiting the number of responses is disabled, then any number of participants can select each of the responses.

6. Enter responses in each choice field. If you require more than 5 fields, click the "Add 3 fields to form" button. You can fill in any number of choice fields—if you leave some blank, they will not be displayed.

7. If you want the question to be available for a limited time, click the "Restrict answering to this time period" checkbox and set the opening and closing dates and times for the choice.

8. Select the miscellaneous options:

Display mode
> Choose whether the responses are displayed horizontally or vertically.

 A small number of responses looks better displayed horizontally, and a large number of responses and/or long responses look better displayed vertically.

Publish results
> You have four options for revealing the results of the choice to students:
> - Do not publish results to students
> - Show results to students immediately after they answer
> - Show results to students only after the choice is closed (if you've set a closing time above)
> - Always show results to students

Privacy of results
> Depending upon your "Publish results" setting, you can choose whether to display students' names with their response in the results.

Allow choice to be updated
> If you want to allow students to change their minds after they've answered, set this to Yes. Otherwise, students will be able to answer the question only once.

Show column for unanswered
> This option determines whether students will see the number of people who haven't answered the question when they see the choice results.

9. Select the common module options:

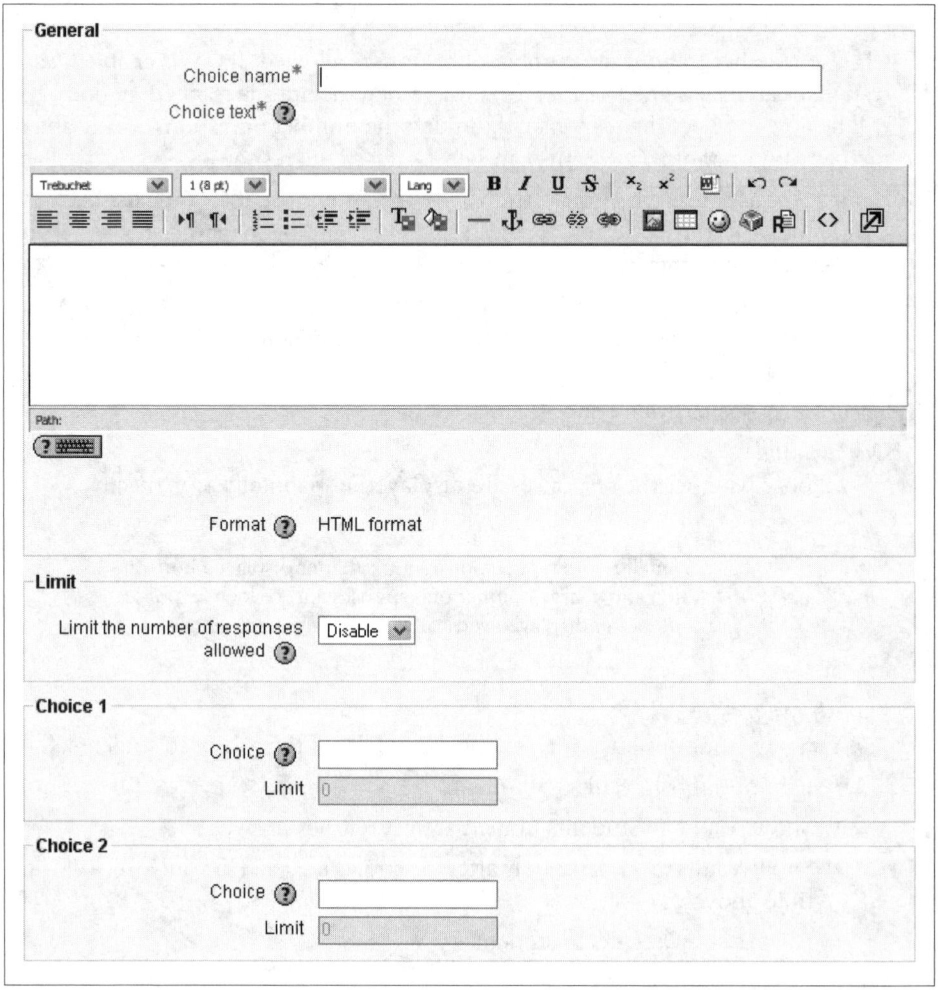

Figure 14-3. Adding a new choice

> *Group mode*
>> This is another location in which to set the group mode for the activity. If group mode is forced in the course settings then this setting will be ignored.
>
> *Visible*
>> This determines whether students may view the activity or not.

10. Click the "Save changes" button.

Once you've created the choice, it will be available to students after the opening time, if you've set one.

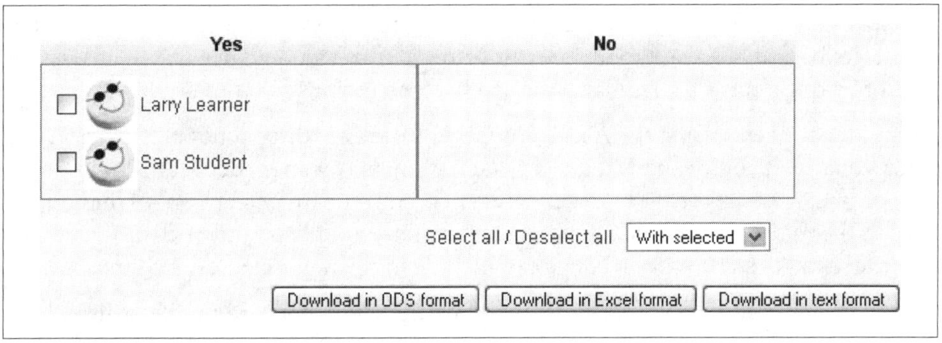

Figure 14-4. Viewing choice responses

Administering Choices

After students have answered the choice, you can see their responses via the "View xx responses" link at the top right of the choice page. Unlike the students' view of the results, irrespective of whether results are published anonymously, you'll see a column for each response with the student's picture and name, as shown in Figure 14-4.

Selected responses may be deleted if you wish. You may like to delete any test response you made.

As for surveys, results may be downloaded in a choice of three formats by clicking the appropriate button at the bottom of the choice responses page.

Choice Capabilities

The choice module capabilities are restricted to managing the responses from students:

Record a choice
    This allows a user to answer the choice.

Read responses
    This allows a user to view other users' responses.

Delete responses
    This allows a user to delete choice responses.

Download responses
    This allows a user to download the full dataset of responses from other users.

Using Surveys and Choices

Surveys and choices represent two different tools for gathering feedback data from students. Moodle surveys are formal and based in theory. Choices are quick and simple for both you and your students. They can both provide useful data about your course and your students' success.

The COLLES and ATTLS surveys are a bit too long to be used frequently. They provide useful feedback if you want to revise your course to meet student needs, but answering a set of 24 questions on a regular basis can become tedious for your students.

Jason: I recommend using the ATTLS or COLLES survey three times per semester (or twice a quarter if you're on the quarter system). You may want to deliver the first survey after the first few weeks to get some early feedback on student perceptions of the course, once at the midterm to make adjustments for the second half, and once at the end of the course to get summative feedback to include in the next semester's course design.

Of the available surveys, the COLLES and Critical Incidents are the most useful for making decisions about your course design. In the COLLES survey, pay close attention to the relevance scores. Student perception of course relevance is very important in determining student satisfaction and learning. If a student believes a course isn't relevant to her life, she will have difficulty spending the time required to be successful. Her performance will suffer, and her perception of the value of the course will diminish.

The Critical Incidents survey can provide useful feedback at the end of a topic or week. If you're trying something new, use this survey to get student feedback on the success of the topic. Because it's only five questions long, you can use it more frequently than the other two surveys.

Choices can be offered much more frequently. Many web sites use quick polls to inform or entertain their readers. Local and national news outlets run informal, nonscientific polls through their sites to gauge public opinion. You can use your choices to do the same. Choices can be about anything from course content to current school events.

Choices can also be used to provide an opportunity to share starting points through which students are encouraged to think about and articulate existing knowledge and understanding of a topic. Choices can encourage students to think in advance of a follow-up related activity, such as a forum discussion or an online text assignment.

CHAPTER 15

Putting It All Together

Now that we've taken a look at all the tools available in Moodle, let's take a step back and look at the big picture. Moodle has a lot of nifty capabilities, but they are only useful if they are applied in the service of effective course design.

If you are a professor in higher education, you are an expert in your field. You know more about your discipline than 99 percent of the rest of humanity. Universities do a great job helping people become domain experts and researchers. They do a poor job of teaching those experts how to teach. Unfortunately, the very process of becoming an expert makes it more difficult to teach novices. Cognitive research has shown that as people become more expert, they lose the ability to explain why and how they do certain basic tasks. The higher the level of expertise, the less conscious access you tend to have to the fundamentals of what you do. To achieve expertise, you need to develop a level of automatic performance for basic skills so you can concentrate your mental resources on the more difficult tasks.

Much of our preparation of teachers assumes teaching comes naturally. Since we've all been to school, we must know how to teach. Unfortunately, this isn't the case. Creating effective learning environments requires training and careful preparation.

In this chapter, we hope to give you some ideas and background from which you can develop your courses. We'll spend some time talking about learning environments in general, then we'll talk about how to apply everything you've learned so far to your courses. We'll also provide some design patterns for different types of courses that research and experience have shown to be successful.

What Is a Learning Environment?

Since we're developing an instructional environment, it would be a good idea to have a definition of what we're hoping to develop. What makes a web-based learning environment different from a web site? How is a web learning environment different from Amazon or Wikipedia?

The answer is: learning goals and feedback.

Learning environments have very specific goals for students. Most other web environments are there for users to achieve their own goals. They provide information, a way to buy things, or a way to connect with other people. People come to these environments of their own volition and can participate at whatever level they choose.

Learning environments are unique because they provide goals for students to achieve, goals they are currently unable to meet on their own. Your course objectives define a set of goals for students, goals they would not normally set for themselves. These goals define how students will interact with the material, other students, and you.

For example, if you are teaching a large survey course, the course goal will be to introduce the main concepts of the field to your students. In an advanced theory course, you will want students to demonstrate the ability to reason critically about advanced topics, and possibly synthesize their own ideas. These goals should be just beyond what your students can achieve right now. They may not even know what goals to set for themselves, so you need to at least suggest goals and performance levels for them.

The second defining feature of learning environments is feedback. Feedback is critical for students to monitor their progress as they pursue the course goals. Goal-oriented feedback is one of the critical defining aspects of a learning environment. If a student doesn't receive feedback, he has no way of knowing if he is closer to achieving the goals of the class or not. Other types of information environments can't provide feedback to their users because the users, not the environment, define their own goals. The only exception is an online game, which defines external goals and measures the player's progress toward them.

Feedback in a learning environment can take many forms. Tests and quizzes are frequently used tools for measuring student progress. They can provide feedback to students in the form of right and wrong answers or a percentage score. Homework can also provide feedback to students about their understanding of the materials. Less formal feedback might include interaction with students in class, conversations with experts, or applying new knowledge in a work setting. The key is to structure the feedback in useful ways so students can measure themselves against the course goals.

These two features make learning environments unique. Moodle provides you with tools to implement these ideas in unique ways. Moodle's educational philosophy guides how those tools are designed and can influence how you structure your learning environment.

Course Design Patterns

Design patterns are abstract solutions to recurring design problems. The term was originally used in architecture, but it has been applied more recently to software design. In architecture, the placement of doors, gates, windows, and other elements are design patterns that recur in many buildings. The idea of a lobby in a large office building is a design pattern. Over time, these patterns become almost invisible to us as we are continually exposed to them. Changing a pattern can lead to the discovery of an entirely new way of interacting with a space.

Instructional design patterns are similar. There are abstract solutions to the design challenges that occur in many courses. We can abstract four basic course types in higher education:

Introductory survey course
> These tend to be large lecture courses designed to expose students to basic concepts, vocabulary, and foundational ideas.

Skills development course
> These courses are designed to apply the ideas introduced in the beginning courses. Labs, recitations, workshops, and second-level courses tend to fall into this category. While there is discussion of theory, applying the theory to problems is the core of the course.

Theory/discussion course
> In more advanced courses, students are expected to think critically about research and theory. Application is typically secondary to the discussion of the theory itself.

Capstone course
> Many programs have some sort of summative experience that enables students to demonstrate what they have learned in their course of study.

While there are variations and combinations of these course archetypes, these categories cover most of the courses taught in most universities.

Understanding the abstract problem types is the first step toward designing a solution pattern. We also need principles of quality that will help us decide which patterns will be more likely to result in a better solution. Every professor develops a response to the course archetypes. The question is, which solutions are more likely to result in a quality course?

Fortunately, the American Association for Higher Education (AAHE) has come up with some recommendations for high-quality university courses. The AAHE has published 12 recommendations in 3 categories:

Culture:

- High expectations
- Respect for diverse talents and learning styles
- Emphasis on early undergraduate years

Curriculum:

- Coherence in learning
- Synthesizing experience
- Ongoing practice of learned skills

- Integration of education with experience

Instruction:

- Active learning
- Assessment and prompt feedback
- Collaboration
- Adequate time on task
- Out-of-class contact with faculty

It would be impossible to apply all 12 of these principles in every class. But a course that integrates as many of these principles as possible will likely be of higher quality than one that doesn't.

Fortunately, many of the tools in Moodle lend themselves well to realizing these quality principles. Let's take a look at how to apply the tools in Moodle to meeting these quality principles in the four class types.

Introductory Survey Course

The introductory survey course tends to be a large lecture course. The primary goal is to expose students to the basic concepts and vocabulary of a field of study. In the best case, this course helps students develop a basic conceptual structure that serves as the foundation for more advanced courses.

There tend to be two primary, related problems to address in these courses. First, their large size makes it difficult to assess open-ended assignments such as projects and reports. Second, student motivation is difficult to maintain due to the course's large size and its nature. Students who are required to take the course may find it difficult to engage in the subject matter, and long lectures are hard for anyone to get excited about.

A survey course might focus on quality measures like assessment and prompt feedback, adequate time on task, ongoing practice of learned skills, active learning, and high expectations. So how can we use the Moodle tools and the above principles to create a successful survey course?

Groups
> The key to success in a large class is the strategic use of groups. To promote active learning, create a group project that students must complete by the end of the semester. Such a project cuts down on the number of submissions you need to grade and provides students with opportunities for collaboration. Moodle has a number of tools to help student groups communicate and collaborate, including forums and wikis, which we'll explore below.

Resources
> Posting your lecture notes before each lecture will help students stay engaged by giving them a structure for taking notes. Before each lecture, post an outline of the

upcoming class to help students plan ahead for that class. Use the data from a short quiz or choice to target your lecture to the areas students find most difficult or interesting.

Alternatively, move yourself from being the source of information in the course to being a helpful tutor. Post your lecture notes, your lecture in MP3, and any reading assignments. Then use the face-to-face time to answer questions, demonstrate problem solving, and provide feedback to students on their work. Moving the information delivery portion of the course online will free up your face-to-face time to provide valuable coaching and support for your students, even in large lecture courses. This will promote active learning and prompt feedback within your course.

Quizzes

Use the quiz tool to provide a small quiz for each reading assignment. This will reward students for completing the reading and allow them to test their understanding of the material. Each quiz should be relatively low-stakes, but all of them taken together could add up to a significant part of the student's score. These small quizzes will provide assessment, prompt feedback, and help students spend adequate time on task. Again, be sure to use the data from the quiz to modify your lecture, or class discussion, to focus on the areas where students need more support.

Forums

A mix of class forums and group forums can be an effective tool for collaboration, active learning, and out-of-class contact with faculty. Forums for questions to the instructors and for general course discussion are great for class discussions. Each group should also have a discussion area for reading groups and lectures. Be sure to seed the discussion each week with a good question that will require students to apply the concepts they've learned during that week. Bring the best questions and discussions to the attention of the whole class to help motivate students. Create a class forum for the submission of final group projects. Everyone can see the projects, and each group needs to post the project only once. You can make this a Q & A forum, so students can't see other students' postings until they post their own.

Glossaries

A good glossary is critical when students are learning a new vocabulary. You can use the glossary to promote active learning by assigning a different group to create definitions for each week or topic. You and the other students can rate submissions based on their usefulness. Be sure to turn on autolinking to get the most benefit.

Databases

While large courses can be difficult to manage, they also provide many minds for collaborative work. In introductory courses, the database module can be a very useful tool. Students can create databases of important figures in the field, collect data for course projects, post quiz questions, or simply create small biographies of themselves. You can leverage the large numbers of students in the course to create rich resources for the students to use as they study.

Wikis

Each group should have a group wiki for their course project that they can submit at the end of the semester. Using a wiki this way promotes active learning and collaboration.

Lessons

Learning vocabulary is difficult without a lot of practice. To provide another opportunity for assessment and feedback, create a series of vocabulary flash cards in the lesson module to help students drill themselves on the new concepts. You could also replace static lectures with lessons on important topics, which will provide students with immediate feedback on the topic, rather than reading something and then receiving feedback later.

Messaging

Students in large-format courses can easily get lost. If students get into trouble with the course material, or simply lose motivation, they may disengage from the course and risk failure. The messaging system gives you a useful tool for communicating with students who are not engaging with the course site. Filter your students by last login, and send regular messages to those who haven't visited the course site in a while. This will let them know you are interested in their success and encourage them to reengage.

Roles and capabilities

In a large-format course, it can be difficult to manage all of the forums, glossaries, and databases yourself. Giving students a level of responsibility for different areas of the course can increase motivation and engagement. Give each group of students moderator privileges on a different forum each week. Students will study harder to make sure they know what they are talking about when it is their turn to moderate. Giving other groups capabilities to approve glossary entries or database entries will give them a sense of ownership in the course.

Combine these tools to create an effective learning environment. Each week or topic should have lecture notes, a glossary, a quiz or quizzes, and a forum. At the beginning of the course, post the course glossary, the course forum, and your syllabus. At the end of the course, post the final-project forum.

Skills Development Course

The skills development course is generally the second-level class in a course of study. The aim of this course is to give students the opportunity to apply the basic concepts learned in the survey course and explore one aspect of the field in more detail. These are usually workshop or lab courses that focus on a project or the repetitive application of important skills. The goals of this course type include development of automaticity in some skills, refining skill performances, and beginning to develop flexibility in skill application.

Skills development courses require continuous feedback and assessment. Engaged students need feedback so they can know if they are performing the skills correctly. They also need resources to help them troubleshoot when they cannot solve a problem on their own. You can create an effective practice environment for skills development with the following tools in Moodle:

Resources

As students practice on their own, they will need information resources to help them diagnose their mistakes. If you can post demonstrations, step-by-step instructions, or other aids for students as they practice on their own, you'll make it easier for them to succeed and eliminate a lot of repetitive questions.

Forums

Forums provide valuable opportunities for your students to help each other. Set up a forum for each topic or week and have students ask each other for assistance with course assignments. Allow post ratings in these forums to reward students who provide assistance to their classmates. This encourages collaboration and gives students an important out-of-class communication channel for support.

You can also use the forums for students to post their work and receive feedback from their peers. With a well-structured scoring guide and good exemplars, students can help each other improve their work with well-reasoned critiques.

Quizzes

If your class is focused on math skills, you can use the calculated-question type to provide your students with unlimited practice opportunities. Create a library of questions for each topic and let students take the quiz as many times as they'd like. Each time, they will see a different set of questions. Other types of courses can use the quiz module to test the students' ability to apply basic concepts, provide graduated practice, and provide an opportunity to practice other types of skills.

Lessons

Well-constructed lessons give students the opportunity to apply their skills and receive immediate feedback. Each page in the lesson should challenge students to use the skills they are developing in the course, and either provide direct feedback or allow them to explore the consequences of their actions in a simulation type of environment.

Databases

There is a lot of evidence to suggest people learn effectively when they are producing new materials for other people. In a skills course, you can use the database to give students a place to create practice assignments for each other, which you can then use in quizzes or lessons to provide additional practice, and spread the work of developing a good course.

Roles and capabilities

As students progress in their capabilities, they can take on more responsibility for their own learning. In a skills course, you may want to give groups of students the ability to develop a quiz for other students, pulling questions from pools developed by you, by a publisher, or ones they write themselves. Set up new lessons for them to add new lesson pages, developing new practice opportunities for other students.

Theory/Discussion Course

A discussion course focuses on readings and the discussion of ideas. These are usually senior or graduate-level courses that focus on discussions of theory and research. There is little practical application. Instead, ideas are discussed, debated, and critiqued. The emphasis is on reasoning, presenting evidence from the research literature, and critical thinking.

Student motivation is typically not a problem in these courses. Students who take advanced courses are usually interested in the subject. However, it can be difficult to create opportunities for active learning and provide prompt feedback. Fortunately, there are a few Moodle tools that can help you overcome these issues:

Blogs

Critical thinking and analysis of theory typically require periods of private reflection along with public discussion. Encourage students to actively engage in these activities by providing them with the opportunity to blog about the course topics. Having students keep a blog in Moodle rather than a journal on paper allows you to give them feedback on their entries without interrupting the writing process. You can encourage students to use their blogs by bringing the most insightful or interesting entries for discussion in class or a forum.

Databases

One of the hallmarks of most theory courses is a large amount of reading, usually from original research. To help your students keep on top of the reading, create a database and ask them to submit a short summary or abstract of the papers they read. This strategy will reward them for keeping up with the reading and encourage them to actively engage with the reading. It will also provide the students (and you) with an annotated bibliography at the end of the course.

Choice

As a stimulation for conversation, include a choice each week. Poll the class about a controversial point in the reading or discussion. Combine this with a forum asking students to explain their responses.

Forums

Forums are one of the keys to a successful discussion course. As we discussed in Chapter 5, forums allow students to compose their thoughts and focus on the content of their responses. Encourage careful, well-reasoned postings in the forum by scoring posts. Encourage more active engagement by assigning groups of students as moderators for different topics.

Wikis

A class wiki can be used to create a shared understanding of the ideas under discussion. After each discussion, students should be encouraged to share their notes on the course wiki for other students to learn from their perspectives on what was important or interesting. At the end of the semester, students will have a synopsis of the entire class to take with them.

Roles and capabilities

In a theory course, the collaborative construction of knowledge and artifacts is the most powerful method for engaging students. Students can create activities, artifacts, and other materials for each other, developing their critical-reasoning abilities through the creative development of learning materials for other students. In a theory course, you can override the student role at the course level to enable students more permissions throughout the course, then set role overrides in those areas where you need to restrict their access. This encourages students to actively construct the course web site for each other.

Capstone Course

Capstone courses are usually focused around a final project that requires students to demonstrate what they have learned during their course of study. In graduate school, these courses are focused around a thesis or dissertation. In undergraduate study, students are expected to produce a paper or other artifact. These project-based courses present challenges for both the instructor and students. Students need to be able to apply skills they may have learned several years ago, and may have not used since. Instructors need to ensure the project is stimulating and interesting. Moodle can provide activities to meet these challenges:

Assignments

You can help students structure the task by assigning a set of deliverables over the course of the semester. Each deliverable should be a one- or two-week project you collect with an assignment. For example, if students are writing a paper, you could collect an annotated bibliography, a subject proposal, an outline, a couple of early drafts, and a final draft.

Messaging

Use messaging as a private feedback channel so students can discuss their work. As they work on each section of the project, they will need to ask questions about the assignment and their performance. A record of all discussions is kept in the message history for each student.

Blogs

Part of a student's capstone experience is reflecting on what he has learned over the course of study. Blogs can act as a tool for reflection and as a project notebook. Encourage students to use their blogs for both activities.

These design patterns are abstract starting points for designing a solution that works in your class. We've tried to recommend patterns that we have seen work, or that other researchers have reported to be successful. They are not the final word on effective course design by any means. But they can provide a useful starting place when thinking about how to use Moodle to promote learning in your course.

CHAPTER 16

Moodle Administration

If you are the administrator for your Moodle site, there are a lot of options at your fingertips. Most of the time, the default settings that come with your Moodle installation will work well. But there are a lot of options for customization and performance that can make your version of Moodle work exactly as you'd like.

The number of administration settings has increased a lot in recent versions of Moodle and it can take a while to understand it all. We can only provide a brief mention of each setting in this book; however, the "Moodle Docs for this page" links at the bottom of each page in Moodle provide access to further information.

This chapter is organized into sections that are the same as the links in the Site Administration block, which you'll find on your Moodle front page when you log in as an administrator. We'll finish with a section on Moodle support, just in case!

 A good way to learn about Moodle administration is to download and install a Moodle package on your own computer. Create some test user accounts and assign them the roles of student and teacher. Try logging in as a student or a teacher in a different browser from the one displaying you logged in as an administrator. You can change an administration setting, then see how it affects students or teachers by refreshing the page (or logging out, then logging in again for role changes).

Notifications

In the middle of the notifications page is the "Moodle Registration" button for registering your Moodle site with *Moodle.org*. Despite the statement "Please register your site to remove this button," the button doesn't go away when you register! It remains in order to enable you to update your registration—simply click the button again at any time. Updating your registration periodically helps improve the accuracy of the global Moodle statistics (*http://moodle.org/stats/*).

Below the Moodle Registration button is your Moodle version number. If you add a bug report to the Moodle tracker (*http://tracker.moodle.org/*), you should state your Moodle version number.

The notifications page may also include a warning that your site might not be secure and a statement if your cron has not run within the past 24 hours. The cron is a script that is run regularly and checks whether certain tasks need performing, such as sending email copies of forum posts.

Users

User management can be one of the most time-consuming jobs for an administrator. As your system grows, the number of users who lose their password or have difficulty creating a new account grows as well. Fortunately, there are a few tools to help make the job of user management easier.

Authentication

One of the first things you need to consider when setting up your Moodle site is user authentication, i.e., enabling people to log in to your Moodle site.

In Chapter 2, we covered how to create a user account using email-based self-registration. You created the account and Moodle sent you an email with a link to confirm your address. While this is an effective and efficient way to create new accounts, particularly for smaller sites, Moodle provides a number of other authentication methods as well. If you are in a university environment and have access to a university email or directory server, you can tell Moodle to use them to authenticate new user accounts instead. External servers prevent users from creating multiple accounts and prevent people from outside your organization accessing your server when they shouldn't.

Authentication methods (also known as authentication *plug-ins*) include:

Manual accounts
    This method requires the administrator to manually create all user accounts. It may be used together with the upload users facility (see following section).

Email-based self-registration
    With this method, users can create their own accounts. They then receive an email at the address they specified in their account profile to confirm their account.

External database
    This method uses an external database to check whether a given username and password are valid. You can choose whether certain Moodle user profile fields are filled with information from the external database.

FirstClass/POP/IMAP/LDAP/NNTP server
> These methods use an external server to check whether a given username and password are valid. If the name and password match, an account with the same username is created in Moodle.

Moodle Network authentication
> Moodle Networking is a new feature in Moodle 1.8, enabling resources to be shared between Moodle sites using a single sign-on. Setup instructions can be found in the Moodle documentation.

No authentication
> Users can create accounts with no external validation. This option should only be used for testing purposes.

Shibboleth
> Shibboleth is open source software that provides a single sign-on across or within organizational boundaries. The *README.txt* file in the *auth/shibboleth* folder of your Moodle distribution contains setup instructions.

To set the authentication method:

1. Click on Authentication in the Site Administration block.

2. On the authentication page, as shown in Figure 16-1, click on the closed-eye icon to enable your chosen authentication plug-in.

   If you want, you may choose to use more than one authentication method. Use the up/down arrow icons to arrange the plug-ins in order, with the plug-in handling the most logins at the top of the page. This will minimize authentication server load.

3. If you have chosen email-based self-registration, select "Email-based self-registration" from the self-registration drop-down menu in the common settings section. Potential users will then be presented with a "Create new account" button on the login page.

4. If you have courses with guest access, set the Guest login button to show.

5. Click the "Save changes" button.

6. Click on Settings opposite the authentication plug-in(s) you have chosen.

7. Configure the required settings and click the "Save changes" button.

Accounts

Each user on your Moodle site has an account that contains profile information, forum posts, blog entries, and activity reports.

Browse list of users

The "Browse list of users" page provides a list of all user accounts.

Site Administration [-]	Please choose the authentication plugins you wish to use and arrange them in order of failthrough. Self registration will be handled by the plugin selected in the 'Registration' column (usually 'email').	

Name	Enable	Up/Down	Settings
Manual accounts			Settings
No login			Settings
Email-based self-registration	👁		Settings
CAS server (SSO)	✌		Settings
External database	✌		Settings
FirstClass server	✌		Settings
IMAP server	✌		Settings
LDAP server	✌		Settings
Moodle Network authentication	✌		Settings

Site Administration menu:
- Notifications
- Users
  - Authentication
  - Accounts
  - Permissions
- Courses
- Location
- Language
- Modules
- Security
- Appearance
- Front Page
- Server
- Networking
- Reports
- Miscellaneous

[Search]

Figure 16-1. Choosing an authentication plug-in

If you are using email-based self-registration and a user has a problem confirming his account, you can confirm his account for him by clicking the confirm link opposite his name.

You can also search for a particular user, using her name or email address as the search term, and then edit her profile. You will need to do so in order to reset user passwords if users are unable to log in. Another reason for editing a user's profile is to disable her email address if you are receiving lots of undelivered mail!

If you want to temporarily disable an account (i.e., prevent a user from logging in to Moodle), you can do so by editing the user's profile page and changing the authentication method to "No login."

Add a new user

The "Add a new user" page allows you to manually create a new user account. The form to add a new user looks just like the new user profile page in Chapter 2 that you used to create your own account. If you create a test account, you can use a made-up email address.

You can always create new accounts manually, regardless of which authentication method you are using.

Upload users

The "Upload users" page allows you to import a list of users via a text file. Moodle creates an account for each user and, if you want, can also enroll students in courses and arrange them in groups.

The user data text file must follow a certain format, as described in the upload users help file. (Click on the question-mark icon.)

By default, Moodle assumes that you will be creating new user accounts and skips records where the username matches an existing account. However, if you set "Update existing accounts" to Yes, then the existing user account will be updated.

User profile fields

A new feature in Moodle 1.8 is the ability for administrators to create additional user profile categories and fields. New profile fields will appear on each user's profile page.

Permissions

As we covered in Chapter 4, the new roles and permissions system provides you with a huge amount of flexibility to manage how students and other users interact. However, teachers can't do much unless you give them the appropriate permissions.

Define roles

The "Define roles" page, as shown in Figure 16-2, has three tabs: Manage roles, Allow role assignments, and Allow role overrides.

The "Manage roles" tab contains a list of roles on your site. The Edit column contains icons for editing and deleting roles, and for moving them up or down in the list (affecting the way that roles are listed around Moodle). Below the table is an "Add a new role" button.

If you wish to modify the capabilities for a particular role, you can do so by editing the role. For example, you may want to allow students to unenroll themselves from a course when using internal enrollment.

To edit a role:

1. Click on Permissions in the Site Administration block, then "Define roles."
2. Click the edit icon opposite the role you want to edit, e.g., student.
3. On the "Edit roles" page, change permissions as required. For example, change the "Unassign own roles" capability from "not set" to "allow."
4. Scroll to the bottom of the page and click the "Save changes" button.

Depending on what you require, rather than modifying a particular role, it may be easier to create a new role. For example, you may want to create an inspector role for providing

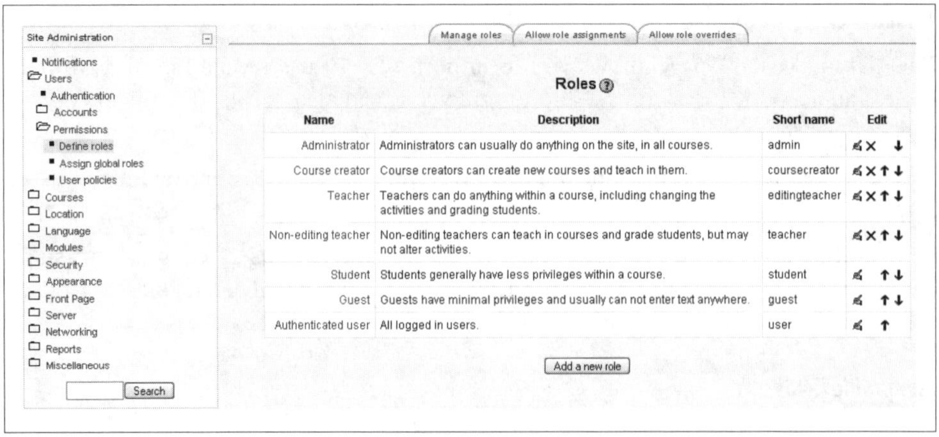

Figure showing Site Administration roles management interface:

Name	Description	Short name	Edit
Administrator	Administrators can usually do anything on the site, in all courses.	admin	⚹✗ ↓
Course creator	Course creators can create new courses and teach in them.	coursecreator	⚹✗↑↓
Teacher	Teachers can do anything within a course, including changing the activities and grading students.	editingteacher	⚹✗↑↓
Non-editing teacher	Non-editing teachers can teach in courses and grade students, but may not alter activities.	teacher	⚹✗↑↓
Student	Students generally have less privileges within a course.	student	⚹ ↑↓
Guest	Guests have minimal privileges and usually can not enter text anywhere.	guest	⚹ ↑↓
Authenticated user	All logged in users.	user	⚹ ↑

Figure 16-2. Managing roles

external inspectors or college principals with permission to view all courses on your Moodle site.

To add an inspector role:

1. Click on Permissions in the Site Administration block, then "Define roles."
2. On the "Manage roles" tab, as shown earlier in Figure 16-2, click the "Add a new role" button.
3. On the "Add a new role" page, give the role a name, e.g., Inspector.
4. Give the role a meaningful short name. The short name is necessary for other plugins in Moodle that may need to refer to the role (for example, when uploading users from a file or setting enrollments via an enrollment plug-in).
5. Give the role a description (optional).
6. Set the "View courses" capability to "allow."
7. Scroll to the bottom of the page and click the "Add a new role" button.

You will then need to assign the inspector role as a global role (as described in the next section).

To test a new role:

1. Create a test user and assign the new role to them.
2. Either log out as the administrator and then log in as the test user, or use a different browser to log in as the test user.

 Role changes only take effect when the user next logs in.

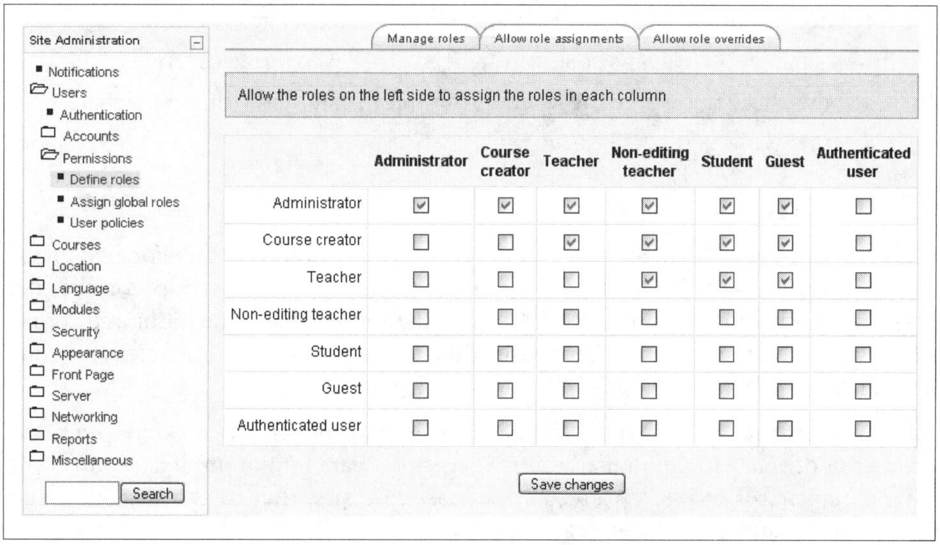

Figure 16-3. Allowing role assignments

You can find setup instructions for other example roles in the Moodle documentation.

The "Allow role assignments" tab, as shown in Figure 16-3, contains a grid for setting which roles each role can assign other users to. For example, by default, teachers can only assign other users the roles of non-editing teachers, students, and guests. If you want teachers to be able to assign other teachers in their course, you can allow the role assignment:

1. Click on Permissions in the Site Administration block, then "Define roles."
2. Click the "Allow role assignments" tab.
3. Click the checkbox where the teacher row and column intersect.
4. Click the "Save changes" button.

The "Allow role overrides" tab looks similar to the "Allow role assignments" tab, with a grid for setting which roles each role can override.

In order for teachers to make the most out of the roles and permissions functionality, it is highly recommended that you enable teachers to set role overrides for students. To do so, you need to first allow the capability to override roles and then to set which role (s) teachers can override:

1. Click on Permissions in the Site Administration block, then "Define roles."
2. On the "Manage roles" tab, as shown earlier in Figure 16-2, click the edit icon opposite the role of teacher.
3. On the "Edit roles" page, change the "Override permissions for others" capability to "allow."

4. Scroll to the bottom of the page and click the "Save changes" button.

5. To set which role teachers can override, click the "Allow role overrides" tab.

6. Click the checkbox where the teacher row and the student column intersect.

7. Click the "Save changes" button.

Assign global roles

Global roles are roles that apply across the whole of your Moodle site. For example, a user assigned the global role of teacher will have this role in every course on the site. Most likely you will only want to assign the default roles of administrator and course creator globally, though you may create additional roles, such as the inspector role, which require assigning globally.

Administrators can do anything and go anywhere in the site. You should limit the number of people with administrator privileges to a bare minimum. If a lot of people have administrator access, it's a recipe for disaster because they can add accounts and courses and change site variables at will.

Course creators can create new courses and assign the role of teacher in them. If you are administering a small Moodle site, enabling your colleagues to create their own courses removes you as a potential bottleneck. If you are running a university-wide site, however, using this extensively is not recommended. On a large site it can become difficult to track who is creating legitimate courses and who is abusing the system. A large number of bogus courses will clutter your system and could lead to performance slowdowns.

Global roles are assigned in exactly the same way as course roles (see Chapter 4), including hidden assignments.

 Assigning users the global role of student will result in them being enrolled in every course.

User policies

The user policies page includes a number of role settings that are generally best left as default. They include the following options:

Default role for all users
> This should be set to authenticated user. If it is set to student, then all students are enrolled in all courses.

Auto-login guest
> If this is not set, then visitors must click the "Login as a guest" button before entering a course that allows guest access.

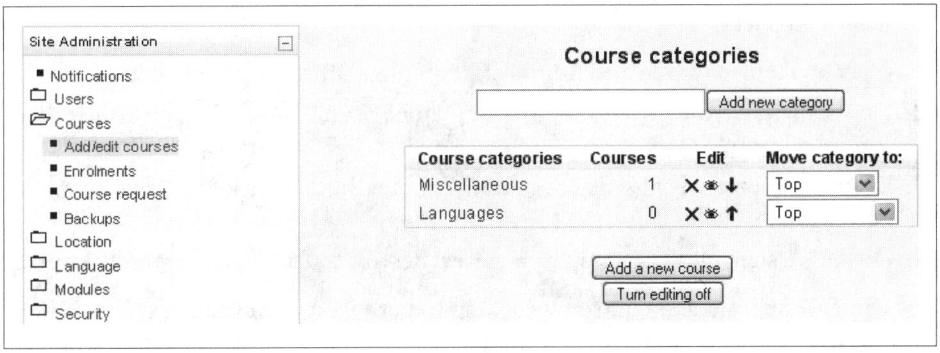

Figure 16-4. Adding a new category or course

Roles that are not synchronized to meta courses
> Meta courses combine enrollments from multiple courses (see Chapter 2). You will probably want users to have the same role in the meta course as in the normal courses. If not, select the roles that should not be synchronized.

Hide user fields
> User fields appear on users' profile pages. You can increase student privacy by hiding selected user fields.

Courses

You, as the administrator, together with any colleagues you have assigned as course creators, are responsible for adding courses to Moodle.

Add/edit courses

Before creating courses, it's sensible to set up some course categories.

By default, there is only one Moodle category: miscellaneous. Although you are certainly free to put all your classes in the miscellaneous category, your students will find it easier to find their classes if they are organized in descriptive categories.

To add a category:

1. Click on Courses in the Site Administration block, then "Add/edit courses."
2. On the "Course categories" page, as shown in Figure 16-4, type the name of your new category in the text box and click the "Add new category" button.

You now have a new course category, which you can move up or down or into an existing category to create a subcategory.

Once you set up a few course categories, you are ready to create a course.

To create a course:

1. Click on Courses in the Site Administration block, then "Add/edit courses."
2. On the "Course categories" page, as shown in Figure 16-4, click the "Add a new course" button.
3. Enter the course settings, as covered in Chapter 2, then click the "Save changes" button.
4. On the "Assign roles" page, click on the teacher role to assign teachers to the course.

You can choose to hide a course by clicking the eye icon opposite the course name. Only users with the capability to view hidden courses, such as teachers, will be able to access the hidden course. Categories can also be hidden, if you want.

Enrollments

By now you should have set up user authentication, i.e., enabled people to log in, created some courses, and assigned teachers to them. The next thing to consider is course enrollment, that is, assigning users the role of student in a course.

By default, students can enroll themselves in whatever courses they choose. They do so by clicking on the course name, then answering Yes to the question "You are about to enroll yourself as a member of this course. Are you sure you wish to do this?" This method of enrollment is called internal enrollment. You can restrict users from enrolling in whatever courses they choose by setting enrollment keys (see Chapter 2).

 If you want to enable students to unenroll themselves from a course as well as enroll themselves, you can do so by editing the role of student (see the previous section).

Whilst internal enrollment is an effective and efficient way of managing course enrollment, particularly if you don't have a lot of courses, Moodle also provides a number of other enrollment methods (or enrollment *plug-ins*). They include:

Authorize.net Payment Gateway/PayPal
> These methods allow you to set up an e-commerce system so students can pay to enroll in a course. If you are running a business selling Moodle-based courses, you can use either of these methods to enable students to use a credit card.

External database
> This method looks up enrollments in another database. You'll need to configure the login settings so Moodle can access the remote server and map the fields in Moodle to the fields in the external database.

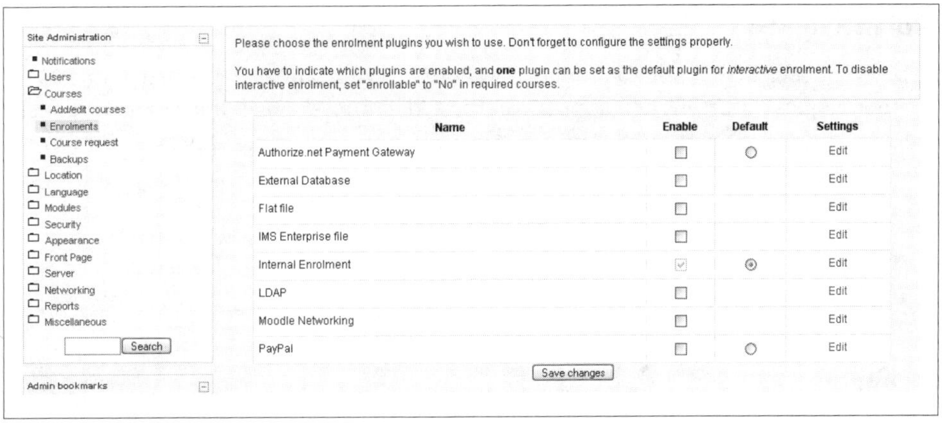

Figure 16-5. Choosing an enrollment plug-in

Flat/IMS Enterprise file

Like the upload users tool, which we covered in a previous section, these methods allow you to import user enrollment data via a specially formatted text file. IMS Enterprise file format is described in a help file, and flat file format is described on the flat file settings page.

Internal enrollment

This is the default enrollment method, as described above.

LDAP

You can use an LDAP server to manage enrollment as well as manage authentication. Setup instructions can be found in the Moodle documentation.

To set the enrollment method:

1. Click on Courses in the Site Administration block, then Enrollments.

2. On the enrollments page, as shown in Figure 16-5, click the enable checkbox opposite your chosen enrollment plug-in.

   As for authentication methods, you may choose more than one enrollment method, if you wish. For example, if you have some courses that students must pay for and some free courses, you can use PayPal and internal enrollment.

3. Select the default plug-in for interactive enrollment. This is when a user has to do something interactively in order to be enrolled, such as clicking "Yes, I do" (internal enrollment) or paying some money (Authorize.net Payment Gateway, PayPal).

4. Click the "Save changes" button.

5. Click on Edit opposite the enrollment plug-in(s) you have chosen.

6. Configure the required settings and click the "Save changes" button.

Course Request

If you want users to be able to request new courses, you can enable course requests. A "Course request" button then appears on the "All courses" page. If users then request new courses, you as an administrator will see a "Courses pending approval" button on the "All courses" page.

 If you enable course requests, you will need to check the "All courses" page regularly for the "Courses pending approval" button. Email notification of course requests is not yet available.

Backups

There's a saying in the computer industry: "There are two types of users, those who have lost data, and those who will." Eventually, a hard drive will fail or your database will collapse on your Moodle server and you will lose data. Fortunately, Moodle has an automated course backup system that you can run on a nightly basis to export all course content for the entire site.

The course backup tool in Moodle actually runs the same functions as an individual course backup. It simply runs automatically on all of the courses on the site at a designated time. It's a good idea to schedule backups for when your server isn't usually busy. Running the backup tool over all the courses can be processor-intensive, so you shouldn't run it when there are a lot of students trying to access the server.

The backup page lets you set the types of content to be backed up. If you are running a nightly full-server backup (which is strongly recommended), we suggest you use the following settings:

Include modules and module user data
  Click both of these checkboxes to preserve all student work for each course.

Users
  Set this to All. If you need to restore your Moodle server from a backup, you don't want to lose any accounts, even if they aren't associated with a current course.

User files
  Check this as well. You want the restored server to look as much like the original as possible, so all user files should be restored.

Course files
  Again, click this checkbox. You'll need to deal with a lot of angry teachers if they have to restore all of their course files after you restore the server.

Keep
  This setting determines how many old backups will be saved. Set this as high as you can without taking up too much space on your server. If you need to restore a course a few days after you run the backup, you'll be glad you have a few weeks' worth of data.

Once you've selected the backup settings, you'll need to set a backup schedule.

To set the backup schedule:

1. Click the Active checkbox. This turns on the automated backup system.
2. Click the days of the week to run the backup. Backing up every day is *recommended*.
3. Set the execution time for the backup process. For most servers, early morning will be the best time.
4. Set the "Save to..." path. If you can, choose a backup path on another machine or on a different drive than the one Moodle is on. You don't want to lose your backups at the same time you lose your Moodle site if the drive fails. If you leave the field blank, then backup ZIP files will be saved in the backup folder of each course files folder.
5. Click the "Save changes" button.

Once you've set up your backup schedule, Moodle will automatically create archives of all the courses on the server at the time you specified. Once the backup is complete, Moodle will send you an email describing the status of the backup. Any courses which are unavailable to students and have not been changed in the last month are automatically skipped in the backup process.

 In addition to setting automated course backups, we strongly recommend that you perform regular site backups, as explained in the Moodle documentation.

Location

The location settings page includes the following options:

Default time zone
   This sets the default time zone for date display. This can be overridden by a user's profile setting unless the default time zone is forced.

Default country
   Select your country so that it appears by default on the new account page.

IP address lookup
   You can experiment to find out which works better for your area, hostip or ipatlas.

Language

One of Moodle's many strengths is its language-handling capabilities. As we mentioned in Chapter 2, you can provide users with a choice of language or force a language in a particular course. Even if you want your site in English only, you may well find the language editing facility useful for making changes to the standard text in Moodle.

Language Settings

The language settings page includes the following options:

Default language
> This sets the default language for the site. The setting can be overridden by users using the language menu, or the setting in their personal profile.

 If a preferred language is set in a user's browser, then this will override the default site language.

Display language menu
> This sets whether the language menu is displayed on the login page and the front page. If it is turned off, the only places where a user can change the language setting are in her user profile or in the course settings if she is a teacher.

Languages on the language menu
> If you want to limit the number of languages students and teachers can select from, enter a reduced list here.

Site-wide locale
> Leave this setting empty, as it's set through each language pack.

Excel encoding
> Leave as default (Unicode) unless you have a particular reason for wanting Latin encoding.

Language Editing

The language editing interface enables you to easily change any word or phrase used on the site. For example, you may want to change the word "Course" to "Area."

To change a word or phrase:

1. Click on Language in the Site Administration block, then "Language editing."
2. Click the "Edit words or phrases" link in the middle of the page.
3. On the "Edit words or phases" page, as shown in Figure 16-6, click the "Switch lang directory" button. A local language folder, *parentlanguage_local*, will automatically be created in *moodledata/lang*. Files of edited strings will then be saved in this folder. This is necessary to prevent changes that you make from being overwritten by a newer language pack when updating.

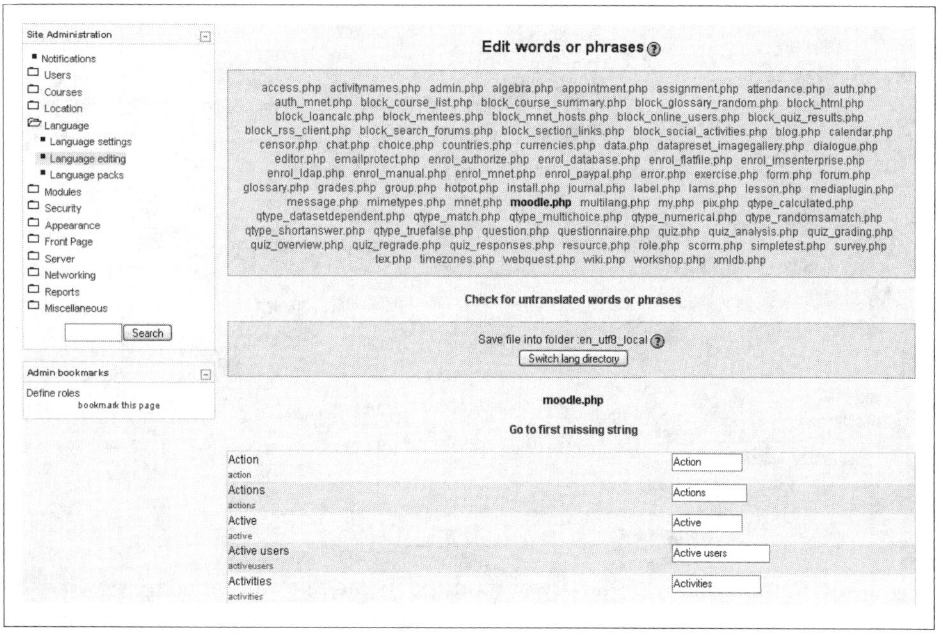

Figure 16-6. Editing words or phrases

4. Choose a file to edit. You may need to search through a few files before finding the file containing the word you wish to change. The file *moodle.php* contains all common site-wide phrases.

5. Change the word or phrase.

6. Click the "Save changes" button. The changed phrase will be highlighted in a different color.

If you wish to make further changes later, be sure to check that files of edited strings will again be saved to the folder *parentlanguage_local*, switching folders if necessary.

Language Packs

At the time of this writing, over 70 language packs are available for you to install on your Moodle site. Simply select the languages you require from the list of available language packs and click the "Install selected language pack" button.

All language packs, apart from English, are stored in the *moodledata/lang* folder.

Modules

As mentioned in the beginning of this book, Moodle is an acronym for Modular Object-Oriented Developmental Learning Environment. It has a modular design.

Activities

Activity module	Activities	Version	Hide/Show	Delete	Settings
Assignment	8	2007020200	👁	Delete	Settings
Chat	5	2007020200	👁	Delete	Settings
Choice	9	2007020200	👁	Delete	
Database	1	2007022601	👁	Delete	Settings
Exercise	0	2007020200	◡	Delete	
Forum	20	2007020202			Settings
Glossary	7	2007020200	👁	Delete	Settings
Hot Potatoes Quiz	4	2007020202	◡	Delete	Settings
Journal	0	2007020200	◡	Delete	
LAMS	0	2007020200	◡	Delete	Settings
Label	30	2007020200	👁	Delete	

Site Administration
- Notifications
- Users
- Courses
- Location
- Language
- Modules
  - Activities
  - Blocks
  - Filters
- Security
- Appearance
- Front Page
- Server
- Networking
- Reports
- Miscellaneous

[Search]

Figure 16-7. Managing activities

In addition to using the wide variety of modules included in the standard download, you can download and install third-party modules and plug-ins from the *Moodle.org* modules and plug-ins database (*http://moodle.org/mod/data/view.php?d=13&rid=22*).

Be aware that third-party modules may have quality issues, may not work correctly, and may not work when you upgrade Moodle. You should test them thoroughly before using them and be prepared to uninstall them before upgrading.

Activities

The activities page, as shown in Figure 16-7, enables you to manage Moodle's activity modules.

The Hide/Show column allows selected modules to be hidden, so they do not appear in any course "Add an activity" drop-down menu and cannot be used in any course. To hide a module, click the eye icon so that it changes to a closed eye.

For various reasons, several modules are hidden by default. For example, the Exercise and Journal modules are old modules that are no longer maintained, but they are included in Moodle for historical reasons.

The activities page also lists how many activities for each module there are on your Moodle site. If you click on a number, the list of courses containing that activity will be displayed.

Apart from the forum, any module can be deleted using the link in the Delete column. There is no reason for standard modules to be deleted. However, nonstandard modules may need to be deleted before upgrading.

To delete a module completely, in addition to deleting it on the activities page, you also need to remove/delete the actual module folder from the *moodle/mod* folder. Otherwise, Moodle will reinstall it next time you access the site administration. This also applies to blocks.

Many of the modules have additional settings, which can be accessed via the links in the Settings column. Settings you may want to change include:

Assignment and Forum
   You can set the maximum file upload size (subject to course and site limits).

Chat
   If you intend to use the chat activity a lot, then you should consider using a chat server daemon to reduce server load.

Database, Forum, and Glossary
   If you have enabled RSS across the site (in the Server > RSS section of the Site Administration block), you will also need to enable RSS in the Database, Forum, and Glossary modules.

Resource
   You may want to allow teachers to create links to files on a local filesystem, such as a CD drive or a common network drive.

Quiz
   You can simplify the "Add a new quiz" page by selecting a number of options to be hidden from teachers by default and only displayed when teachers click the "Advanced settings" button.

Blocks

The blocks page, which looks similar to the activities page, enables you to manage blocks in Moodle. As for activity modules, you can show, hide, and delete blocks.

To reduce the length of course "Add a block" drop-down menus, you should hide blocks that will not be used, such as global search (unless you have enabled the global search feature in the Miscellaneous > Experimental section of the Site Administration block), mentees (unless you have added a mentor role), and network servers (unless you are using Moodle Networking).

The blocks page also lists the number of instances of each block. Clicking on a number results in the list of courses containing that block being displayed.

Some blocks, such as the HTML block, can be used more than once on a course page. You can choose whether or not to allow this by clicking the change link in the Multiple column.

A few blocks have additional settings, which can be accessed via the links in the settings column. Settings that you may want to change include:

Remote RSS feeds

You may want to allow teachers or even everyone to be able to add new RSS feeds. If not, then teachers will have to contact you to add new RSS feeds.

To add a new RSS feed:

1. Click the a "Add/edit feeds" link at the bottom of the "Remote RSS feeds settings" page.

2. On the "Add/edit feeds" page, add the news feed URL and a custom title (optional).

3. Click the Add button.

Filters

Filters allow for the automatic transformation of entered text into different, often more complex forms. For example, the titles of resources can automatically become hyperlinks that take you to the relevant resource, or URLs pointing to MP3 files can become Flash controls embedded in the web page that let you pause and rewind the audio. There are a number of standard filters included with Moodle and many more specialized filters available from the *Moodle.org* modules and plug-ins database (*http://moodle.org/mod/data/view.php?d=13&rid=22*).

The filters included in the standard download are:

Activity Names Autolinking

This filter scans text for activity titles that exist in the same course. Where found they will be highlighted and linked to the activity.

 To use this filter effectively you should use descriptive titles. For example, a title of "Test" is poor because any use of the word "Test" in the text will be linked regardless of what it refers to.

Database Autolinking

This filter scans text for database entry titles and works in the same way as the Activity Names Autolinking filter.

Glossary Autolinking

This filter scans text for glossary entry titles and works in the same way as the Activity Names Autolinking filter. In addition to this filter, individual glossary entries should have the "This entry should be automatically linked" box checked.

Resource Names Autolinking

This filter scans text for resource titles and works in the same way as the Activity Names Autolinking filter.

Wiki Page Autolinking

This filter scans text for wiki page titles and works in the same way as the Activity Names Autolinking filter.

Algebra Notation

This filter converts algebra code into GIF images. It requires the TeX notation filter to be enabled.

Word Censorship

This filter "blacks out" words from a list in the word censorship settings.

Email Protection

This filter scrambles email addresses in user profiles so that outside search engines and guests can't see users' email addresses. This protects your users from spammers and other attackers.

Multimedia plug-ins

This associates uploaded multimedia files with the correct media players.

Multilanguage Content

This enables resources to be created in multiple languages (as covered in Chapter 3). When turned on, it looks for `<span lang="xx" class="multilang">` tags, which indicate that a text contains multiple languages. Then it selects and outputs the best language for the current user. The language of the resource will change when the user changes his selected Moodle language.

TeX Notation

Another mathematics markup tool that allows you to use TeX notation and display it correctly in Moodle.

Tidy

This filter checks whether HTML code is XHTML-compliant, tidying where necessary. To make this filter work you need to have PHP compiled with the libtidy option. See *http://www.php.net/tidy* for more information.

To enable a filter:

1. Click on Modules in the Site Administration block, then Filters.

2. On the filters page, as shown in Figure 16-8, click the eye icon opposite the filter you want to enable, so that it changes to an open eye.

3. Use the up/down arrow icons to arrange the filters in the order in which they should be applied.

Certain filters have additional settings, which can be accessed via the links in the settings column.

Filter settings that apply to more than one filter can be found in the Appearance > Filter settings section of the Site Administration block.

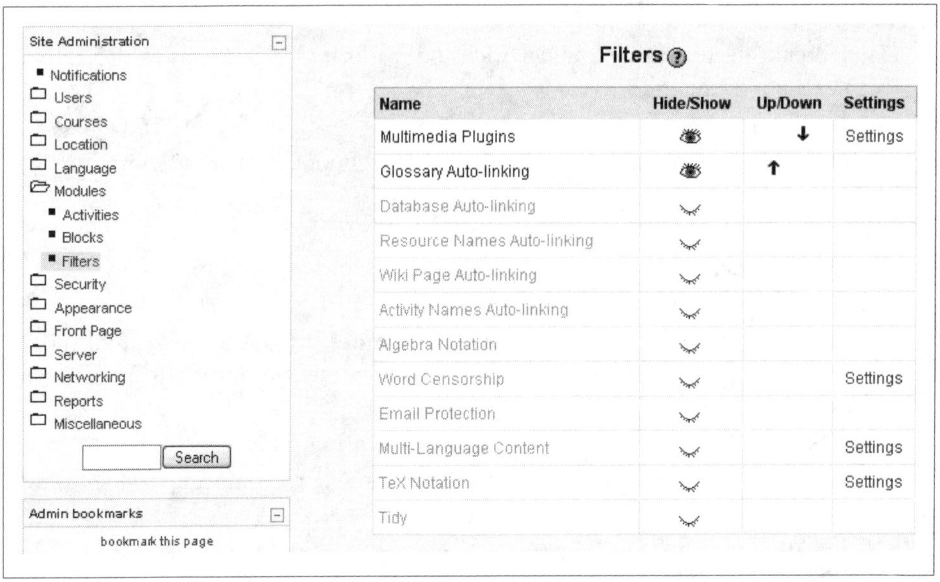

Figure 16-8. Managing filters

Security

The Moodle project takes security seriously and is continuously improving Moodle to fix any security issues that may arise. We recommend that you take the following basic security measures:

- Update Moodle regularly on each release. Published security holes draw crackers' attentions after release. The older the version, the more vulnerabilities it is likely to contain.
- Disable register globals. This will help prevent against possible XSS problems in third-party scripts.
- Ensure that administrators and teachers use strong passwords. This protects against "brute force" cracking of accounts.
- Only give teacher permissions to trusted users and avoid creating public sandboxes with free teacher accounts.

Further security advice can be found in the Moodle documentation.

Site Policies

The site policies page includes the following options:

Open to Google
   Enabling this setting allows Google's search spiders guest access to your site. Any part of the site that allows guest access will then be searchable on Google. In

addition, people coming into your site via a Google search will automatically be logged in as a guest.

Maximum uploaded file size

Probably the most frequently asked question in the *Moodle.org* forums is, "How do I increase the upload file size limit?"

Upload file sizes are restricted in a number of ways—each one in this list restricts the following:

1. The Apache setting LimitRequestBody
2. The PHP settings post_max_size and upload_max_filesize
3. The site-wide maximum uploaded file size setting in the Security > Site policies section of the Site Administration block
4. The course maximum uploaded file size setting in the course settings
5. Certain activity module settings

Enable messaging system

Click the checkbox to enable the messaging system (see Chapter 5).

If you enable the messaging system, all users will be able to send and receive messages at any time. Teachers can't choose whether or not messaging is allowed between students in their particular course.

Maximum time to edit posts

This sets the editing time for forum postings. The editing time is the amount of time users have to change forum postings before they are mailed to subscribers.

Blog visibility

To enable blogs (as covered in Chapter 11), select the level to which user blogs can be viewed. By default, all site users can see all blogs. Blog visibility may be restricted so that users can only see blogs for people with whom they share a course or a group.

HTTP Security

The HTTP security page contains just one option:

Use HTTPS for logins

HTTPS encrypts the user's login data, so it's difficult to sniff out a user's username and password on the network. You will need to enable HTTPS on your server before you turn on this setting, or else you will be locked out of your site.

Every web server has a different method for enabling HTTPS, so you should check the documentation for your web server.

Module Security

Certain activity modules can be set so that they do not appear in the "Add an activity" drop-down menu for teachers. The setting only applies to teachers—administrators are always able to add any activity to a course.

To disable an activity module completely, click the eye icon in the hide/show column in the activities page.

Notifications

The notifications page contains the following options:

Display login failures to
> Set this to Administrators to be warned of anyone attempting to steal student or teacher logins. When set, a link stating the number of failed logins appears in the top-right corner of the page when an administrator logs in. Click the link to access the login error page.

Email login failures
> If you're concerned about login failures, you can set up email notification for administrators.

Threshold for email notifications
> This sets the number of failed logins for a given user from a single computer that will trigger notification.

Anti-Virus

To make use of Moodle's anti-virus feature, the open source virus scanner ClamAV should be installed on your server. See *http://www.clamav.net* for more information.

Appearance

Themes

A theme sets the appearance—colors, fonts, and icons—for your Moodle site.

Theme settings

The theme settings page includes the following options:

Allow user themes
> If enabled, users can select their preferred theme on their "Edit profile" page. All Moodle pages will be displayed in the user's theme, apart from courses where a course theme has been set.

Allow course themes

If enabled, teachers are provided with a "Force theme" option on their course settings page. The course will always be displayed in the theme specified in the course setting, with the user and site themes being ignored.

Theme selector

Moodle has a number of themes for you to choose from using the theme selector, including an interactive theme called Chameleon. Chameleon uses Ajax technology to enable you to easily design your own theme or enhance an existing theme. Further information on Chameleon can be found in the Moodle documentation.

Alternatively, you can download a theme from the *Moodle.org* themes database (*http://moodle.org/themes*).

To install a theme from the *Moodle.org* themes database:

1. Unzip the theme on your computer.
2. Copy the folder to the *moodle/theme* directory on your server.
3. Click on Appearance in the Site Administration block, then Themes > Theme *selector*.
4. Click the Choose button opposite your new theme. (If your new theme is missing from the list of themes, check that the new theme folder in the *moodle/theme* directory doesn't contain another folder with the same name, as this may occur with some ZIP utilities.)

Calendar

Moodle's calendar displays the following events:

Site

These events are created by administrators and are viewable in all courses.

Course

These events are either created by teachers or are a result of setting closing dates for activities such as assignments and quizzes, or repeating chat sessions. Course events are only viewable by course participants.

Groups

These events are created by teachers and are only viewable by members of a group.

User

These are personal events that a user can create and are only viewable by the user.

The days and events to look-ahead settings are for displaying events in the Upcoming Events block. If the Upcoming Events block becomes too long, you can reduce the number of days and events to look-ahead.

Filter Settings

The filter settings page contains the following options:

Text cache lifetime

Text filters can take a lot of processor power to analyze. If you have a large number of courses, the filters may slow your system. The text cache lifetime determines how often the filters run. If you set them to run too frequently, your system may slow down. If you set them to run too infrequently, analyzing new content will take too long and users will notice. You should experiment to find the correct amount of time for your server.

Filter uploaded files

Moodle can also apply filters to uploaded HTML and text files, as well as content entered directly into Moodle itself. Again, you will need to balance the increased load imposed by filtering more files against the added usefulness of applying filters more widely.

Filter match once per page or text

This setting affects the Glossary, Database, Resource, and Activity Names Auto-linking filters. If checked, only the first match on a page, or in a block of text, will be converted to a link.

Filter all strings

If checked, headings and titles can be displayed in different languages using the Multilanguage Content filter (see Chapter 3).

 Settings for particular filters can be found in the Modules > Filters section of the Site Administration block.

HTML Editor

The HTML editor is a word-processor interface for formatting text and inserting images, tables, links, and smileys (see Chapter 3), which teachers generally find useful.

You can customize the HTML editor and change the background color, fonts, and font sizes, and hide selected buttons. If you want the HTML editor to have a spellcheck button, you need to install aspell 0.50 or later on your server, and enter the correct path to access the aspell binary in the Server > System Paths section of the Site Administration block.

Moodle Docs

By default, teachers and administrators have "Moodle Docs for this page" links at the bottom of each page in Moodle for accessing context-specific documentation.

You may find that teachers prefer the documentation to open in a new window, so they can easily return to their page in Moodle. If so, click the "Open in new window" checkbox.

My Moodle

My Moodle is a customizable "dashboard" front page that provides users with links to their courses and activities within them, such as unread forum posts and upcoming assignments.

To enable My Moodle, click the "Force users to use My Moodle" checkbox.

By default, users can add and delete blocks from their My Moodle page. If you don't want users to be able to do so, you can edit the authenticated user role and change the "Manage My Moodle" page blocks capability from "allow" to "not set."

If you want certain blocks to appear on every user's My Moodle page, they can be set as sticky blocks (see the later section "Sticky Blocks").

Course Managers

The course managers setting allows you to control who is listed in the course description. (Course descriptions are displayed in course lists.)

By default, users with the role of teacher in a course are listed in the course description for that course. If a course has several teachers, the course description can become rather long. In this case, you can create a role (e.g., head of subject) with no capabilities set and assign it to selected users in addition to their teacher role. If you then select only the head of subject role in the course managers setting, the course descriptions will be shorter.

Sticky Blocks

Sticky blocks are blocks that you, as an administrator, can set to always appear on course pages and/or on users' My Moodle pages.

To configure sticky blocks:

1. Click Appearance in the Site Administration block, then "Sticky blocks."
2. Choose whether to configure My Moodle or course pages.
3. Select the required blocks from the "Add a block" drop-down menu. Configure each block as desired.
4. Reposition blocks using the arrow icons in the block headers.

If you add a block that is already present in a particular course page or My Moodle page, then it will result in a duplicate block. Course pages contain a number of blocks by default. Instructions on changing the default arrangement of blocks on course pages can be found in the Moodle documentation.

Front Page

Your site front page is similar to a course page. You, as an administrator, can edit the front page by clicking the "Turn editing on" button in the top-right corner of the front page.

Front Page Settings

Front page settings include the following options:

Full site name
> This name appears at the top of every page above the navigation bar.

Short name for site
> The short name appears at the beginning of the navigation bar as a link back to your site front page.

Front page description
> This is an optional setting enabling you to add short message to your users in a block on the front page.

Front page and front page items when logged in
> The center of the front page can display any combination of the following: news items, a list of courses, a list of course categories, a list of categories, and courses or none. If you choose to display a list of courses when logged in, then students are provided with a list of only the courses they are enrolled in.

 An alternative option for logged-in users is My Moodle (see earlier section).

Include a topic section
> This adds a topic section to the center-top of the front page. When editing is turned on, resources and/or activities can be added to the topic section using the drop-down menus, in the same way as on a course page.

 The label resource can be used to add text and/or an image to the center-top of the front page.

News items to show
> This setting only applies if the front page is set to display news items or if you are using the Latest News block.

Front Page Roles

You can assign roles and set up role overrides for your front page in exactly the same way as for a course (see Chapter 4).

To enable users to engage in front page activities, you need to either assign all users the front page role of student or set up authenticated user overrides. For example, if you want users to be able to view forum discussions and reply to posts, you can override the authenticated user role and allow these permissions.

 If you have a site news forum in which everyone is forced to be subscribed, you need to assign all users the front page role of student in order for them to receive email copies of forum posts.

Front Page Backup

You can back up your front page with or without user data in exactly the same way as for a course (see Chapter 4).

Site Files

Site files are basically the course files for the front page. Any images you want to display on the front page can be uploaded to the site files folder.

Don't be afraid of the note at the top of the site files page: "Files placed here can be accessed by anyone." This simply means that, unlike course files, which require a user to have appropriate rights in order to access them, anyone who has the URL can access the files within the site files folder.

 The site files folder can be used for uploading a course backup ZIP file prior to restoring it.

Server

System Paths

The system paths page includes the following options:

GD version
> GD is a graphics library that manipulates graphics. It's used to create thumbnail images from uploaded files and other graphics on the fly. If you don't know what version is installed, leave this on the original setting.

Path to zip and unzip
> If you are running Moodle on a Unix or Unix-like server (Linux, Solaris, BSD, Mac OS X), you may need to specify where the zip program is located. Zip and unzip are used to compress and decompress ZIP archives such as the backup folder.

Path to aspell
> To use spellchecking within the HTML editor, you *must* have aspell 0.50 or later (*http://aspell.net/*) installed on your server, and you must specify the correct path to access the aspell binary.

Email

The email page includes the following options:

SMTP hosts
> SMTP stands for Simple Mail Transfer Protocol. The SMTP host is an email relay that will take the email from Moodle and send it to users. You will need to set this only if your server does not allow mail relay. Otherwise, PHP will send out the mail using its built-in mail server. All the email sent by forums and other modules will be sent through this host.

SMTP username
> If you set an SMTP server and it requires authentication, enter the username for the account that will be relaying the email from Moodle.

SMTP password
> Enter the password for the SMTP user you set previously.

No-reply address
> Email sent from Moodle needs to have a return address or many servers will reject it as spam. Some users also want to keep their email private, so Moodle sends all of its email using the no-reply address you set here.

Allowed and denied email domains
> Authentication can be restricted to particular email domains when using email-based self-registration so that, for example, only students with a university email can log in.

Hour to send digest emails
> Moodle allows mail digests from the forums, so users get only one email per day instead of an individual message for every posting. This setting specifies when digests are emailed to users. Users set their email digest type in their profile page.

Session Handling

The session handling page includes the following options:

Timeout

Once someone logs in to your Moodle server, the server starts a session. The session data allows the server to track users as they access different pages. If users don't load a new page during the amount of time set here, Moodle will end their sessions and log them out.

Be sure this time frame is long enough to cover the longest test your teachers may offer. If students are logged out while they are taking a test, their responses to the test questions may be lost.

Cookie prefix

Most of the time, you can leave this blank, unless you are running more than one Moodle site on the same server. In this case, you will want to customize the name of the cookie each Moodle site uses to track the session. This enables you to be logged in to more than one Moodle site at the same time.

If you change the cookie prefix you will need to log in again, as the change takes effect immediately.

RSS

The RSS page contains only one option:

Enable RSS feeds

Certain modules can send RSS feeds to users' news readers. RSS feeds are headlines that notify users of new content in Moodle. Users subscribe to RSS feeds by clicking the orange RSS button and copying the address in the browser bar to their RSS reader software.

In addition to enabling RSS across the site, you also need to enable RSS in the module settings for each module with RSS capabilities (forum, database, and glossary). Teachers also need to enable RSS in the activity settings.

Debugging

Debugging messages are intended to help Moodle developers. If you have a problem with your Moodle site and ask for help in a *Moodle.org* forum, a developer may ask you to turn debug messages on, in order to locate the cause of the problem.

Statistics

If you enable site statistics, Moodle will gather statistics about each course and for the whole site and produce graphs displaying them.

To enable statistics:

1. Click Server in the Site Administration block, then Statistics.
2. Click the "Enable statistics" checkbox.
3. As stats processing is quite resource-intensive, you should set the stats processing to start in the early morning.

 Set the stats processing to start an hour before your automated course backups are scheduled to start, then set the maximum run-time to one hour. This ensures that stats are not being processed at the same time as course backups are being made.

4. Click the "Save changes" button.

HTTP

The HTTP page contains the following options:

Frame name
> If you've developed a web wrapper for Moodle and you want to include Moodle in a larger frame, set the name for the Moodle frame here.

Use slash arguments
> You will need to change this setting only if you are having trouble viewing files or images. Most of the time, Moodle will display files and pictures with no problem using the slash arguments. If you get errors when you try to view pictures or files from within Moodle, your PHP server doesn't allow the slash argument method and you will need to use the file argument method instead.

Proxyhost and proxyport
> Your Moodle server may need to access the Internet through a proxy server, depending on your network configuration. If you're not sure about whether you need a proxy server, contact your network administrator or ISP.

Maintenance Mode

Maintenance mode is for preventing any users other than administrators from using the site while maintenance is taking place.

When users attempt to access a course when your site is in maintenance mode, they receive a message informing them that the site is in maintenance mode. If you wish, you can create a customized maintenance mode message, perhaps stating when the site will be available again or giving the reason for doing maintenance.

The front page of your site will appear as normal when your site is in maintenance mode. Users will only see the maintenance mode message when they attempt to access a course.

To put your site in maintenance mode:

1. Click Server in the Site Administration block, then Maintenance mode.
2. Click the Enable button.

 An alternative way of putting your site in maintenance mode if you're unable to access the web interface is to create a file called *maintenance.html* and save it in the folder called *1* in your *moodledata* folder. A customized maintenance mode message can be entered in the *maintenance.html* file.

Cleanup

The cleanup page contains the following options:

Unsubscribe users from courses after
> To help keep lists of participants up-to-date, you can tell Moodle to unenroll any student who hasn't logged in for a certain amount of time. Be sure to keep this time long enough so students aren't unenrolled accidentally while they still need access to the course.

Delete unconfirmed users after
> If you're using email-based self-registration, users must confirm their account within a certain time frame. Once the time set here has passed, any account that hasn't been confirmed will be deleted. Seven days is a good setting.

Keep logs for
> Moodle keeps extensive logs of user activity. Eventually, however, the logs will become so large that they begin to clog your server. Limiting the length of time logs are kept for will reduce database table size. Generally, a year is enough time to keep logs for.

Environment

The environment page enables you to check that your server meets all system requirements for your current and future versions of Moodle.

 You should check that your server meets all system requirements before upgrading your site.

PHP Info

The PHP info page provides information on the version of PHP your server is running, including PHP compilation options and extensions, server information, and the PHP environment and OS version information. If you have a problem with your Moodle site and ask for help in a *Moodle.org* forum, you may be asked to provide some information from this page.

Performance

Moodle can be made to perform very well, at small usage levels or scaling up to many thousands of users.

If you're happy with the performance of your site, leave the performance settings as default. If you want to improve the performance, you can refer to the Moodle documentation for advice.

Networking

Networking is a new feature in Moodle 1.8, enabling resources to be shared between Moodle sites using a single sign-on. Additional information, including setup instructions, can be found in the Moodle documentation.

 Your server must have Curl and OpenSSL PHP extensions installed in order to use Moodle Networking.

Reports

Just as teachers can obtain detailed logs and reports of student activity in their course (as covered in Chapter 4), as an administrator you have access to logs and reports for the whole site.

Course Overview

To obtain course overview reports, you must first enable statistics (see the "Statistics" section earlier). You can choose to view reports of the most active courses or the most participatory courses over a certain time period. Results are displayed in a bar chart and in a table.

Logs

You can select any combination of course or site, participants, date, activity, and actions and choose whether they are displayed on the logs page or downloaded in text, ODS, or Excel format.

The "Live logs from the past hour" link opens a pop-up window listing all course activity in the past hour, which refreshes every minute. You can use it to gauge server load and to get a snapshot of how students and teachers are using the site.

Statistics

To obtain statistics reports, you must first enable statistics (see the "Statistics" section earlier in this chapter). You can select any course or the whole site and choose to view reports of all activity, all views, all posts, or all logins over a certain time period. Results are displayed in a line graph and in a table, which contains links to course logs.

Miscellaneous

Experimental

The experimental page lists features that require additional testing and bug-fixing, such as the global search. We recommend you use a test server for testing experimental features before enabling them on your production site.

XMLDB Editor

The XMLDB editor is a tool for developers to easily edit tables/fields/keys/indexes in *install.xml* files.

Moodle Support

Hopefully you won't have any problems with your Moodle site. However, just in case you do, Moodle support is available in the following ways:

Moodle documentation (http://docs.moodle.org/)
    At the bottom of each page in Moodle is a "Moodle Docs for this page" link for accessing context-specific documentation.

Community discussion forums
    Moodle has a large and diverse user community which provides free support via discussion forums on *http://moodle.org/*. You can search for answers to questions other users have already asked, or post a new question of your own.

Commercial support and other services

   If you need urgent, complicated, or ongoing help, we recommend that you contact a Moodle Partner—see *http://moodle.com/support/*.

Happy Moodling!

Index

We'd like to hear your suggestions for improving our indexes. Send email to *index@oreilly.com*.

style function, 33
submit assignment capability, 126
subscribe (forums), 73
subscript function (HTML editor), 33
subscriptions, 70
superscript function (HTML editor), 33
surveys, 2, 203–206, 209
   administering, 204
   capabilities, 205
   creating, 204
   introductory courses, 214–216
system administrators, 9, 39
   multilanguage content, adding, 40
   statistics and, 66
system contexts, 53

T

table tool (HTML editor), 33
talk in a chat (chat module), 87
teachers, 131
   explaining tasks, 211
   roles, assigning, 227
templates (database), 175
   CSS, 185
   editing, 180–185
   JavaScript, 185
   RSS, 184
TeX text filter, 105, 239
text, 13
   filters, 105
   page, composing, 30–32
themes, 242
   database, 176
theory/discussion courses, 213, 218
threads, 70
threshold for email notifications option, 242
throttling applies (forums), 80
tidy filter, 239
TIFF files, 44
time delay between attempts option, 96
time limit option, 96
time limits for lessons, 144
time spent (minutes) option, 146
time zone, 13
timeout option, 249
toggle text function (HTML editor), 34
tool-centric systems, 5
topics format, 17
true/false questions, 101

turn editing on tool, 15
   Blog Tags block and, 170
   chat sessions, creating, 85
   choices, creating, 206
   forums, adding, 71
   front page and, 246
   glossaries, creating, 132
   labels, adding, 30
   lessons, 144
   linking to files or web sites, 34
   messages, 90
   surveys, creating, 204
   wikis, 157
tutorial support (messaging systems), 93

U

UK Open University, 47
underline function (HTML editor), 33
undo action, 33
Uniform Resource Locator (see URL)
update this glossary button, 135
updated pages (wiki links menu), 163
upload a single file assignment type, 123
upload a single file option, 127
upload_max_filesize setting (PHP), 241
URL (Uniform Resource Locator), 7
use advanced features button, 194
use HTTP for logins option, 241
use this lesson's settings as defaults options,
   147
user backup option, 62
user contexts, 53
user files backup option, 62
user files setting (backup page), 232
user policies page, 228
user profiles, 10–14
usernames, 9
users, 222–229, 224
Utah State University, 47
UTF-8, 8

V

versions, tracking, 42
video files, 44
view any ratings (forums), 79
view assignment capability, 126
view blog entries, 171
view discussions (forums), 78

About the Authors

Jason Cole is a product development manager at the Open University in the UK, where he works on the development of the OU's Course Management System. Prior to joining the OU, he was the academic technology manager at San Francisco State University, where he initiated the process of upgrading the university from Blackboard to Moodle.

A member of the Moodle community, he has developed a student data integration tool for the system and contributed to discussions regarding a document management system and object model for Version 2.0. Jason earned a Ph.D. in educational technology from the University of Northern Colorado.

Helen Foster is a Moodle administrator for the site with the most users (over 300,000 at the time of this writing)—Moodle.org—and holds a key Moodle role of documentation steward. Helen is a facilitator for the Using Moodle course, which provides free 24-hour support for Moodle users worldwide.

Prior to relocating to Belgium, Helen was the Information Learning Technology Manager at Alton College in the UK, where she implemented Moodle and managed the development of the third-party Object module and other Moodle code. Helen has a B.S. in Mathematics from the University of London and a Postgraduate Certificate in Education from the University of Cambridge.